SMART GIVING

Is Good Business

HOW CORPORATE PHILANTHROPY CAN BENEFIT YOUR COMPANY and SOCIETY

CURT WEEDEN

JOSSEY-BASS
A Wiley Imprint
www.josseybass.com

Published by Jossey-Bass
A Wiley Imprint
989 Market Street, San Francisco, CA 94103-1741—www.josseybass.com

Jossey-Bass books and products are available through most bookstores. To contact Jossey-Bass directly call our Customer Care Department within the U.S. at 800-956-7739, outside the U.S. at 317-572-3986, or fax 317-572-4002.

Jossey-Bass also publishes its books in a variety of electronic formats. Some content that appears in print may not be available in electronic books.

Library of Congress Cataloging-in-Publication Data

Weeden, Curt.
  Smart Giving Is Good Business: How Corporate Philanthropy Can Benefit Your Company and Society
/ Curt Weeden.
    p. cm
  Includes bibliographical references and indexes.
  ISBN 978-0-470-87363-2
  1. Corporations—Charitable contributions—United States. 2. Investments—Social aspects—
United States. 3. Social responsibility of business—United States. I. Title.

  HG4028.C6W44 2011

  361.7—dc22

                                                                                    2010048705

Printed in the United States of America
FIRST EDITION
HB Printing   10 9 8 7 6 5 4 3 2 1

Contents

Introduction

Why More Corporations Are Giving Less

"Don't tell me how much we have to give because that turns charity into a tax. Tell me what's worth giving to and why. If you can sell me, we can start talking dollars and cents."

During my ten-year stint with Johnson & Johnson, my CEO was what I called a yardstick kind of guy. If you brought a proposition to Ralph Larsen, it had to measure up. It didn't matter if it happened to be a business opportunity or a plan to help the company meet its social obligations.

"Make the case," Ralph would demand. Then the yardstick would come out.

When it came to corporate philanthropy, Ralph measured twice before cutting (a check) once. First, he wanted assurance that company contributions were legal and ethical and would be going to the most appropriate charitable organization possible. And second, a proposed cash or product donation was subjected to this sometimes gut-churning question: "Why is this contribution relevant to the company?"

An outsider might come to the wrong conclusion that Ralph used his yardstick to suppress Johnson & Johnson's giving. After all, how many contribution recommendations could stand up to this double-barreled type of scrutiny—particularly question number two? As it turns out, many requests can and do. Ralph's intent wasn't to use his yardstick to stifle philanthropy. Rather, he used it like a shepherd's staff to guide a potentially undisciplined outpouring of gifts into a more logically directed stream of social investments.

Over the years, I have worked with dozens of senior executives charged with running some of America's largest businesses. Only a few have been as demanding as Ralph Larsen in requiring that corporate contributions have social value *and* have clear relevance to their businesses. CEOs who don't insist on keeping charitable commitments close to a company's mission and business objectives represent the first of three reasons why American corporate philanthropy has periodically been stuck in neutral or, even more troublesome, has edged downward for nearly three decades in a row.

The "Big Three" Trouble Spots for Corporate Philanthropy

1. *CEO myopia.* Business leaders at the top of the private sector food chain who simply don't get it.
2. *Muted middle management.* Company personnel charged with planning and carrying out philanthropy activities who don't have or who are prevented from using a loud enough voice to be effective.
3. *NGO misfires.* Proposals or "pitches" by nonprofit organizations that lack the "business relevance" factor.

There's a reason why CEO near-sightedness makes it to the top of this list. If chief executives don't recognize the potential of creative and conditional grants as resources to enhance a company's mission and business objectives, then corporate philanthropy drifts into a "difficult to justify" zone. Ralph Larsen didn't let that happen. He understood it wasn't his money he was doling out to charity—it belonged to shareholders. Hence, each contribution decision had to be footnoted with a logical, persuasive *business* rationale.

As the "Big Three" list points out, corporate philanthropy is plagued by other problems aside from narrow-thinking or totally clueless CEOs. The men and women who have line management responsibilities for planning and executing corporate giving too often aren't given a long enough leash to do their jobs—or, in some cases, are simply not prepared or competent enough to turn a gift into an impressive business social investment.

Then there are the nation's one million-plus 501c3 charities parked at the receiving end of the corporate giving continuum. How could these non-private-sector entities share a portion of the blame for a slowdown or decline in corporate philanthropy payouts? Answer: when nonprofits use a tin cup approach to companies—when they beg for money without remembering that businesses are not set up to be charitable wellsprings—their "same old, same old" fundraising tactics usually fall short of prompting a business to be more responsive to social challenges. Far too few nonprofit groups have come to understand that it makes more sense to approach a company with a *deal* rather than an *appeal*.

The Decline of Corporate Philanthropy

This book opens with a claim that corporate charitable giving has been heading south for years, interrupted only by a few brief periods of stagnation. How can that be? What about all those generous and well-publicized donations companies pump out after a natural or manmade disaster? One case in point is the huge corporate response to the 2010 earthquake in Haiti.

Within forty-eight hours after the 7.0 magnitude earthquake shook much of one of the poorest countries on the planet into ruins, businesses responded with over $100 million in charitable contributions. The first wave of donations came fast, and many business gifts were larger than even those made to the three other most devastating catastrophes of the twenty-first century's opening decade: 9/11, Hurricane Katrina, and the South Asian Tsunami. The cruise company Carnival donated $5 million. Deutsche Bank gave $4 million. There were million-dollar checks from Google, Hess, UPS, MorganStanley, and a host of other businesses. ADM supplied seven hundred tons of rice, and a million cans of water came from Anheuser-Busch. Donations included medical supplies, water filters, Crocs shoes, backpacks, solar lights, mattresses—a mind-boggling inventory of donated goods and services.

This extraordinary benevolence was indicative of the ongoing philanthropic practices of the nation's largest corporations. Right? Wrong.

Actually, the response to the tragedy in Haiti was more a blip on a not-so-stellar corporate philanthropy continuum. Here's a reality check: when measured as a percentage of profits, business grant making has actually been on a bumpy decline for well over two decades.

The erosion in corporate giving runs counter to the assumption many people have that companies are more supportive of nonprofit causes and programs now than they have been in the past. That's understandable, since the mainstream media include news stories and advertisements that point to businesses positioning themselves at the front of the line to provide help after some notable crisis. And in many instances, corporations do stand tall with their philanthropy. But too often, appearance looms larger than a company's actual responsiveness.

Even during the recession that officially began chewing up the U.S. economy in 2007, corporate grant making—with some notable exceptions—was notoriously sluggish. Although an abundance of companies (especially many of the 5.7 million smaller, privately held corporations that employ one or more workers) sustained or even increased their contributions during the two-year recession, many larger corporations—including highly profitable businesses—pulled back their philanthropy.

For companies that collapsed or operated in the red, it was reasonable to expect grant making to come to a halt (although some businesses such as Chrysler continued their philanthropy even while experiencing prolonged losses). But the recession didn't wipe out the earnings of the vast majority of U.S. corporations. Quite the contrary: in 2008, the nadir of the recession, U.S. companies earned $1.3 trillion in pretax profits, which gave them the capacity to be far more generous than they were that year. Instead of ramping up their giving to meet the mounting needs of those communities where they had a presence, too many of the country's largest businesses used the recession to challenge the fundamentals of corporate philanthropy by asking questions such as

- How can we possibly defend making charitable donations when we're laying off our own workers?
- Why should we continue matching employee (and sometimes, retiree) gifts when we are cutting other benefits?

- What's the point of supporting the United Way when we hear how many United Way organizations are dysfunctional or are overpaying their staffs?
- Why promote employee volunteerism when we need all hands on deck to keep our business afloat?
- Recession or no recession, why should corporations be making charitable contributions at all? We're in business to make a profit—shouldn't we be passing along our earnings to shareholders and owners so they can make their own donations?

These are not new questions for American businesses. They have lingered below the surface for decades and may help explain why over the past twenty-five-plus years, America's private sector *cut its charitable giving as a percentage of its profits by half.*

For some highly profitable businesses, the recession became a handy excuse to make even deeper cuts in their giving. Other companies were not as quick to slash their contribution budgets but became genuinely confused about what the appropriate level of charitable support should be.

A Stronger Business Case

The recession made it more obvious than ever before that a much more compelling *business* case for corporate contributions is badly needed—a case that definitively addresses the following:

- *Why* a business should carve out a portion of its earnings to assist nonprofit causes and programs
- *How much* of a company's pretax profits should be used for such purposes
- *What conditions* should be in place in order to justify the use of corporate resources for support of nonprofit organizations

In other words, a case that will measure up to Ralph Larsen's two-sided yardstick.

This is the underlying intent of *Smart Giving Is Good Business*—to give businesses a roadmap that will enable them to make a convincing case for corporate philanthropy—one that legitimizes when and how a company should use profits to pay for strategically positioned "conditional" contributions.

While doing consulting work for companies such as General Motors, Merck, Xerox, and Bank of America, I made a curious discovery. Top executives were struggling with several questions about corporate philanthropy—and most sounded remarkably similar. After I hired on with Johnson & Johnson to run its philanthropy program in the 1990s, the same questions surfaced. When I left J&J to launch a national trade association of corporate contributions professionals in 2000, ditto. Identical questions again flew over the transom from 150 different member companies. More recently, having returned to the corporate consulting world, I field inquiries from client companies such as Target, Novartis, Bausch & Lomb, Starbucks, and several others that all are echoes of the past.

I realized that whether a corporation is a huge multinational with revenues in the billions or a small mom-and-pop operation, executives tend to have very similar inquiring minds when it comes to framing a plan—*a case*—for giving away money, products, or employee time. Business leaders want concrete answers that will allow them to

1. Determine why a company should be in the corporate giving "business" at all
2. Decide what the minimum price of entry should be (assuming corporate philanthropy can be justified as a generally accepted business practice)
3. Identify value-added options for going beyond the "minimum" and the risk-benefits of being more than marginally generous

As noted, these are hardly new concerns. One of my first consulting clients, Tom Donohue, who managed the U.S. Chamber of Commerce Foundation, voiced them loud and clear. Tom would eventually leave the Chamber to climb the executive ladder at other trade associations and then return to the Chamber as its president and CEO. Tom presented me with a chance to get a crow's nest view of the private sector, and even thirty years ago, it wasn't hard to spot trouble brewing. The business of corporate philanthropy, it seemed, wasn't a business at all—it was too often viewed as a bottom-drawer function that rarely got much attention or respect by a company's line and staff. Yet Donohue, who has a tough exterior that covers up a goodly amount of compassion, thought corporate philanthropy deserved better. He helped me see that when effectively managed, the donation of company money and employee time could be more than a social tonic—the resources could also help a corporation advance its own business interests.

That perspective took on greater clarity during my many years of consulting when I worked with a mix of businesses in different industry sectors, including the health care giant Johnson & Johnson. At the time, J&J was among the most respected companies when it came to philanthropy. And for good reason. The corporation's simple but profound four-paragraph mission statement called its *Credo* mandated philanthropy as a business requirement. One of those paragraphs read (and still reads):

> We are responsible to the communities in which we live and work and to the world community as well. We must be good citizens—support good works and charities and bear our fair share of taxes. We must encourage civic improvements and better health and education. We must maintain in good order the property we are privileged to use, protecting the environment and natural resources.

It was J&J's strong commitment to the "support of good works and charities" that convinced me to join the corporation as a V.P. charged with handling its contributions program. I signed on for a five-year tour of duty, but nine years later, I was still at the company's impressive I. M. Pei–designed headquarters in downtown New Brunswick, New Jersey, managing a $150 million contributions budget, trying to fend off up to a hundred unsolicited donation requests a day, and having the time of my life.

The Tide Is Still Out

Just before the start of the new millennium, my professional conscience nagged me out of one of the best jobs in America. At about the same time my career clock was winding down, something else was inching downward as well. From 1990 through

1999, corporate contributions in the United States were shrinking. During the 1980s, corporate charitable giving was averaging about 2 percent of pretax profits (the decade-long range ran from 1.5 percent to 2.3 percent of before-tax earnings). When the 1990s arrived, business generosity started slipping until it nosedived to around seven-tenths of 1 percent. To put things in a more emphatic perspective: *on the basis of a percentage of earnings, for every $2.50 a company set aside for corporate philanthropy in the early 1980s, only $1 was earmarked for giving at about the time the new millennium arrived.*

It was time to at least try to turn the tide.

I left Johnson & Johnson the same year my book *Corporate Social Investing* was released. The book got a fair amount of attention thanks to prefaces written by legendary investment guru Peter Lynch and the late actor and entrepreneur Paul Newman. If the philanthropic world had a Hollywood Boulevard, these two men would be immortalized on the contributions Walk of Fame. When it comes to figuring how symbiotic corporate philanthropy can be to corporate success, these two truly understood the connection.

A year after the release of the book, it was apparent that the power of the pen had its limitations. Corporate giving—again, as a percent of profits—continued to sink. Paul Newman decided enough was enough. He joined with retired deputy secretary of state and retired co-chair of Goldman Sachs John Whitehead to launch an organization more exclusive than Augusta National Golf Club. Open only to corporate CEOs or chairmen, the group's purpose was to move the corporate contributions needle in the right direction.

I sat in on one of the earliest meetings of the Newman-Whitehead organization, where the still strikingly handsome movie star and king of his own line of salad dressings wondered out loud why his business (Newman's Own) could direct *all* its profits to worthwhile causes but U.S. corporations on average could barely scrape together 1 percent of their pretax profits for charity. For a time, Newman's new organization pondered setting a contributions spending target for U.S. companies but abandoned that idea when several CEOs pushed back. That development came as no surprise because almost every industry captain I have come to know sings the following refrain: don't turn charity into a tax.

Although Newman had to be disappointed that businesses couldn't agree on a minimum level of annual giving, he and Whitehead, along with the cadre of other CEOs who joined the organization (now called the Committee Encouraging Corporate Philanthropy), did manage to move the issue a little closer to the front of the stove.

Capacity Building Where It Counts the Most

While Newman and Whitehead were working the front office, I went about testing a different theory. Maybe, I thought, if the staffs charged with overseeing corporate contributions programs were afforded more business management skills, they could become more influential in convincing companies to increase their annual giving. The theory rested on a few untested suppositions:

- Suppose corporate philanthropy and community relations managers were to be put through a mini-MBA program customized to meet their particular job requirements?
- Suppose these staffers were given the kind of leadership skills that would amplify their voices and give them added standing so as to get senior management's serious attention?
- Suppose these middle managers could demonstrate how to leverage social investments to generate as much or more business benefit as advertising or marketing initiatives?
- Bottom line—suppose these people became such polished business professionals that they wouldn't be viewed as extraneous to the P&L interests of the corporation?

That theory and its interconnected suppositions led to the launch of the Contributions Academy—a venture that brought together small clusters of corporate giving administrators and pushed them through an intensive three-day program that included everything from budgeting to evaluation methodology, from strategic planning to leadership development.

Five years after the Academy was born, a group of graduates proposed recasting the loose-knit enterprise into a stand-alone, independent professional organization. Executives from Hasbro, Sony Electronics, Tupperware, Boeing, Northwestern Mutual, Becton Dickinson, Verizon, Johnson & Johnson, Novartis, and Chrysler took the lead and hammered together the framework for the Association of Corporate Contributions Professionals (ACCP). The organization grew with extraordinary speed, and within two years its membership stood at over 150 businesses representing more than $20 billion in annual cash and product contributions. I left ACCP in 2008 to return to the consulting world, but the organization continues to provide unparalleled professional training thanks to an exemplary board of directors and an outstanding management team.

With Newman and Whitehead working the top tier of business and ACCP grooming the professional staffers within the ranks of larger corporations, one would think companies would push the pedal on their philanthropy programs.

Such was not the case.

Questions: A Baker's Dozen

Just before the economic upheaval struck the United States and the world in 2007, business contributions continued to slip downward. In spite of Newman, Whitehead, and ACCP; in spite of philanthropy programs sponsored by the Conference Board, U.S. Chamber of Commerce, and the Council on Foundations; and in spite of higher education programs that addressed corporate giving issues at schools including Indiana University, Boston College, and UC-Berkeley—company grant making stayed stuck in low gear. Only because profits took such a beating in 2008 and 2009 did corporate philanthropy consume a slightly larger chunk of company earnings—but clearly that was an unintentional "benefit" of the sub-prime fiasco and the crumbling of Wall Street.

So where are we? With the exception of a few blips, businesses have fallen into a comfort zone where an acceptable level of corporate giving equates to doling out around 1 percent of before-tax profits. But here's the kicker—larger businesses are often spending *far* less than this on average. Yes, there were—and are—noteworthy exceptions. Some sizeable companies continue to spend 2 percent to 5 percent of their profits for good works. But these corporations are truly outliers. What has become obvious is that most U.S. businesses have not taken to heart what former Chase Bank chairman and CEO David Rockefeller told the New York Economic Club in 1996:

> "Business leaders appear to have devoted themselves to making more and more money and find themselves with less and less time to devote to civic and social responsibilities and to sinking roots in their communities...."

What appears to be standing in the way of a serious corporate philanthropy turnaround are a cluster of those previously mentioned hurdles that can so easily put a damper on efforts to bring the level of company giving back to where it once was. There are thirteen of these hurdles, a baker's dozen that *Smart Giving Is Good Business* has translated into the following questions:

1. Why should a company even consider making a charitable contribution?
2. Assuming a case can be made for corporate philanthropy, how much should a company give, minimum and maximum?
3. Who should decide which nonprofits get funded, and what criteria should be used to make those decisions?
4. What's the most effective role for a CEO when it comes to grant making?
5. Where should a company's contributions program be parked inside a company, and who should have the day-to-day responsibility of overseeing the giving process?
6. Should a company have a foundation?
7. Should corporations be donating products, services, or both—possibly as a preferred form of giving over cash donations?
8. How should businesses handle the onslaught of dinner and special event (such as golf outing) requests?
9. Should a company fund the United Way, or are there better options?

10. How should a company respond to a natural or manmade disaster?
11. Is it possible to measure the impact of a grant—including its impact on the company?
12. How much should a company say about its contributions, and when does promotion morph into out-and-out bragging that triggers negative public reaction?
13. How should a corporation handle its philanthropy if its profits tank?

Conditional Grant Making

Many of the answers to our baker's dozen hinge on a concept that for the past few years I've been calling "conditional grant making." The premise is based on this fundamental principle:

> Businesses have an obligation to shareholders, employees, and other stakeholders to be exceedingly careful and responsible in any contributions decision they make.

As Ralph Larsen was prone to remind me—when a company hands out a contribution it's doing so with someone else's money. A corporation could use those funds for an array of other business purposes. In some cases, that would include hiking a dividend to shareholders so *they* could make their own charitable choices.

But how can a company best ensure that its philanthropy is properly aligned with its business purposes? As a starter, make certain three basic *conditions* have been met before even thinking about making another contribution. These are the three essential lynchpins that can make the difference between a lackluster, largely irrelevant giving program and a vibrant, meaningful social investment venture.

Conditional Grant-Making Requirements

1. A crystal clear strategy and process that ensures corporate contributions are relevant to both society *and* the company (Ralph's yardstick)
2. A CEO and other senior executives who openly endorse smart giving—the donation of cash, product, and employee time

that yields a beneficial return on investment for society *and* the business itself

3. A day-to-day administrative system that provides for competent oversight of company contributions to ensure good intention doesn't dissipate into a bad outcome

By meeting these conditions, a company builds itself a platform for the kind of corporate philanthropy program that is more likely to expand than contract.

Intervention Time

The past couple of decades provide us with plenty of evidence that the future won't bring about much change in how the private sector thinks or acts in respect to corporate philanthropy. Corporate giving probably will stagnate at its current low level or possibly sink even lower. Unless—

- Forward-thinking CEOs rally for change. We need a new crop of David Rockefeller–type business leaders who will take the lead in advocating for responsible (a.k.a. conditional) corporate philanthropy on the part of all companies large or small.
- Businesses fully commit to smart giving. Adopting the principles presented in this book will get companies past the thirteen impediments that too frequently stand in the way of a corporate philanthropy rebound.
- Nonprofit organizations solicit businesses differently. Nongovernmental organizations (we will call them NGOs throughout this book) can do a lot to prime the corporate philanthropy pump if they come forward with the right kind of business-relevant proposals.

If corporate giving is resuscitated, businesses will be in a position to mine the benefits of a resource that regularly gets underused or totally ignored. NGOs will stand to gain big time. If *Smart Giving* funding recommendations are widely implemented, an estimated *$8 billion in cash* will get added to what companies annually allocate for nonprofit programs and activities.

But these end benefits won't be realized if the hurdles in our baker's dozen loom large and aren't cleared. If company leaders conclude that corporate giving really is nothing more than a self-imposed tax, game over. If the validity of corporate philanthropy is challenged more aggressively and executives don't have the right defense in place, for sure there won't be a surge in philanthropy spending. If NGOs pepper companies with generic appeals that have nothing to do with the business, don't look for a wave of new company contributions.

America's corporate philanthropy is currently mired in a not-so-impressive place. To get it unstuck, thirteen irksome questions need thirteen persuasive answers.

Why Should a Business Give at All?

This is what Nestle SA Chairman Peter Brabeck said during a London television interview:

> "I am personally very much against corporate philanthropy. You shouldn't do good with money that doesn't belong to you."

Brabeck is not alone in his thinking. Far from it. His reservations were echoed in a prominent *Wall Street Journal* article written by a University of Michigan professor who argued "The Case Against Corporate Social Responsibility." Aneel Karnani undoubtedly struck the right chord with some business leaders when he wrote:

> Managers who sacrifice profit for the common good also are in effect imposing a tax on their shareholders and arbitrarily deciding how that money should be spent.

There is no denying that a contingent of company senior executives would just as soon see corporate philanthropy disappear. But there are also CEOs who are willing to go along with company grant making if the level of giving is kept *way* under the radar. In my own unscientific surveying, I have found that most business leaders fall into a third category: company executives who think corporations should have the latitude to support charitable programs and causes but are looking for clear-cut guidelines to justify such expenditures and a framework for deciding what the most appropriate level of giving should be.

A lot of people have asked me, "Is corporate philanthropy something CEOs and other top executives actually even think twice about?" With everything that gets thrown on an executive's plate, it is difficult to conceive that grant-making issues could possibly work their way into the front office. But surprisingly they do.

"It's not that charitable contributions rank up there with mega-merger decisions or figuring out how to shut down a plant," one CEO told me. "But you can't escape them. People or organizations looking for donations eat up time and attention. And because solicitations are often made by friends or even family members, it's easy to get backed into a corner."

Most high-level company executives I have met over the years share the same complaint. They can't escape being hustled by family, friends, business acquaintances, golf club members, high school alumni—all of whom assume the executive should have no trouble putting a hand into the company's very deep pocket.

Executives don't relish being pestered (sometimes plagued) by unsolicited requests for company donations. But even more troublesome is dealing with an unhappy shareholder, a laid-off worker, or an inquisitive journalist looking for an explanation of why the company is making a charitable contribution when money could be used for so many other purposes seemingly more important to the corporate P&L.

The "Why?"

It is this last concern that brings us to the lead question drawn from our baker's dozen list:

Question 1: Why should a company give at all?

Answer: There are three primary reasons.

Moral and Social Responsibility

With all due respect to Peter Brabeck and the University of Michigan professor who views corporate social responsibility as deeply flawed, businesses do have an elemental obligation to do the right thing. And acting philanthropically is proper business behavior *if* a company is following the three principles for conditional grant making as outlined in our introduction.

This answer gets easier to grasp if you think about the similarities people and businesses have when it comes to philanthropy. People generally support causes and programs that are most meaningful to them. Corporations should do the same. Consider this: Americans who make charitable contributions each year donate 2.7 percent of their adjusted gross income to charity (for those over age sixty-five, the average giving level jumps to over 3 percent). Is it too much to expect a business to donate 1 percent to 2 percent of its profits (not its income)? The answer is "no—it's not" as long as a company's giving is directed toward business-relevant programs and activities.

To Benefit the Company

To some, this answer to "Why?" may not make sense. How can a charitable commitment benefit a donor and still be a legitimate contribution? The U.S. tax laws seem to make this kind of *quid pro quo* impossible. The Treasury Department says companies or individuals wanting to take a charitable tax deduction must make sure funds or properties are "transferred to a qualified organization without the donor's expectation that there will be a financial or economic benefit commensurate with the donation being made." So what benefit(s) can a company accrue without violating the tax code?

Properly directed, company donations can be used to affect conditions that influence a corporation's ability to function. Examples include enhanced company or brand name recognition, basic research that is a door-opener to discoveries that may have long-term commercial potential, community services that improve a plant location so it becomes a more desirable site for new hires, and the list goes on. The direct benefit a corporation receives may not be "commensurate with the donation being made." But the *indirect* advantages that come from making the right kind of contribution can be substantial.

In 2007, McKinsey & Company surveyed 721 executives to get a better perspective as to what business benefits should accrue from social efforts carried out by a corporation. Only 12 percent of respondents said there should be no business goals linked to a company's philanthropy activities. What executives *did* say they wanted from a corporation's social spending were

- Enhanced reputation for the company, brand, or both (70 percent)
- Bolstering of employee skills (44 percent)
- Improved employee respect and pride for the company (42 percent)
- A differentiation from competitors (38 percent)

If answering the "Why?" doesn't include an explanation about how corporate philanthropy affects a business, then we are circumventing our conditional grant-making principles. There *has* to be a defined connection between a gift and a business. Otherwise it probably shouldn't be made.

To Benefit Society

Businesses aren't exempt from playing a role in addressing social problems and challenges. So "Why?" has to include a statement that corporations are committed to leveraging contributions to make a difference to society. But the key is to aim donations of cash, product, and even employee time at causes and issues relevant to the company.

Go back to our company-is-like-a-person analogy. If you or a loved one is unfortunate enough to have cancer, you're inclined to make a donation to one of the more than seven thousand nonprofit organizations in the United States that work to prevent or cure cancer. In making the donation, your hope isn't that the gift will lead to a treatment breakthrough that will be helpful just to you. The contribution comes with a hope that it will be advantageous to anyone suffering from cancer. Apply that same line of thought to a company.

For example, during the 1990s, Johnson & Johnson, along with dozens of other pharmaceutical companies, put a high priority on finding a drug that would slow down or prevent Alzheimer's disease. But research was stymied because there were no mice that had the genetic make-up needed to carry out essential experiments. J&J awarded "basic research" grants to medical schools—funds used to breed mice that had the characteristics necessary for Alzheimer's research.

Because basic research findings are non-proprietary, whatever discoveries the grant produced would be in the public domain. Certainly J&J had a strong interest in developing mice that would move its own research forward. At the same time, the company recognized how important these mice would be to an array of other scientific experiments totally outside its commercial interests. The grants were legitimate charitable contributions that turned out to be a win for the corporation and a win for society.

Corporate Social Responsibility—A "Why?" or a "Way Out?"

Missing from our list of answers to "Why give?" is a call for businesses to live up to their corporate social responsibility (we'll call it CSR). The omission might seem strange to some. After all, CSR is a widely touted business notion that on the surface seems to be a bugle call for an increase in conditional grant making. In reality, too often CSR has had just the opposite effect on corporate philanthropy. With some exceptions, it has been a drag on the growth of smart giving. To understand why this has happened, here is a brief explanation of the often-confusing concept of CSR.

The idea that businesses have responsibilities that transcend their corporate walls has been around a long, long time. But during the 1970s, the concept began a more open relationship with business ethics, and by the 1980s and 1990s, the two had coupled and became all the rage—particularly in the academic community.

In the classroom, CSR (also called corporate citizenship, sustainable responsible business, and a host of other terms) is a thing of beauty. Public interest blends with corporate decision making and gives an added zing to the "triple bottom line": people, planet, and profit. When CSR hits the road, though, things change.

Over the years, I have pressed dozens of corporate executives to give me their take on CSR. "What does it mean to your company?" I would ask. Here are some of the answers I jotted down:

- Mainly showing we have decent environmental standards
- First, you have to be responsible to your own employees—reasonable labor practices
- Just doing the right thing all the time
- Quality control for whatever products we make
- Sustainable development
- Live up to fair trade policies
- Worker health and safety—mainly safety
- Ethics training for all employees

In other words, CSR has no consistent definition within the real corporate world. Attempts have been made to bring some agreed-upon clarity to the concept. For example, the Geneva-based International Organization for Standardization has come up with a proposed global set of standards for corporate responsibility called ISO 26000. And a few companies hold up "Deming's 14 Points" as the recommended standard for CSR. (Deming was an American statistician whose fourteen management action points became the foundation for the TQM or Total Quality Management movement.) But in spite of these efforts, CSR is largely amorphous and assumes different shapes and sizes depending on a company's interpretation of the concept.

One of the more comprehensive CSR reports that at least tries to link general CSR activities with contributions spending is produced annually by ExxonMobil (the company calls its statement, which usually runs fifty pages or more, a *Corporate Citizenship Report*). The central theme is "sustainability," which ExxonMobil defines as a balancing of economic growth, social development, and environmental protection. But what exactly does that mean?

ExxonMobil uses a third party (Lloyd's Register Quality Assurance) to validate its efforts to address several "citizenship focus areas." These include

- Corporate governance
- Safety, health, and the workplace
- Environmental performance
- Managing climate change risks
- Economic development
- Human rights and security

Part of the company's report is a breakdown of its philanthropy (what it calls "community investments"). In 2009, ExxonMobil awarded $235 million in grants, or about seven-tenths of 1 percent of its pretax profits—about the average level of giving for larger companies that year. The report attempted to show how these contributions as well as employee volunteerism intersected other CSR categories throughout the year. The attempt fell short in a few areas—but ExxonMobil deserves credit (as do a few other businesses) for at least trying to demonstrate what should be a connection between contributions and other CSR interests.

The BP Case

CSR critics complain that too many companies use corporate responsibility rhetoric as a cover—that words and hype mask genuine commitment and meaningful action. (In his *Wall Street Journal* article, Professor Aneel calls the tactic "greenwashing.") Nothing helped that argument more than the Gulf of Mexico crisis that vilified the oil giant BP as the culprit most responsible for America's worst environmental disaster.

Ironically, years before a series of accidents that led up to the Gulf pipeline calamity, BP had branded itself as a global CSR leader. Lord John Browne, who led the company from the mid-1990s until his resignation in 2007, promoted BP as the leading "green" energy business. The corporation developed a green logo and produced slick publications that trumpeted its CSR advocacy.

In addition to numerous inside-the-company CSR initiatives, BP also ballyhooed its external social responsibility efforts. Here are excerpts from a 2002 speech by the company's VP for global social investment:

> Today the over-arching social goal that inspires us everywhere is the concept of sustainable progress. Clearly the definition of this progress can vary. In some places it means supporting capacity building. In others it means helping education or health care reform. Or it may mean underwriting job creation schemes or conservation projects or moves to achieve greater self-sufficiency.

> Last year we invested nearly $95 million on social initiatives globally... One-third of BP's contributions went to community development, 30% to education and 15% to environment and health.

> The range of projects is vast—everything from aiding small farmers in Colombia to underwriting female adult literacy in Angola, heightening environmental awareness among children in China, teaching corporate governance in Zambia, encouraging clean business in Poland and comforting cancer patients in Egypt. Not to mention scores of initiatives in Europe and North America.

Sounds good, right? With a $95 million contributions program, no wonder BP cited itself as a frontrunner in the CSR field. But let's add some perspective to this story. BP's contributions payout for 2001 equaled seven-tenths of 1 percent of the $13 billion in pretax profits it earned for the year. The payout wasn't that out of line with what many other mega-sized corporations were spending on philanthropy that year. But note that this was about *half* the average level of corporate giving for 2001 (the business community in total donated around 1.3 percent of its aggregate pretax net income).

For those looking to debunk CSR, BP served (and still serves) as a classic case. When a company shouts about its response to social challenges but doesn't even make par with its social investments, then it has wandered into risky territory. Of course, BP could probably point to other CSR projects conducted outside the contributions arena that probably cost more than $95 million. And that comeback is exactly why CSR has contributed to the downward trend in corporate grant making.

CSR "In Lieu Of" Corporate Contributions

CSR efforts that are largely internal in focus—for example, employee ethics training, environmental improvements, diversity outreach, workplace safety changes, and so on—can be expensive. A business can easily rationalize that these often costly initiatives have just as much value—maybe even *more* value—than any program folded into its contributions program. "We need to ensure the safety and well-being of our employees before we worry about funding the local symphony so it can add a bassoonist," the corporation might conclude.

And that's the CSR jab to the corporate contributions jaw that's been a problem over the years. I have had conversations with executives who complain they are under so much pressure to pay for CSR-prompted internal changes that even thinking about a hike in corporate giving borders on absurdity.

My counterpunch to these statements is that when considering what to spend on grant making, don't lump corporate contributions with whatever else a company may have bundled under the CSR umbrella. Most all the internal CSR-related adjustments are carried as usual business expenses and taken into account before a company figures out its profit and loss for the year. A company's conditional grant-making payout should be tied directly to a company's pretax earnings—earnings that are calculated after all other internal CSR expenses have been paid.

Smart Giving and CSR

Where corporations too often fall short in their CSR strategic planning is to overlook how grant making can be used as a fuel line for at least some of the firm's most important social responsibility activities. It would behoove any company to identify all its CSR objectives and then think creatively about how smart giving could address those goals. For example, suppose BP had spent more of its annual contributions on funding environmental protection methods and standards at universities and research institutions known for their expertise in oil and mineral exploration. Such basic research grants may have generated information useful to the petroleum industry as a whole—and who knows, they possibly might have prevented the crisis in the Gulf of Mexico.

BP's retort might be that the company *does* make these types of grants. True—*after* the Gulf oil spill, the company pledged a half billion dollars for a Gulf of Mexico research initiative, including three grants totaling $25 million to southern universities working on oil and dispersant technologies. But a review of the company's publicly reported giving *prior* to the Gulf crisis shows similar commitments to be relatively minor.

"But had this kind of sharply focused conditional grant making been going on before the oil spill, it might have resulted in a reduction of BP support for adult literacy programs in Angola or projects to help farmers in Colombia," some would complain. If the company had kept its giving level at a comparatively low level, yes, that's probably what would have happened. It's the reality of any kind of philanthropy—choices have to be made. For businesses, smart giving means making smart choices.

So CSR *could* be added to our list of answers for "Why give?" *if* companies (a) clearly identify what those CSR objectives are; and (b) use conditional grant-making principles to find ways of directing resources (contributions and employee time) to address those CSR issues.

When "Why?" Goes Awry

There's a right answer to "Why give at all?"—

> We carefully manage our corporate philanthropy as a unique type of business resource. We use cash and product donations to address critical problems and quality-of-life issues and to advance important opportunities that have a clear relevance to our business. Managed this way, our philanthropy is beneficial to both society and our company.

And there's a wrong answer—

> We support causes and organizations on behalf of our senior management and other employees. We view contributions as an added employee benefit with special consideration given to our highest-level executives.

The ugly truth is that the "wrong answer" is sometimes the dominant (albeit nontransparent) answer within certain businesses. The corporate giving pot sometimes gets turned into a slush fund for top-tier executives and on occasion even outside board members. The rationale is that contributions become inducements for retaining high-quality talent.

The slush fund shouldn't be confused with set-aside funds for employee matching gifts—limited and controlled commitments that ride on the back of employee or retiree donations. These are vastly different from free-standing $25,000, $50,000, or $100,000 unrestricted gifts that are fired off to the CEO's alma mater as a way of giving the executive added status (plus a V.I.P. box seat at the fall homecoming game).

Peter Brabeck has every right to be critical of a corporate philanthropy program that in essence is a CEO's personal cash drawer. His displeasure with corporate philanthropy is also understandable if a company simply "gives for the sake of giving" and doesn't have a conditional grant-making management model in place.

Even for smaller businesses, a corporate philanthropy program doesn't have to be (and shouldn't be) a private cash register for upper-tier management. It can be (and should be) a much more powerful resource that brings added value to the company and society.

Widget Worldwide and the "Why?"

In running workshops and speaking to both business and non-profit audiences, I have used a brief quasi–case study to underscore two points: (a) how top corporate executives sometimes are driven to the brink by—of all things—corporate contributions and (b) how to come up with an acceptable answer to the question "Why give at all?"

The following case is an amalgamation of many experiences I have had with senior managers over the years. The company is a fictional *Fortune* 500 manufacturing firm with its headquarters in New York City. But the business could be just about anywhere in the United States, and the CEO you will meet next could be Peter Brabeck or maybe the frazzled, pressured individual running a company you work for.

THE WIDGET CASE

"Do we have to?" Charles "Chuck" Gilfant asked me. Six months in the hot seat at Widget Worldwide, Inc., and a profit squeeze had the CEO bottom feeding for nickels and dimes.

"Nope, you don't have to," I answered. "This isn't a tax."

"Isn't it?" Chuck wasn't buying it. "As far as I'm concerned, it's a self-inflicted tax. Businesses making gifts to charity—I mean, what the hell is that all about? We're *not* philanthropists, you know. So why is it that every Mr. Good Shoes running a charity thinks companies should be giving the store away?"

There was a reason Chuck Gilfant wasn't in a benevolent mood. Widget hadn't met analyst expectations for the second quarter in a row. Sales were flat, and profits, although still respectable, weren't respectable enough for analysts, which meant Chuck had to start cutting costs even if it meant looking for loose change in all the wrong places.

"Your top line hasn't been growing the way you might like, but you're still making money and a lot of it," I reminded Gilfant. Widget had pretax profits of $940 million last year.

"Not enough," Chuck responded quickly. "Since sales are going nowhere, I need to cut costs to move my next quarter's profit in the right direction. And I'm talking about *all* costs. Corporate contributions won't get a pass. No matter how pretty you package them, donations are still expenses, and they're on the block."

"Suppose contributions were expenses that improved the business?" I asked. "Suppose they helped put into place the right conditions so Widget had a better shot at improving sales?"

"Yeah, right," was the comeback. "And suppose Wall Street starts regulating itself. Some things aren't meant to happen. Fact is, we've got hundreds of charities sucking millions out of us each year. I want as many of those hustlers as possible to get their fingers out of my cookie jar. Can that be done?"

"Sure," I advised. Like most consultants, I learned long ago never to say no to a client. "But how about taking a breath before swinging the hatchet?"

Widget's top dog gave me one of those looks usually reserved for McKinsey or Booz Allen Hamilton when they pushed for more billing hours.

Why Should Widget Give at All?

"A couple of minutes ago, you asked if Widget had to give to charity. Rephrase the question: *Why* should Widget Worldwide be making any tax-deductible charitable contributions?"

"Exactly!" Chuck yelped. *"Why?"*

"Once you tackle that question, it will be easier to sort out what donations you should be making and what others should be dropped."

Gilfant asked what needed to be done to answer the "why." A two-hour meeting with senior managers from line operations, R&D, public affairs, legal, tax, and public relations would be a good way to start, I told him.

"My office?" Chuck wanted to know.

"Nope," I said. "You're not involved."

Gilfant looked apprehensive but relented. Two weeks later, I was sitting in a conference room with nine of Widget's top-drawer executives. After a few preliminaries, I walked to a flipchart and drew four imperfect squares. I spelled out one word in each panel. Strengths. Weaknesses. Opportunities. Threats.

There were a few muffled moans, and it was obvious that a couple of managers were about to run for a pee break. The group was being subjected to another "SWOT" exercise—the over-used management analytical process developed by a Stanford University professor back in the sixties. SWOTs were as commonplace to seasoned executives as internal audits—and sometimes just as aggravating.

"Sit through this and you get to name Chuck Gilfant's next grandkid," I joked, and the room relaxed.

The ``SWOT`` Exercise

"Top of mind, give me a few items to fill in the squares," I requested. In less than five minutes, the squares were full.

SWOT

Strengths

- Widget number one in sales in three product categories
- Strong brand recognition
- Solid senior management leadership

Weaknesses

- New product development—lackluster pipeline
- Attracting/retaining high-caliber workers

- Lack of respect (not on *Fortune*'s "Most Admired Companies" list)

Opportunities

- Business growth outside the U.S. (especially China)
- Expanded U.S. government contracting
- Second-generation product launch of Widget's most popular product

Threats

- Competition
- Government regulators
- Environmental restrictions

"Tell me what corporate contributions have to do with anything you see on the flipchart," I said.

A chorus of "absolutely nothing" filled the room. I ripped off the SWOT page and taped it to the conference wall. "So if Widget Worldwide's contributions program has nothing to do with this—" I waved at the sheet, "why does the company keep mailing checks to a slew of different charities?"

I used a blank flipchart sheet to catch the responses until I ran out of room:

- Dinner fundraisers
- Golf outings
- CEO and outside board member pet causes
- Appeals made by big customers
- United Way arm twisting
- Employee matching gifts
- Other local CEOs make the "ask"
- Meeting diversity obligations
- General public relations
- Tax deductions

I pulled the second sheet from the flipchart easel and taped it next to the SWOT page.

"Any connection between one page and the other?" I asked.

"Maybe a little," the marketing VP answered. "But not much."

I nodded in agreement and sat down.

"Now let me ask each of you something personal," I said. "What's your favorite charity?"

A flurry of reactions came from all parts of the room. American Heart Association. M.I.T. Kit Carson Museum. Habitat for Humanity. I stopped them when the list grew to fifteen organizations.

"What about making personal contributions to other causes that aren't at the top of the list?" I asked.

There was another volley of responses.

"Church."

"Salvation Army".

"Red Cross—if there's a disaster."

"Boy Scouts."

"My kid's school fund-raisers."

I could have scribbled for another five minutes. But I had culled enough information to get to the point.

"Each of you has a pretty solid answer to *why* when it comes to your personal charitable giving. Your highest priority is connected to something you define as very important to your own life and interests. Then there's a second tier of giving that's triggered for different reasons—like a sense of obligation or maybe a neighbor who won't take no for an answer."

There were chuckles, nods, and shrugs. I stood and walked back to the two taped flipchart pages hanging on the wall. "But when you look at these two sheets, priorities and giving practices don't line up the same way," I stated. "The *why* isn't at all clear for Widget Worldwide except when the company caves in to an obnoxious customer every once and awhile."

No one argued the point.

"So other than a nice thing to do for a few folks inside the company—including your CEO, I might add—or trying to make a customer or two feel good, we come up short on figuring out *why* Widget is spending money on contributions at all."

This was a group of high-level execs who probably gave corporate philanthropy no more than five minutes' worth of attention during the course of a year. As expected, there wasn't a single person in the room who pushed back.

"Since the *why* is fuzzy at best," I continued, "it's not surprising Chuck Gilfant is ready to do major surgery on the company's giving program. Right?"

Widget's philanthropy spending was no skin off anyone's nose in the room. As long as the corporation's gifts and grants had no direct impact on an executive's own budget, the general attitude was one huge *"Who cares?"*

Inserting Business Relevance into the ``Why?''

Now it was table-turning time.

"But suppose Widget's contributions program *did* happen to be connected to the company's business mission," I conjectured.

"Then it wouldn't be charity," the VP of finance contended.

"Charity's always been a loose concept," I replied, glancing at the tax man seated at the end of the conference table. "For example, in the eyes of the IRS, a donation that adds to Harvard's multibillion-dollar endowment is charity. It gets the same charitable tax deduction benefit as a gift to a nonprofit that feeds the poor. See what I mean?"

Widget's top financial guy scrunched his eyebrows. He wasn't quite sure if I had just insulted his alma mater or was simply making the point that the IRS definition of a public "charity" was akin to the wide open spaces where a million education, religious, scientific, literary, public safety, and even some amateur sports organizations dotted the crowded landscape.

"What if we put together a contributions strategy that points Widget's donations—or at least a good chunk of those donations—toward its biggest problems or its best opportunities for growth?"

Skepticism took over the room. I grabbed a Sharpie marker and drew a thick line under the SWOT subhead "Weaknesses," and then another line under "New Product Development."

"If you had a million dollars a year to spend on research in the product development field," I asked the R&D head, "could you use it?"

No hesitation. "Yes."

"What if the money had to be used for *basic* research, which the tax law says is the advancement of scientific knowledge not having a specific commercial objective? Now, understand—basic research means that whatever discoveries are made are up for grabs. Everyone and every company gets a crack at what comes out of the lab. Absolutely no proprietary rights for the company making the donation. Even under those conditions, could you still use the money?"

"Definitely," the R&D chief nodded. "The trick is to use basic research as a kind of scan. You get a first-hand look at what's promising, and if you find something interesting, switch gears. Shift from basic research to contract research. Once you get protected rights, start massaging a discovery into a commercial opportunity."

"You think you could find universities and nonprofit research institutes interested in doing the kind of basic research that might eventually open up new business avenues for Widget?"

"I already have a couple of candidates in mind."

The Earmarking Process

For the next half hour, the group pulled apart the SWOT list and mapped out a contributions option for each entry under the "Weaknesses," "Opportunities," and "Threats" listings on the flipchart.

- Weakness: attracting/retaining high-caliber workers

Widget Worldwide consistently had trouble getting first dibs on recruiting the best and brightest graduates from targeted universities. Widget's attractiveness as an employer could be affected by a few strategically placed donations, the HR vice president predicted. As for retaining workers, employee-centered programs such as matching gifts could make a difference if they were more widely promoted. Right now, the VP acknowledged, matching gifts were mainly perks for upper management.

- Weakness: Absence from *Fortune*'s "Most Admired Companies" List

A company can't buy its way onto this oft-referenced list using contributions. However, by getting information about Widget's contribution accomplishments to the hundreds of executives annually polled by researchers on behalf of *Fortune,* Widget might be able to climb its way up the magazine's sub-category list of companies admired for their "social responsibility." Funding the right programs and communicating Widget's efforts at the right time to the right audience is what it would take, I advised the group.

- Opportunity: Business growth in China

Calling on qualified nonprofit organizations in the United States as funding conduits, Widget could underwrite programs (approved by appropriate government ministries) in key locations within China that would build company name awareness ahead of planned product launches. The executive vice president charged with international market development asked for organization examples. "King Baudouin Foundation, Charities Aid Foundation, U.S. Committee for UNICEF and a long list of others all have tax standings in the United States that will allow Widget to route a donation to another country and still get a domestic charitable tax deduction," I answered.

- Opportunity: Expanded U.S. government contracting

In developing and launching an awards-based programming strategy, Widget could acknowledge high-performing nonprofits that would be recognized at ceremonies in Washington or at selected state capitals. The events would give Widget significant exposure in front of key government decision makers, with award recipients reminding elected officials and their staffers that Widget is a decent corporate citizen. The government relations and public affairs director looked intrigued.

- Opportunity: Second-generation product launch

By capitalizing on liberal tax deductions that come from donating certain products to qualified nonprofit groups, Widget could get around disposal and inventory carrying charges if the company contributed first-generation products prior to the introduction of a new line.

With only a few minutes of meeting time left, I polled the room. "What do you think?"

"If our contributions program actually looked like this, it shouldn't be cut," the CFO stated. "But the problem is, your whole scenario is fiction."

"Doesn't have to stay that way," I replied. "And frankly, it shouldn't."

The PR vice president had been unusually quiet throughout the meeting—maybe because the corporate contributions administrator was his direct report. "You forget that we're already making contributions to hundreds of charities. They may not line up with our business goals, but to chop them off at the knees will stir up the kind of community stink that can hurt us big time."

"You're right," I conceded. I had learned long ago that you don't argue publicly with a public relations pro. "So let's not chop. Instead, why not ask at least some of these organizations to come to Widget with requests that are consistent with a new set of contribution guidelines—guidelines that mesh with the company's business priorities."

"And if they can't?" the chief counsel, and the only woman in the room, asked.

"Then in the kindest and sometimes most gradual way possible, they should be moved off the list."

I could tell the PR vice president had the feeling I was chewing away at his authority. After all, corporate philanthropy was supposed to be his domain. And here I was, Chuck Gilfant's alter ego, revamping the rules of the philanthropic game. The ball had to be bounced back to PR—and fast.

"What I'd like to tell Chuck is before anyone tampers with Widget's giving program, your department should have a shot at piecing together a plan that ties philanthropy to the company's business priorities. What do you think?"

Clout Trumps a Cut

A month later, Chuck Gilfant called me to his office. "This is freakin' unbelievable!" he squawked. "PR turned in spending projections for next year and they've got corporate contributions up by 20 percent!"

"Terrific work, isn't it?" I volleyed back.

"You were supposed to help them *cut* contributions!"

"They made some cuts," I confirmed.

"Yeah, but they *added* a boatload of new donations!" Gilfant whined.

"All hooked up with some of Widget's most important business goals."

"Look what's happened!" Chuck gritted his teeth. "You've pushed our contributions total to nearly 1 percent of this year's pretax profit forecast!"

"And well worth the investment," I said.

Here's the moral of this purposely exaggerated story.

Answering "Why should a company give?" makes a lot more sense if the corporation's philanthropy relates to its own interests and purposes. If a company's policy is to simply "give for the sake of giving" or makes donations based on the personal inclinations of its management, board of directors, or others, then it is far more difficult to make a case that justifies a corporation allocating resources for outside nonprofit organizations.

This statement does, however, need a caveat.

Company Size and Structure Have an Impact on the "Why?"

If a company is solely owned or closely held, contributions might legitimately reflect the personal interests of the owner(s). In effect, a corporate donation becomes an extension of (or, in some cases, a substitution for) a direct personal gift. The early days of Paul Newman's company, Newman's Own, is a good example. The company started as a garage operation by Newman and his friend, author Aaron Edward Hotchner. The pair decided that all profits from the sale of products ranging from salad dressing to spaghetti sauce would be given to charity. Most of the organizations picked to get Newman's Own donations were those charities favored by the owners. This is not that hard to do when those who control the company can fit around a kitchen table.

But when a corporation expands its owner base, trying to satisfy the charitable interests of its shareholders gets challenging. Warren Buffett's company, Berkshire Hathaway, is a classic case study of a business that went overboard in trying to accommodate the philanthropic concerns of its multiple owners. The company ran a "shareholder-designated" contributions program from 1981 until 2003. Under the plan, holders of the company's class A shares could designate a per-share amount that the business then donated to up to three 501c3 organizations each year. Nearly $200 million was distributed through the program, with funds going to a diverse assortment of nonprofits. With no ability to control where shareholder-designated donations were directed, Berkshire eventually stepped into quicksand—notably the pro-choice, pro-life squabble. After coming under fire from protestors, Berkshire announced that it was shutting down the program.

Businesses that have a multitude of shareholders typically make an extra effort to navigate away from donations to controversial causes or organizations. Given what happened to AT&T in 1990, it's understandable why businesses are gun shy about taking chances with their contribution dollars. The giant phone company had been a long-time supporter of Planned Parenthood until pressured by pro-life groups to cease and desist. When the company cut its $50,000-a-year grant, Planned Parenthood awakened the pro-choice forces with full-page ads that read, "Caving in to Extremists, AT&T Hangs Up On Planned Parenthood." Pro-life advocates fired back and the company found itself caught in a crossfire. The episode has become an epic case study of how businesses need to circle around groups or projects that have the faintest scent of controversy.

The Doing Good-Business Success Link

Since 1935, when Congress gave businesses the prerogative of taking a charitable gift as a tax write-off, some philanthropy advocates have contended that a company's generosity can and often does have an impact on its overall P&L performance. A lot of anecdotes have been used over the years to back up that point of view. But in 2006, researchers dug deeper to find if there really is a correlation between philanthropy and business achievement.

When a trio of accounting professors from New York University and the University of Texas conducted a study encompassing 251 businesses to test the theory that philanthropy had an effect on sales and earnings, a lot of corporations and charities paid attention to the findings and continue to do so. As well they should.

Using a kind of credible scientific data analysis rarely applied to the corporate contributions field, here is the key take-away from the study:

> The analysis we perform supports our conclusion that charitable contributions by U.S. companies enhance future revenue growth.

Predictably, the study found consumer companies benefit the most by "doing good." Consumer-focused businesses (particularly retailers and financial services) tend to leverage contributions in a way that promotes revenue growth. The researchers found less evidence that philanthropy has any significant impact on the financial performance of business-to-business corporations. By my observation of scores of companies, this is largely because B-to-B firms simply do not work as hard as consumer businesses to wring value out of their philanthropy programs.

Harvard Business School's Rosabeth Moss Kanter, a long-time corporate researcher, has come to the conclusion that business performance and societal contributions are intimately connected. In her book *Supercorp*, Kanter says this:

> Societal initiatives undertaken largely without direct profit motives are part of the culture that builds high performance and thus results, ironically, in profits.

Kanter calls corporations that have figured out the value of hooking business practices with social responsibility *the vanguard*. I call them *comprehensive corporate citizens*. Regardless of the label, the point is that top-performing companies have figured out how to marry social responsibility—including an acceptable level of conditional grant making—with their pursuit of revenue and earnings.

"Why give at all?" prompts many valid answers that debunk Peter Brabeck's aversion to corporate philanthropy. Frankly, there simply is no excuse for a company to circle around corporate giving if it adheres to our conditional grant-making principles. Far more challenging questions include "How much should we give?" and "How can we get the most bang for our buck?" Check the following chapters in *Smart Giving Is Good Business* for answers.

IN SUMMARY

Question 1: Why should a company give?

Answer: Like any concerned and responsible citizen, a corporation has a moral obligation to support charities and socially important initiatives. However, businesses must meet this obligation by making philanthropy decisions based on conditional grant-making principles. When doing so, corporations will address those social needs that are aligned with the company's purposes and interests.

2

What's the Right Amount to Give?

Of all the questions on our baker's dozen list, this is the one that gets asked the most. Senior executives are perplexed by how much or how little to put on the table for charitable giving purposes.

"To me this is a no-win deal," a CEO once told me. He agreed that companies should be philanthropic, but just *how* philanthropic was his dilemma. "I approve a budget that's too heavy with contributions, and I get shareholder complaints. I cut our giving level, and the company is accused of being a cheap, socially irresponsible business. I have to pick my poison."

What would *really* make a difference, this same CEO said (and many of his peers agree) is being able to fall back on a generally accepted *standard* that *all* businesses could use to establish their annual giving payouts.

Smart Giving Is Good Business is here to help.

The Comprehensive Corporate Citizen

There are many criteria used to judge a company's overall social responsibility—fair treatment of employees, environmental practices, quality of its products or services, general ethical conduct, and so on. Sometimes corporate philanthropy is on that list. Sometimes it isn't. It should be.

Most companies I have encountered contend they are respectable corporate citizens and then back up those claims with a few impressive examples. Even if corporate philanthropy isn't top of mind as a social responsibility "must," businesses can always point to an illustration or two of how effective their contribution program happens to be.

Here's the problem—

A company that spends a smidgeon of its pretax profits for grant making will often tout its philanthropic efforts just as loudly as a corporation far more financially committed to philanthropy. Somehow it doesn't seem fair that a firm notoriously cheap when it comes to making contributions gets to stand on the same "decent corporate citizen" platform as a business that's much more generous and usually a lot smarter with its giving.

The answer to our second question is, in effect, a turnstile. It allows companies that meet a minimum giving standard to join a community of what we will call *comprehensive corporate citizens*. The contention is that businesses can ballyhoo their corporate responsibility all they want (virtually every business already does this)—but to be a *comprehensive* corporate citizen, a business has to commit to funding its philanthropy at a level specified in the answer to our next question.

Question 2: What's the right amount to give?

Answer: A minimum cash commitment of 1 percent of a company's anticipated current year pretax profits, which entitles a business to be labeled a comprehensive corporate citizen.

For some companies, this answer is going to mean a major overhaul of their contributions budgets. Given that likelihood, let me make the strongest plea possible for making this "1 percent" target an accepted giving standard for all businesses.

Why Base Giving Targets on a Percentage of Pretax Profits?

Giving as a percentage of pretax profits is the yardstick that for a long time has been commonly used to gauge corporate contributions. It is considered to be a fair means of assessing where a company stands relative to what other businesses are doing in the philanthropy field (although there are definitely critics of this means of comparing corporate giving programs). When all business donations nationwide are added up for a year and all corporate pretax earnings are aggregated for the same time period, we are able to get a clear picture of corporate philanthropy trends in the United States.

Corporate contributions—on average—have slipped to around 1 percent of pretax income, and with the exception of the blip caused by the 2007–2009 recession, there has been very little upward movement in the level of company grant making (Table 2.1).

Although the national average for corporate philanthropy hovers around 1 percent, keep in mind that many businesses (especially many larger corporations) have contribution payouts far below 1 percent of pretax profits. At the other end of the contributions spectrum, there are a few businesses that have giving programs four or five times more sizeable than the country's average.

Most companies tend to view contributions with a kind of herd mentality. By staying in the middle of the pack, they lower the

Table 2.1. Corporate Giving as a Percentage of Pretax Profits.

Year	Pretax Income ($ billion)	Charitable Contributions ($ billion)	Percentage of Pretax Income
2001	720.8	11.7	1.6
2002	762.8	10.8	1.4
2003	892.2	11.1	1.2
2004	1,195.1	11.4	1.0
2005	1,609.5	16.6	1.0
2006	1,784.7	15.3	0.8
2007	1,774.4	15.7	0.9
2008	1,462.7	14.5	1.2
2009	1,427.6	14.3	1.1
2010	Actual/expected contributions level:		1.0

Sources: Bureau of Economic Analysis—U.S. Dept. of Commerce; National Bureau of Economic Research; Giving USA Foundation; IRS Statistics of Income.

risk of being criticized for unconventional behavior by a horde of special interest groups that continuously circle the private sector. When it comes to deciding how much—or how little—a company should spend on charity, being a "minnow in the middle" is a preferred place to be for many businesses.

The Internal Revenue Service allows corporations to deduct up to 10 percent of their pretax profits for qualified charitable donations. Few ever reach that level of giving. However, back in the mid-1980s, the percentage-of-pretax giving average *was nearly* twice *what it is today.* Why? There is no particular reason except that different years spawn different safe harbors where herds tend to migrate.

Corporations spend a lot of time keeping tabs on one another. You can't be sure where the middle is if you don't regularly check on where your cohort happens to be. So "benchmarking" becomes a commonplace phenomenon, with company surveys and industry comparisons used to pluck out information that's kept readily available in case a CEO asks the inevitable, "Where does our giving program stand in comparison to our competitors?"

While the percentage-of-pretax income calculation has become the common metric for comparing corporate contributions, it creates issues for some businesses. Take highly profitable companies as an example. Pushing some of these well-to-do corporations to keep pace with the national corporate philanthropy pretax percentage "average" would require a *really* large financial outlay, in some cases so large that top executives worry about charitable contributions morphing into a red flag that might uncork shareholder distress.

The 1 Percent Logic

Making a business case for moving *all* corporations to commit a minimum of 1 percent of their forecasted current-year pretax earnings for contribution purposes does not seem out of line *if* the case rests on our three conditional grant-making principles:

- A strategy and process to ensure all contributions are relevant to both society and the company

- Open CEO and senior executive endorsement of smart giving decisions that yield a return on investment to society and the corporation
- An administrative system that provides for competent business-focused, day-to-day oversight of a company's contributions program

Even if a business is committed to these principles, coming up with a budget equal to 1 percent of projected current-year earnings will be a high mountain to climb. The reason is that earnings projections are usually considered top secret. Ask anyone working in the company's finance department for that information, and you'll probably hear, "We keep our sales and earnings predictions for the year under lock and key. There's no way those numbers are going to be leaked to the contributions manager."

This a financial reality for most businesses. Corporations are disinclined to release earnings forecasts for the year—even to those inside the company. So if you can't get this carefully guarded or constantly moving number, than how can you get close to targeting a 1 percent contributions budget? There is actually a mathematical way around this obstacle—more on this later. But before outlining this new approach, consider two more points that help make the case for our 1 percent recommendation.

1 Percent: A Reasonable "Ante-Up" Minimum

Anybody who's ever played poker knows that the usual way of getting into a game requires putting money in the "pot." The price of playing is an up-front commitment of a predetermined amount of cash. If you don't "ante up," you don't get cards.

The "ante up" for businesses in the corporate philanthropy field should be a budget commitment of 1 percent of the current year's projected before-tax profits. This is the level of charitable giving that "buys" a company the prerogative of calling itself a comprehensive corporate citizen. Businesses motivated to allocate even more than 1 percent can add to the pot. These additional commitments are all optional and can come in different forms. But give careful attention to this point: *the "ante up" is an all-cash deal.*

As will be spelled out in later chapters, a corporation can define a contribution in many different ways. A donation can be a check, product, land, a building, or even a service or volunteered time. There are many tax and public relations benefits that come from making donations other than cash. However, not every company has access to these non-cash giving options that include attractive tax benefits (for example, banks and insurance firms don't have any "product" to donate other than dollars and cents, whereas manufacturing companies have a slew of product-giving choices). That being the case, it seems reasonable to expect those businesses with product-giving potential should kick in an "entry fee" *in cash* before capitalizing on these supplemental benefits.

While corporate equity is one reason why cash is the required "ante up," fairness to the nonprofit world is another. As mentioned, donating product and certain types of services can yield lots of advantages for a company. Nonprofit organizations that accept non-cash donations don't always walk away with as many benefits. The following story is an example.

PRODUCT GIVING'S BENEFITS AND BURDENS

An international relief organization is contacted by a large pharmaceutical company that has several pallets of an over-the-counter drug one year away from being phased out to make room for a second-generation product. The company wants to donate the pallets to the relief agency.

The drug has a fair market value of $1 million, which is an attractive lure for the international organization (a nonprofit can declare the fair market value of donated goods as revenue). But the nonprofit agency will incur a lot of out-of-pocket cash expenses in going forward with the deal—shipping, handling, inventory cost accounting, reporting, finding overseas clinics and hospitals that will use the drugs appropriately, and so on.

The company, on the other hand, is richly rewarded for the deal. It will get a very handsome added tax deduction and avoid an expensive drug disposal charge or an inventory carrying charge.

The example points out that while there's nothing wrong with product donations, the business benefits that stem from these contributions are so substantial that the process can stretch the meaning of "charitable intent" to its limits. This underlines the recommendation that corporations looking to donate products should include a minimum cash "ante-up" component as part of their giving programs.

Something else shouldn't be counted as part of the "ante-up" minimum—the estimated value of employee volunteer time. Some businesses use Labor Department statistics to calculate how much a nonprofit organization would have to pay in order to hire the manpower a company's employee volunteers provide. A few corporations then fold this dollar estimate together with whatever cash or product donations they make to come up with a contributions total. Since current tax laws don't allow volunteer hours to be expensed as charitable deductions, they need to be off the "ante-up" table.

First Rung on a Corporate Citizenship "Ladder"

By "anteing up," a company moves across an important charitable giving threshold. For some and probably even most businesses, budgeting contribution payouts to equal at least 1 percent of projected current-year profits will be sufficient to fuel their comprehensive contributions programs going forward. Many corporations won't be motivated to go beyond this point. But for other businesses, the "ante up" will just be the starting point for building a much larger philanthropy program.

Corporations looking to use their contributions as a way of generating greater market awareness, polishing their reputations or solidifying or opening customer channels may make significantly larger investments via their respective philanthropy programs. By going beyond the 1 percent funding level, these firms put themselves on a pathway for moving from—as author and consultant Jim Collins might put it—good to great. But ratcheting up a philanthropy program budget only makes sense if there is a likely beneficial return on that investment, not just for society but for the company as well. Just throwing extra dollars or even donated

product or volunteer time at the nonprofit world without a pur-
poseful plan isn't a winning strategy. When a business figures out
how to leverage a larger-than-normal philanthropy payout, it can
win big. Take, for instance, the example set by Target.

TARGET'S 5 PERCENT TRADITION

The huge retail chain capitalizes on its deep-rooted tradition of
philanthropy as a marketing point of difference in competing with
other monster retailers such as Walmart and Kmart. You probably
have seen TV or print ads which are reminders that Target donates
$3 million *a week* to communities where it has a presence. In
addition, the company gives a percentage of charges from its
Target Visa card to schools designated by consumers.

Using contributions to underscore its concern for a community's quality of life and, in particular, local education is a terrific
business decision. The typical Target shopper is a woman who's
forty-one years old (younger than the consumer norm for other
competitive discount stores). About half the females walking in
and out of a Target store have children at home. All other factors
being more or less equal (price, store access, and so on), Target
creates customer loyalty by jogging Mom's memory (and Pop's too)
about how the company is pouring money back into the education
infrastructure of the consumer's town or city.

It isn't surprising that Target is among the cutting-edge companies in the philanthropy field. The company got its start in
Minneapolis when George Dayton opened a dry goods store in the
city. That was in the early 1900s, and ever since, the business
(which took on the name Target in 1962) has been a beacon for
corporate responsibility. It annually donates 5 percent of its pretax
net income and has been an inspiration for 134 other companies in
the Minneapolis–St. Paul region to do the same.

Adding more cash to the philanthropy budget isn't the only
way a company can move beyond its "ante-up" investment. As
noted, corporations that have product to donate can tack on the
value of those contributions once the minimum cash commitment has been made. These contributed products can elevate a

company's overall giving total *way* above the "ante-up" minimum (see Chapter Seven).

The 1 Percent Pushback

Some of the nation's most profitable corporations are far below the national norm for charitable giving when contributions are measured as a percentage of profits. To bring them up to the national average would mean, in some cases, pouring hundreds of millions of additional dollars into their contributions programs. And that's something many CEOs of high-profit companies don't want to do—mainly for the following three reasons.

Calls Too Much Attention to High Profits

Here's another brief case that puts you in the driver's seat of ExxonMobil during the high-profit year of 2007.

WHEN CORPORATE PHILANTHROPY BECOMES A RED FLAG

ExxonMobil is racking up record-breaking earnings on a quarterly basis. The PR department churns out one press release after another reminding Main Street that the oil industry profits are cyclical and that today's highs can easily sink to tomorrow's lows. That doesn't placate Joe Consumer, who goes ballistic each time his local gas station adds a few cents more to the price of regular or premium.

As CEO, you decide to lie as low as possible so that the extraordinary amount of money your company is making doesn't anger Joe to the point where he begins thinking a windfall profit tax isn't such a bad idea. The goal is to muffle news about your earnings—except, of course, to your investors.

On your calendar today is a meeting with the head of your corporate philanthropy management team. The group recommends that ExxonMobil increase its 2007 contributions. Three options are presented. First, increase charitable giving by 25 percent over last year's total. Second, increase the contributions budget so it equals the average level of giving by those corporations that take a charitable tax deduction on their federal tax returns. And third, hike ExxonMobil's philanthropy total to 5 percent of its projected annual pretax profits, which would match what a few other front-running businesses do each year.

As CEO, you ask the requisite first question: How much will each option cost? Put another way, how much will have to be added to what ExxonMobil has budgeted in 2007 for charitable gifts and grants? Here are the answers:

Option 1 (25 percent increase): add $36 million

Option 2 (move to national average): add $498 million

Option 3 (go to 5 percent): add $3.7 billion

Remember—one of your objectives as CEO is *not* to stoke consumer unrest over soaring profits. Moving your company contributions program to the national average would mean *tripling* what you plan to spend for charitable giving during 2007. To raise the level to 5 percent would make ExxonMobil's contributions program more than twice as large as that of any other business (the most generous corporate donor in 2007 was Pfizer at $2.4 billion, with product accounting for 99 percent of its total—see Chapter Seven).

These expensive choices smell like the kind of gas that could ignite a lot of consumer unhappiness. Even the option to increase giving by 25 percent could be a reminder that ExxonMobil was flush with cash.

So what do you do?

If you want to play it safe (and most CEOs do just that), you will wave off any of the three options, choosing instead to grow your company contributions program at a much slower pace. You may come to the conclusion that it is more prudent to risk taking the heat for being a parsimonious corporate citizen than to let your company's generosity remind the public how profitable your business happens to be.

Not all CEOs follow this course of action—particularly chief executives of less profitable businesses who *do* manage to carve out at least 1 percent of earnings for charity. As one displeased CEO of a mid-sized business told me, "1 percent isn't a lot to ask no matter what the profit line looks like. If our company can do it, so can the big boys.''

For businesses at risk of being criticized for reaping too many profits, there's no denying that the 1 percent ante up does put more light on a company's earnings.

Accustoms Charities to Unsustainable Giving Levels

For all the goodwill that can come from giving big, a company's reputation can get badly scratched if a corporation decides to end or deeply cut back its financial support of a nonprofit organization. At least that's the thinking of some businesses—especially those that have fluctuating profits. For those corporations, the strategy is clear: don't get charities accustomed to higher giving levels no matter how profitable the business might be.

I've talked to nonprofit executives about this ''donate low and steady'' approach, and their response is predictable—give us more money in the ''up'' years and we'll understand if you have to pare back your philanthropy in the lean years. Reasonable enough except that on occasion, companies actually have been burned by nonprofits after a corporation's altruistic spigot was turned off.

For example, during my Johnson & Johnson years, one of the company's operating units stopped sending donations to a women's shelter. When the shelter didn't get its usual annual donation, it raced to the local newspaper, and the end result was a very nasty story. In spite of a long history of funding the shelter, Johnson & Johnson—usually known for its generosity, particularly to causes linked to mothers and children—was accused of turning its back on battered women. The negative media coverage stung, and it took some doing to repair the corporation's reputation in central New Jersey, where J&J is headquartered.

One lesson learned from the women's shelter debacle was that ending a contributions relationship with a nonprofit requires a carefully crafted divorce strategy. Terminating a philanthropic connection to a nonprofit with little or no notice isn't very smart. Neither is closing the funding door without a compelling reason, which should go far beyond ''sorry, we have limited resources this year'' or ''regret to inform you that the company is shifting its giving priorities.''

So, yes, there have been occasions when companies have been scarred because they used the wrong approach in withdrawing financial support to nonprofits that have enjoyed many years of funding. But this is not a common occurrence. When "give low and steady" businesses use the argument that donating large amounts of money exposes them to too much risk if funding has to be pulled back, they overstate the danger. When a company feigns that kind of paranoia, it's usually because it's fundamentally cheap.

Ignores the Milton Friedman Factor

Although Milton Friedman died in 2006, his memory still lingers. The Nobel Laureate economist issued what has become one of the most frequently quoted phrases in the history of corporate philanthropy. In a 1970 *New York Times Magazine* article titled "The Social Responsibility of Business Is to Increase Its Profits," Friedman contended that corporations have only one purpose—to maximize shareholder value. Corporate philanthropy had no place in Friedman's world. He argued that money should be passed along to stockholders, who could make their own call about which nonprofits deserve a donation and which don't. If there is any doubt that Friedman's words still resonate, read the 2010 article in *The Wall Street Journal* titled "The Case Against Corporate Social Responsibility."

I wish Friedman were still alive because I think he would come around to agreeing that *conditional* charitable giving isn't just okay, it could and should be a preferred business practice. That may seem to be too big a leap for a man who during his later years became a captain of capitalism and the darling of the conservative world. But if Friedman came to understand the conditional grant-making principles, he would be sending out a different message than he did in the 1970s. If, however, Friedman uncovered evidence that corporate donations are primarily a charitable slush fund for senior management, then he would revert to his hardcore stand that the private sector should steer clear of philanthropy. And, frankly, he would have a point.

So there are predictable pushbacks to our 1 percent recommendation. But various arguments fall away if a company is holding to the principles of conditional grant making. A larger challenge is coming up with a way for a business to set a giving target of 1 percent of an elusive current-year profit projection.

The Sabsevitz Ante-Up Formula

As noted, a corporation's financial team is unlikely to disclose a company's profit projections for the current year—and for good reason (to cite one, how about aiding and abetting an insider trading scheme?). So it becomes necessary to look to some other method of forecasting a corporation's current profits.

Without invading a company's confidential financial files, there are obtainable data that can give us a clue as to what a corporation's current year profits are likely to be. Over the past twenty-five years or so, the mean increase per annum in corporate profits has been 8.8 percent. With business earnings having taken a tumble after the start of the recession in 2007, one might assume that percentage had to have dropped considerably. But keep in mind that corporate profits jumped 15 percent from 2004 to 2005 and 17 percent the next year. And in 2006, corporate profits were at their highest level since 1929! When the ups and downs are taken into account, per annum business earnings average between 8 and 9 percent.

With this information in hand, I asked a long-time friend, mathematician and systems expert Art Sabsevitz, to develop a mathematical formula that would pinpoint a percentage multiple that could be applied to the pretax profits a company earned two years earlier in order to move that corporation's contributions program to around 1 percent of pretax earnings for the current year. Art developed a new formula (see below) which says that when a company multiplies its before-tax profits from the previous year by 1.2 percent (actually 1.184 percent, which has been rounded up to 1.2 percent), it will yield a number that comes close to what is likely to be 1 percent of its pretax profits for the next year.

Sabsevitz "Ante-Up" Formula for Budgeting Corporate Contributions

Ante-up formula is based mathematically on a compound interest calculation where

$$(t*P \ (1+r)**n)/P = t(1+r)**n$$

with r = the rate, n = the number of years, and t = the target contribution rate. Using 8.8 percent mean growth in corporate profit as r, target contribution rate of 1 percent as t, and n = 2, 1.184 percent of a company's pretax profits two years earlier is the result.

Source: Arthur L. Sabsevitz

Hold it—something seems out of whack here. Why go back to *last* year in order to calculate a 1 percent giving total for *next* year? Why not use this year's pretax profits to figure out next year's contributions budget? That would be ideal if it weren't for the realities of the budgeting cycle of most corporations. Here's an example of the budgeting timetable that applies to most corporations:

Anteing-Up and the Budget-Planning Process

- It is May 2013 and you are given the responsibility for developing a contributions budget for next year—fiscal year 2014 (January–December).
- You want to peg your company's giving to 1 percent of projected pretax profits for 2014 in order to be counted among the "comprehensive corporate citizens."
- You visit the finance department to ask for profits projections for next year. That is confidential information, you are told. Okay. So what about profit estimates for this year? Nope—also confidential. You find out that profit forecasts are more closely guarded than the Hope Diamond.
- You have no choice but to go back to last year's (2012's) publicly reported financials to use as a base for calculating the 2014 budget.
- You apply the Sabsevitz Ante-Up Formula to the 2012 pretax profit number (which should be easily obtained since company financials are generally available three to four months after the close of a corporation's fiscal year).
- You submit your budget recommendations for 2014.

We can boil this down to a very easy way to remember how to apply this budgeting strategy. We'll call it the Sabsevitz Ante-Up Formula:

Sabsevitz Ante-Up Formula

Multiply 1.2 percent times last year's pretax net income to set the minimum cash giving budget for next year's contributions program.

To some, there may seem to be a fundamental problem with this budgeting methodology. If a corporation's profits were sky high last year but projected to tank next year, the 1.2 percent multiple will kick out a contributions budget way in excess of 1 percent of next year's before-tax profits.

Absolutely correct.

But fast forward two or three years. When the company's profits are (hopefully) once again in high gear, the 1.2 percent multiple used against the poor profit performance of previous years will yield a contributions budget below the 1 percent of pretax level. In either case, a business has the option of paring back its giving because of reduced earnings (see Chapter Thirteen) or supplementing its annual giving in order to stay as close as possible to the giving target of 1 percent of current year pretax earnings.

No matter what the explanation, some companies aren't going to like the 1 percent target or the Sabsevitz Ante-Up Formula. Not at all. They will contend that creating this kind of funding platform is, indeed, a giant step toward a de facto tax.

To overcome this resistance, some companies are going to need extra encouragement.

Pressure Points for Change

Any company turning a profit can easily afford to "ante up." But let's get real. Convincing a majority of corporations that have contribution commitments far below the recommended "ante-up" level to inflate their donation payouts will be nothing less than a Herculean task. These businesses are going to require encouragement. And a lot of it. Shareholders, employees, and retirees can nudge corporations in the right direction.

Shareholders

If a company is publicly held (there are more than thirteen thousand of these businesses, including most of the largest corporations in the nation), then its lifeblood and bane is—the shareholder. The trade-off for allowing you as an outside investor to become a part owner of a company is that the business also has to answer to you. Obviously, the leverage you have as an "owner" only goes so far, especially if you're hanging on to only a fistful of the millions of outstanding shares issued by a company. Still, as a stockholder, you have "standing," which is something you can leverage.

Companies are well practiced in fending off shareholders who batter the corporate doors with unrealistic expectations. They know how to deal with total whack-jobs and constant whiners. However, businesses will listen to ideas from shareholders if comments and recommendations are credible. Valid requests and suggestions usually get a response, albeit not necessarily the answer you might want to receive.

Asking about whether "your" company has a cash giving total of at least 1 percent of expected pretax earnings this year by budgeting at least 1.2 percent of pretax profits recorded two years ago is a perfectly reasonable question for a shareholder to ask. To make this kind of inquiry, go to the company's website and click on *investor relations*. Scroll down to *investor contacts* and you will usually find the name of an investment relations manager along with a phone number and email address. Call or write the manager with this message:

> I am a company shareholder and want to be sure our corporation is keeping pace with other businesses in the corporate philanthropy field. Can you tell me if our company's cash giving is budgeted at or above 1 percent of what we expect in pretax profits this year? Will our cash contributions equal or exceed 1.2 percent of pretax profits our company earned two years ago, which I understand is a way of approximating a 1 percent giving level for this year? If our cash giving is likely to be below 1 percent of pretax earnings this year, could you please inform me about

plans to move our company to this minimum level of cash giving and how long it will take to reach this goal?

When the company receives this message, here's what is likely to happen. If the company is at the 1 percent or higher level of projected pretax earnings, you will get a prideful answer. Case closed. If the company is lagging in its minimum giving, it will respond with a slippery statement full of "we benchmark our giving to be sure it's in line with competitive companies....," or "we appreciate your interest in our philanthropy, and you can be assured that we make donations based on community needs taking into account our own financial status and projections....," and so on. Then your note or phone message will be dumped into a folder along with emails and letters asking the company to stop discriminating against Pygmies and criticizing the corporate logo because it looks too much like a pornographic picture if you turn it sideways.

If that's what is likely to happen, why go to all this trouble?

It's all about volume. If the company gets a few of these "ante-up" emails and phone calls, it begins paying attention. The messages will be forwarded to the department handling corporate contributions. There may be more defensive posturing on the part of the company, but if enough messages show up, the corporation's contributions program gets scrutinized. The CEO worries about going to the annual shareholder meeting and being bombarded with questions about the company being philanthropically challenged. Even worse, management gets nervous about being folded into an Associated Press story focusing on corporations that aren't particularly good corporate citizens.

Employees and Retirees

Whether a corporation is publicly or privately held, it is commonplace for those who are on the company payroll to be clueless about how much their employers spend or should spend on contributions. If a business has a matching gifts program or runs an aggressive United Way or similar campaign (see Chapter Nine), workers may be familiar with bits and pieces of their company's philanthropy. But as a general rule, I have found that employees and retirees know little about their employer's charitable giving.

The typical employee is overwhelmed with so much other information related to company business (workplace expectations, safety and security, and so on), that philanthropy news can't penetrate the clutter. Retirees are sometimes open to learning more about the company's charitable ventures but only after they have waded through pension, medical insurance, and other retirement issues.

This disconnect between employees and corporate philanthropy is odd, considering that building and sustaining employee morale is widely cited as a primary reason for carrying out a contributions program. Since creating an employment environment that makes workers feel good about their company is acknowledged as a *raison d'être* for a corporation's philanthropy, one would think businesses might do a better job of communicating their philanthropy initiatives (Chapter Twelve). Even in the absence of a majority of workers not knowing enough about a contributions program to press a company to "ante up," there are always a few workers and pensioners who are *very* concerned about a company's community involvement—usually because they are involved with nonprofit organizations they feel should be on a corporate donor list. Interestingly, when it comes to answering questions about corporate philanthropy, it is this group of individuals who will often get more attention than outside shareholders. Without sounding like a kook or malcontent, an employee can email any member of the company's foundation board of directors or trustees or contributions committee and pose this question:

> I'm a volunteer working with the United Way (or some other nonprofit organization). I was recently asked about whether our company's cash donations are budgeted at a minimum of 1 percent of this year's expected pretax earnings—or if our cash giving is equal to 1.2 percent of our pretax earnings two years ago, which I understand is a method of approximating a 1 percent level of cash giving for the current year. Apparently many socially responsible companies are at this minimum level of giving. Could you help me get back to the United Way (or other organization) with an answer?

For retirees, it would be productive to use the same approach. Blowing off a retiree is something companies do with regularity (ask any benefits manager who deals with retirees). But when a retiree is asking for information that could affect a company's reputation (particularly in or around its headquarters location), the individual is less likely to get a runaround.

The Payoff

The Sabsevitz Ante-Up Formula delivers big on two fronts. First, it rides over a dilemma many CEOs complain about by putting into place a fair method of calculating business contributions. Second, if widely adopted, it will mean a significant infusion of new corporate grants. If all corporations were to move their cash giving to at least 1 percent of pretax net income (our ante-up goal), an estimated *$7 billion to $8 billion in new funding would flow into the nonprofit world.*

As a way of emphasizing this point, I researched thirty-eight companies with large contributions programs but that have cash donation allocations less than 1 percent of their before taxes income. If just these thirty-eight businesses were to hike their cash giving to 1 percent, *an additional $2.6 billion would be added to the corporate philanthropy "pot."*

Since corporate contributions so often come wrapped in employee volunteerism and other added-value benefits, moving the corporate cash contributions needle in the right direction will have an enormous impact on the thousands of organizations working in the social services, education, cultural, and health care fields. But companies will also win big if they make sure they keep their contributions aligned with our conditional charitable grant-making principles.

IN SUMMARY

Question 2: How much should a company give?

Answer: A minimum of 1 percent of its current year's projected pretax net income using 1.2 percent of the company's earnings from two years ago to estimate that number. The minimum spending target should be all cash, should be allocated in accord with the conditional grant-making principles, and should be considered the "ante-up" requirement for comprehensive corporate citizenship.

3

Who Decides What Gets Funded?

Estimates vary, but the number of nonprofit "charities" actually functioning in the United States ranges from around 600,000 to 800,000 (not counted are those nonprofits that are dormant or which have gone belly up but still get included in the list maintained by the IRS of 1.2 million 501c3 organizations). The Treasury Department does its best to track the ebb and flow of the nonprofit tide. But understand that it's *really* easy to become a not-for-profit organization (ask the IRS for Publication 557 and just follow the instructions). So while an indeterminate number of nonprofits die off each year, there are about 100-plus new nonprofit charities that are hatched *every single day!*

With so many funding options available to a company, which should be singled out for support and which should be turned down? And, as one of our baker's dozen questions asks:

Question 3: Who decides what gets funded?

Answer: A group of senior executives with key business responsibilities who are handpicked by the company CEO should select high-impact grants and establish policies for core grant administration. Decisions should be reviewed by the CEO and amended if necessary.

Does this answer mean that every $50 to $500 gift request must get screened and scrutinized by an expensive senior management team? Absolutely not. The recommendation is for a high-ranking group of executives to set policies and standards that the day-to-day contribution manager(s) can use to handle what are called "core" contributions—generally smaller and often regularly renewed donations. That same group of executives should also weigh in on "high impact" grant possibilities—large company contributions that usually consume a smaller percentage of contributions funds but deliver a strong return because they can be pointed at opportunities or concerns important to the business itself.

An argument might be made that enlisting senior executives to spend even two minutes on philanthropy issues is unrealistic and unwarranted. That's bad reasoning. The more top management distances itself from a company's contributions goals and processes, the less likely grant making will generate benefits to a business or society. It comes down to making senior executives part "owners" of a corporation's philanthropy efforts.

The Ownership Factor

From my interaction with over two hundred businesses (most fairly large), it's clear that companies that engage upper-level management as "owners" of parts of the contributions program tend to come out on top in the philanthropy field. When influential executives have responsibility for extracting the most value possible out of certain pieces of the program, more often than not they meet high expectations. This only works, though, when these top-end managers are connected to the most *strategic* parts of the philanthropy program.

Picture a corporate contributions program as having two essential parts (see Figure 3.1). *Core* giving encompasses the requisite donations that almost all companies make—United Way or similar workplace-linked gifts, smaller grants to community nonprofits, employee matching gifts, and so on. Typically these core donations will consume at least two-thirds of a larger corporation's annual contributions payout.

Figure 3.1. High-Impact, Core Contributions Model

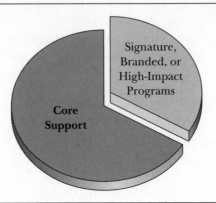

High-impact grants usually yield a stronger return for the business even though they consume a lesser percentage of the company's cash giving (generally around one third of the total budget for businesses with more highly regarded philanthropy programs).

If a clear contributions framework has been approved by senior management, a lower-level corporate contributions administrator—whether full time or part time—can oversee *core* donations because they don't require a lot of strategic overview. Where senior executives can be most valuable is in the planning, conduct, and evaluation of *high-impact* grants.

The senior executive "owners" of a company's contributions program will vary from business to business. The following case is a look at the Johnson & Johnson "ownership" structure that was in place during my years with that company.

CONTRIBUTIONS PROGRAM ``OWNERSHIP´´

J&J's CEO "invited" twelve corporate executives to serve on a corporate contributions committee. These were among the most talented leaders in the company, drawn from the pharmaceutical, consumer, and professional sectors along with staff functions including R&D, public relations, finance, government relations, and human resources. In spite of their challenging schedules, members met every other month for a couple of hours with an average 80 percent attendance record. But even more impressive, most members also took on time-demanding ownership responsibilities for different high-impact programs funded by contribution dollars.

Each contributions committee member became the "face" of the program he or she was leading. Over time, executives established very strong connections to high-impact initiatives and regularly showed up at outside functions and events linked to these programs. During the annual budget cycle when the next year's contributions allocations were being planned, committee members turned into rabid advocates for the programs they "owned." A representative from a nonprofit seeking support could not have argued so passionately for continuance or expansion of a grant that fueled a committee member's high-impact program.

The J&J contributions committee also set the parameters for the company's core giving—and periodically reviewed those parameters. Day-to-day managers fielded or solicited donation requests that fell within the contribution walls built by the committee. A list of proposed core grants was sent to each committee member for inspection. Rarely did the committee request a core grant be held up for further discussion. Because core giving standards were so clearly defined, J&J's high-level executives were only infrequently diverted into a discussion about smaller donations that had less business impact than larger social investment. Time and energy were mostly directed toward high-impact grants.

Granted—not every company has the ability to bring together a dozen top executives to focus on philanthropy. Nor does every company have the wherewithal to pour millions of dollars into high-impact programs (most of J&J's high-impact grants topped $1 million each). Still, *the fundamentals of this model are relevant for any business of any size.* Carve out a portion of the money to be used for philanthropic purposes for high-impact grants and allow executives who are in the best position to leverage that money to own the programs funded via these contributions.

Tools for Decision Makers

Once a company has set up the best possible grant-making structure, it should equip decision makers with the right tools. Why? Because the sheer number of requests that strike businesses by the day can easily push the best philanthropy intentions off the track.

Unless one stands inside a company and experiences the almost unimaginable barrage of appeals that get fired at a corporation, it's difficult to grasp what a high-volume enterprise grant-making management usually is. Publicly held companies are particularly vulnerable to unsolicited requests. They stand out as perceived deep-pocket targets because these firms report financial information, which equates to meat on the bone for fundraisers.

The staggering number of solicitations hurled at these larger businesses (particularly those in the *Fortune* 500 category) has prompted some corporations to post warning signs that uninvited requests are about as welcome as lice.

- UPS announced in 2007 that it "no longer accepts or responds to unsolicited proposals." Microsoft "rarely grants financial support on the basis of unsolicited requests."
- Dominion Resources, FedEx, and several other firms will only entertain solicitations if they are sent via the Internet and only if prospective grantees can pass a rigorous test to determine if they are eligible for funding.

Large corporations commonly use two tools to either fend off unwanted appeals or scout out prospects they *do* want to review: (a) "guidelines for giving" and (b) requests for proposals (RFPs). For businesses anxious to control—rather than be controlled by—the contributions process, these are useful resources.

Guidelines for Giving

Keep in mind that for every one contribution a company makes, it has to say "no" to dozens of other hopeful charities. For obvious reasons, then, the art of rejection can be vitally important. Think about Walmart, JCPenney, Bank of America, or any of the other thousands of businesses that sell directly to consumers.

These companies are swamped with solicitations, some of which come with an implied (and sometimes even overt) threat: make a contribution to our cause or our constituents are going to boycott your products or services.

The least damaging way of handling unwanted appeals is to make the rejection *objective* rather than *subjective*. And this is where guidelines for giving can prove so helpful. A true story will help make this point.

KEEPING REJECTIONS OBJECTIVE

An insurance company called me after it had been pelted with a half dozen proposals asking for large, multiyear grants to be used to endow company-named chairs at colleges and universities located in states where the firm did business. The insurer had a few loose statements about its philanthropy interests posted on its company website, none of which offered a clue as to whether the company did or didn't support higher education endowments.

After a quick conversation with company management, it became clear the firm wanted nothing to do with naming chairs or funding capital campaigns of any kind. But no such message was broadcast as part of its posted guidelines.

Using alumni who had bubbled up to high-level executive positions in the insurance company, universities were able to schedule front-office visits during which they pitched proposals directly to the CEO.

The insurer found itself painted into an uncomfortable corner.

The company couldn't possibly afford to underwrite every endowment appeal (these contributions are typically very large and commonly are paid out over a three- to five-year period). But since there was no predetermined statement that said "we don't do endowments," each request had to be turned down on the basis of what university leaders concluded was a *subjective* decision made on the part of the CEO and others at the top of the company. A turndown meant (in the eyes of the colleges asking for money) that the CEO or other key players in the executive suite had *personally* killed the appeal.

This is not the kind of impression a company wants when it is competing for a university's health insurance business.

The lesson to be learned is that if the insurance firm had had a tight set of giving guidelines, including a "no endowments or capital campaigns" statement, university fundraisers probably wouldn't have bothered soliciting the company in the first place. Even if colleges did arrange to meet with company executives, the insurer could have used the guidelines as an impenetrable line of defense.

"I wish the company could help, but our philanthropy guidelines— which, by the way, have been developed with input from our outside board—just don't give us the latitude to make this kind of grant . . . ."

This is an *objective* rejection. It wasn't hatched on the spot or in some back room by the manager handing out the bad news. It is a company judgment that applies to any endowment or capital campaign. When a turndown is categorical and not just aimed at the one prospecting organization, some of the sting goes out of the "no."

What makes for an effective set of corporate giving guidelines? Almost every company includes the same few provisions about people and groups that won't be considered for support. Boeing's *Guidelines for Grant Applications,* for example, includes "we don't fund" categories found in nearly every other business-issued guidelines statement:

- Individual persons or families
- Political candidates or organizations
- Religious activities that further religious doctrine

Over and above these three restrictions, companies tend to customize their "no" lists. For example, Roche, the pharmaceutical company, says it won't consider requests for goodwill advertising or "the purchase, construction, expansion or modification of facilities."

Guidelines aren't just useful in warding off unwanted requests; they can also be helpful in attracting appeals a company *does* want to receive.

- Water stewardship, health, active lifestyles, community recycling, and education are the kind of interest areas Coca-Cola will consider funding.

- The medical technology company Medtronic's philanthropic focus areas include chronic disease, science education, and improving or sustaining quality of life in communities where the company has a presence.

A workable set of guidelines can be both a lure for the right type of proposal and a repellent for the appeals a company would just as soon never see.

A company's giving guidelines can be enormously useful if they hold to these three basic rules:

1. *Create the narrowest keyhole practical and possible.* Guidelines should clearly shout "don't bother" or "come on in" to any nonprofit likely to solicit a business. The smaller the opening through which qualified solicitations can gain entry to the company, the more efficient the corporate contributions program is going to be.
2. *Revisit guidelines at least every three years.* Company objectives and external conditions consistently change. Guidelines should not be cut in stone but should be modified to keep pace with new corporate interests and concerns as well as shifting social needs.
3. *Get the word out.* Keeping guidelines close to the vest (which some companies do) doesn't make a lot of sense. Post the guidelines on the company website. Enclose printed copies of the guidelines when rejecting uninvited requests. Publish the guidelines as part of any annual statement on corporate citizenship.

The last word on guidelines is *hypocrisy.*

If a company uses its giving guidelines to exclude certain organizations or funding categories but then does an about face and "makes exceptions" by sending checks to nonprofits that are presumably out of bounds, the corporation might as well rip up its guidelines.

For example, a company declares it doesn't support religious or religiously affiliated organizations. Then it makes donations to Habitat for Humanity for a home-building project in Mississippi, Catholic Medical Mission Board for earthquake relief in

Indonesia, and MAP International for a women's health program in Guatemala. All are respectable nonprofits doing good work in this country and abroad. But all are Christian-based organizations. The company either stops funding these groups or revises its guidelines to read, "requests considered from faith-based organizations for nondenominational projects or services but not for support of sacramental or theological programs or events."

If a company has giving guidelines, they should be specific. And once such guidelines are in place, a corporation should stick to those giving parameters.

Requests for Proposals (RFPs)

Grant making is a lot like Internet dating. Scores of candidates knock on your door or check your Facebook site looking for a "meaningful relationship," but rarely do any of them give you the rush you want and expect. To find Mr. or Ms. Right, you have to launch your own search-and-find mission. Ditto for many businesses.

Instead of bar hopping or signing up for a speed-dating session, companies research a list of organizations that match a "most desirable" set of criteria. Then the company either directly or through a third party invites handpicked nonprofits to submit a proposal.

Rather than deal with a flood of unsolicited appeals, the RFP strategy allows a business to use an evaluation screen to judge just a few proposals. While this approach has advantages and can be effective, a corporation needs to be vigilant about how far it goes in pushing a nonprofit organization to manufacture a proposal that meets the explicit requirements of the company. Unintentionally or otherwise, a corporation can convert a grant into a contract and can do so without fully understanding the difference between the two.

If a business establishes the terms and conditions of a relationship with a nonprofit, particularly if that relationship includes an expected *quid pro quo,* then the deal turns into a contract. In other words, the company has contracted with the nonprofit to deliver outcomes, services, and so on that the corporation specifies as a funding condition. A charitable grant comes with no hard and fast *quid pro quo.* Consequently, the nonprofit has the latitude to use company funds in a much less restrictive way.

The line between a contract and a grant can be fuzzy at times. But those nonprofits smart enough to snag a grant often don't worry about boundaries because they have learned how to play the contribution-contract game. On paper, a charitable donation puts the recipient nonprofit in the driver's seat. In reality, though, the nonprofit does pretty much whatever the business wants as long as its actions aren't so over the top that the IRS gets curious. Why would a nonprofit be so willing to do a company's bidding? Because if it treats a corporate payment as a quasi-contract and goes as far as it can in lending a hand to the company, then the chances of getting the grant renewed go up exponentially.

Here is another important point regarding contracts and grants: companies can write off a payment to a nonprofit as either a charitable contribution or an ordinary business expense. There are some minor differences between the two, but for all practical purposes, *a charitable donation and an ordinary business expense give a corporation the same tax benefit.*

If a company accountant thinks a funding commitment to a nonprofit might trigger an auditor's curiosity, that payment can be classified (or reclassified) as something other than a charitable gift on the company's annual tax return. I can tell you first hand that it's an eye opener for many corporate contributions administrators to discover that at least some of the grants they thought were being logged as charitable donations actually had been converted into other kinds of business expenses by the tax department (the exceptions are grants made through a company foundation that are all categorized as charitable gifts).

I have been challenged by a number of corporate contributions managers who insist this kind of behind-the-scenes switching doesn't happen. But if they are able to gain access to a company's annual federal tax filing, I urge them to check line 19 ("charitable contributions deductions") on federal form 1120. I try not to sound surprised when I pick up the phone and hear, "I can't believe those guys changed the numbers!"

If a company does log what is presumed to be a grant as a different type of business expense, the tax consequences to the business are usually nil. But if a nonprofit accepts a check from a company for an activity or project considered to be outside its charitable mission, the payment could fall into the "unrelated business income" pool. And this *could* be a problem—for the nonprofit. This income is potentially taxable, which could mean a hefty chunk of a company's grant would have to be handed over to the IRS for payment of a "UBIT"—unrelated business income tax. So the grant-contract dilemma is one in which the nonprofit is more at risk than the company.

RFPs work for those companies with the capacity to put together the right invitation list and plod through the review process once proposals have been received. The approach is definitely gaining in popularity among larger businesses, but for mid-size to smaller companies, it's not a strategy that's been widely adopted.

More About "Who" Should Decide

Right now, there is no consistency in the way companies currently make contributions decisions. But there should be. Some firms let lower-level employees hand pick which nonprofits get donations and which don't. This egalitarian approach to grant making is at best a lost opportunity for a company and at worst a recipe for trouble. Workers who are deep down in the corporation may know community needs but are less cognizant of business priorities. They could easily make donation decisions that run contrary to a corporation's best interests.

Less risky but still not capitalizing on the full value of a contributions investment is the "CEO vest pocket approach," when most of the giving comes from the front office. This is commonplace among smaller businesses. But whether a company has a hundred employees or a hundred thousand, recruiting a few senior managers to assist the CEO in mapping out a core and high-impact giving strategy can go a long way in pumping up the power of gifts and grants.

How many senior executives should be involved? The number will vary depending on the size and make-up of the corporation. More important than head count is a clear understanding of the group's mission regardless of size. Staying focused on high-impact opportunities and not getting dragged into the weeds where small gift requests lurk by the score is key. It is very easy for a senior management team to get sidetracked. A North Jersey company that asked for my consulting help a few years ago underscored that point.

HIGH-PRICED TALENT–LOW-PRIORITY DECISIONS

"We meet once a quarter," the contributions program manager explained during my first visit to the company. The woman was only two years into her job but clearly knew what she was doing.

"Who's 'we'?" I asked.

"The CEO, chief financial officer, executive VP for domestic sales, head of R&D, the HR vice president, and my boss, who's general counsel for the company," she answered.

I raised my eyebrows. "That's a roomful of talent." *And boatload of expensive executive time,* I thought.

"They're all officers of the company foundation," she explained. "The bylaws state that they have to meet annually."

"But you said they meet four times a year. Why?"

"To review grant requests," she replied and handed me a thick briefing book complete with an appendix listing contribution requests that had been received by the company over the past couple of months. The book opened with an administrative overview that detailed the foundation's year-to-date spending, minutes of the committee's last meeting, and other information written more for the record than it was for easy reading. I could smell law department all over the document.

"The board reviews all of these?" I asked, thumbing through pages of small gift appeals. Most were in the $500 to $2,500 range.

"That's their job," the manager said.

"Uh, huh." I flipped through the briefing book hoping to find information about the larger grants the company made. The corporation funded over a dozen organizations at an annual level of $500,000 each. "What about the big kahunas? How much time does the board spend on the high-priced grants you make?"

"Not a lot," she replied. "Those are in pretty good shape. Several are multiyear grants and don't need much attention. It's the smaller donations that can eat up the time."

"So a request for $1,000 can become the topic of the day at some of the board meetings?" I asked.

"Absolutely," the woman said.

"How long are these board meetings?"

"Three hours–but that includes lunch."

"How much time do you think each board member spends looking over the briefing book and other materials you send out before each meeting?"

The manager thought for a few seconds before responding. "I'd say about an hour or so."

"With meeting and prep time combined, that's four hours per meeting times four meetings a year," I calculated, while pulling the company's proxy statement from my briefcase. "Know what the hourly rate is for the people running this company?" I asked.

"Not really."

I flipped to the executive and director compensation summary table at the back of the proxy statement. Pay and benefits were disclosed for four of the executives serving on the company foundation board. I grabbed a blank sheet of paper and wrote the following:

Executive	Salary and Stock	Divided by 230 Work Days	Divided by 10 hours
CEO	$2.1 mill.	$9,100	$910
CFO	$1.1 mill.	$4,800	$480
Gen Counsel	$1.1 mill.	$4,800	$480
VP Sales	$1.3 mill.	$5,700	$570

"I didn't add in the value of the options awards or any non-equity compensation like certificates of executive compensation," I pointed out. "Of course, senior executives are going to pooh-pooh these hourly rate calculations, claiming that they work a lot more days and put in a lot more hours than are shown on the chart."

The manager smiled.

"But even if the chart's not 100 percent accurate, it's close enough," I continued. "Add up the numbers in the last column."

The woman did the math. "$2,440."

"For just these four foundation board members, the company is investing $2,400 an hour for managing its contributions. Four hours per meeting times four meetings a year–that's over $38,000 per year. And we haven't added in the cost of other executives serving on the board, not to mention the time your department puts in preparing these detailed briefing reports."

The manager blew out a low whistle.

"Nearly $40,000 spent on worrying about a few low-end grant requests?"

"I get the point," the woman said.

The problem is that a lot of corporations don't. They allow core giving issues to dominate the agenda when some of the most costly executives are brought together to discuss contributions matters. The company could and should expect these executives to focus on ways to leverage high-impact grants for the benefit of both society and the business.

Following are the "rules of the road" for company foundation boards or corporate contributions committees that I have found to be notably effective.

Focus on what matters most. A contributions committee or foundation board should be a business brain trust. The company's most intelligent and experienced leaders should take aim at how best to link its philanthropy to the interests and objectives of the corporation—and to do so within the parameters of the charitable giving regulations.

Exclude the CEO. Even if the chief executive is technically an officer of the company foundation, keep him or her away from contribution planning meetings. A group of senior managers tends to function differently and more effectively if the CEO isn't in the room. Ideas are more creative and discussions are more open. It also helps to have the CEO as a clearinghouse for committee or board recommendations—in other words, the CEO has the option to amend (which could mean anything from tweaking to discarding) whatever recommendations are put forward by a board or committee.

Assign ownership responsibilities. While the collective thinking of a board or committee can be powerful, having each member (or at least most members) "own" a part of the contributions program can be just as beneficial to a company. And ownership has to be real, meaning that it should stand the test of the "2 C's"—control and credit.

Empower the contributions program manager. Let the board or committee set the parameters for managing a company's core giving program and then give the contributions program manager the authority to do the job within the policy boundaries. Yes, senior executives need to be certain the right checks and balances are in place. However, those steps don't have to consume large amounts of meeting time. Having core program managers who distribute periodic reports that include a list of proposed core grants and a note that reads, "Here's what we intend to do—let me know if you have any questions or concerns . . . ." usually does the trick.

Keep marketing and sales executives off the contributions decision-making team. The pharmaceutical and medical device industries have adopted guidelines designed to prevent company philanthropy programs from being abused by marketing or sales staffs. These industries are under intense scrutiny for even a hint of kickback practices. Having a sales rep dangle the possibility of a company gift to a customer's favorite charity is a definite no-no (it's called a "subterfuge for bribery" by some watchdogs). While most other industries are not as prone to this kind of outside scrutiny, it still isn't a bad idea to keep marketing or sales people—who do tend to push the contributions envelope from time to time—off to one side.

Keep the CFO or his or her office involved. Although not always the case, CFOs tend to be more difficult to convince about the merits of a carefully planned and managed contributions program. Yet if the finance department does get fully engaged in developing and carrying out grant-making activities, the results are impressive. Enlisting a CFO to play an active role in the contributions process isn't easy (CFOs frequently are among the top execs on a company foundation board—but that doesn't equate to a high level of interest). What seems to work for many businesses is having the CFO assign a direct report to serve on the contributions committee or foundation board. The trick is to make sure the CFO's office is not left on the outside looking in. That is a recipe for trouble.

Remember: the more high-level executives perceive that they "own" prominent parts of a company's contributions program, the more successful the overall program is likely to be. While executives can meet collectively as a contributions committee or as a foundation board to chart a course for the company's philanthropy, executives acting independently can be even more influential when carrying out responsibilities tied to specific high-impact initiatives each of them "owns."

IN SUMMARY

Question 3: Who decides what gets funded?

Answer: A team of senior executives with key business responsibilities handpicked by the company CEO establishes grant-making policies and procedures subject to CEO review and amendment. The same team makes high-impact grant decisions—which the CEO also reviews. Core contribution decisions are made by day-to-day contributions managers and are based on approved grant-making priorities that are communicated as part of the company's giving guidelines.

4

What's the Right Role
for the CEO?

Months before the BP drilling disaster in the Gulf of Mexico, I wrote a *BusinessWeek* op-ed that slammed the largest U.S. oil companies for under-funding their corporate philanthropy programs. The article uncorked a wave of emails, some of which were supportive (for example, "Please write more articles like this one . . . " signed JLL; "Cheap bastards! I work for one of the oil companies and I am embarrassed!" from defox) but most of which ranged from angry to out-and-out nasty. Here's a sampling (and these are unedited, actual comments):

- "I don't give a rat's rear end if a company gives to charity! I'll decide what charity I want to reward!!!"
  —Chamberlin
- "The author is a sanctimonious creep. Makes my skin crawl."—Dave
- "I don't invest in a company to make charitable decisions for me. Pay it out in dividends and let me decide if/where the money can do the most good."—Erick
- "ExxonMobil pays a lot of taxes. This is compared to firms like the Big Three (auto companies), who give a lot to charity but pay nothing into the Treasury. If General Motors focused more on running its business and making

a profit but didn't give a nickel to charity, America would be a lot better off.''—Robert

- "I DO NOT want a socialist company distributing MY profits to charities that I do not like. I refuse to shop at Target precisely because they give 5% which is 5% higher prices I have to pay so they can use their 'charity' as advertising . . . .''—John
- "Charity is nothing more than another capitalistic institution created by mongers to profit on the demise of an individual."—Christian
- "The author is a buffoon . . . .''—Mike
- "The author is a dumb-a**! What a putz this guy is!''
- "I think you've been smoking the first four letters of your last name . . . .''—Bill

Aside from being called a buffoon, a pothead, and a sanctimonious creep, I wasn't irked by most of the responses to the *BusinessWeek* op-ed. The reactions proved there is a segment of the public that needs a *lot* more information about how an effectively managed contributions program isn't a slippery slope into a welfare state.

Quite the contrary: if corporate philanthropy stays faithful to our conditional grant-making principles, it can make a business more successful and actually bolster an investor's return. I believe most (not all) of *BusinessWeek's* irate readers could be brought around to recognizing that conditional corporate philanthropy can be a good deal. But making that case takes time and a certain amount of decorum, which doesn't always come easy to someone who's just been called a dumb-ass putz.

Now put yourself in a CEO's seat. Why would any sane chief executive want to promote a company's philanthropy knowing that such a move is likely to trigger a firestorm? Sure, a CEO who understands the value of conditional grant making could probably go one-on-one with irritated shareholders and show them the light. But given all the other issues most chief executives have to handle, this isn't the kind of education campaign that rises to the top of the "must do" pile. The result is a private sector populated with CEOs who strive to keep their company's philanthropy as under cover as possible.

But that's not necessarily what CEOs *should* be doing, as is evident from the answer to our next question drawn from our baker's dozen list.

> **Question 4:** What's the right role for the CEO?

> **Answer:** Most companies with superior contributions programs have CEOs who do four things: (a) demand a business and social return on investment from the company's carefully managed contributions program; (b) say the right words at the right time about program goals and purposes; (c) build the right team to develop, oversee, and evaluate the program; and (d) pick a competent day-to-day manager to steer the contributions process.

CEOs Set the Tone—Good or Bad

Remember Chuck Gilfant, the harried head honcho of Widget Worldwide whom we met in Chapter One? He is a compilation of everything good and bad that a CEO brings to the table when dealing with a company's contributions program. Chuck had enough horse sense to let his senior management team pound out a philanthropy plan that hooked conditional giving to Widget's business goals. And, albeit with a good deal of reluctance, he not only pulled the paring knife away from the philanthropy program's jugular but even showed some willingness to at least consider adding a few dollars to the contributions budget.

On the dark side, Chuck had a near zero understanding as to the purpose and potential of Widget's grant-making efforts. His actions and words suggested he viewed philanthropy as something peripheral to the business and, in the scheme of things, not at all important. Lurking in the back of his mind, there may also have been a deep-seated fear of being skewered by unhappy shareholders who might brand him as a closet socialist.

I've met my share of Chucks over the years. Then, too, I have met a lot of other CEOs who came equipped with a much greater grasp about what it takes to be a comprehensive corporate citizen. In every case—no exceptions—the CEO sets the tone for a company's giving philosophy. If the top executive signals philanthropy is a useless digression or is apprehensive about saying too much about a company's grant making, that attitude permeates the business like buckshot. If the CEO sends out a sincere message (and sincerity is the key) that the company considers philanthropy a business opportunity as well as a vital corporate responsibility, the whole workforce gets the message.

Here's what I have found in working with a long list of companies: if a CEO doesn't carry the flag when it comes to building a stronger conditional grant-making program, not much happens. Furthermore, the chief executive doesn't just have to be on board, he or she has to be out front.

What's interesting about so many CEOs I have come to know over the years is that most of them have strong personal philanthropic inclinations. Those personal beliefs and behaviors become more obvious the closer a CEO gets to the date of departure from a company. Take, for instance, Leonard Schaeffer, whom I met in 2005 when he was leaving his post as head of WellPoint Health Networks, a large health insurer headquartered in Thousand Oaks, California.

A CEO'S CHARITABLE CORE

One evening, Leonard Schaeffer invited me to dinner. I expected to sit down with a man who didn't have a care in the world. Why would I think any differently? Schaeffer had recently captained a complicated and controversial merger between WellPoint Health Networks and the Indianapolis-based insurer Anthem. The $17 billion deal combined the two businesses into the largest health insurance organization in the United States, providing coverage to twenty-eight million members.

For his efforts, Schaeffer had been paid well. Very well. According to SEC filings, he received $27.5 million in severance pay and a special executive pension worth around $10.5 million. Schaeffer was also walking off with stock shares and options estimated at about $250 million. On top of that, his country club membership would be covered for four years and he would be provided financial counseling, office space, and secretarial support for five years.

The night we had dinner, though, Schaeffer wore an expression that hardly suited a mega-millionaire.

"Need some advice," he opened. For the next couple of hours his conscience took over, and I listened to a man who wanted counsel on how much of his wealth should go to charity. More important, he was looking for a few tips on how to point his donations in a direction that would actually make a difference to the people he wanted to help.

Schaeffer was hopeful that his giving could be as effective as WellPoint's corporate contributions initiatives, which had been instrumental in winning over California state regulators whose approval was essential to closing the merger with Anthem. Well-Point had published a handsome (and expensive) corporate citizenship report replete with information about how the company's charitable commitments had made health care accessible to the medically underserved and improved the quality of life for a countless number of Californians. The self-promoted story about the company's good citizenship scored big points.

While Schaeffer seemed to recognize the power of strategic philanthropy within his own company, it wasn't a top-of-mind issue for him, according to other senior executives inside WellPoint. But as the clock wound down on Schaeffer's time in office, his attention (like that of so many other CEOs whose careers are about to close) tilted toward matters that had less to do with day-to-day P&L performance and more to do with humanity both inside and outside the company. Leonard Schaeffer was a helpful reminder to me that behind the sometimes crusty exteriors of many CEOs, there is a charitable intent. But for a lot of CEOs, encouraging their own companies to be more philanthropic—even if grant making is conditional—remains simply too perilous in the absence of any broadly accepted rules of the road.

That mind-set on the part of so many CEOs led me to pose this question to some of them: Supposing a cross-section of businesses representing all industry segments were to agree to commit a specific percentage of their pretax income for donations and grants—with the requirement that such payments would be in line with our conditional grant-making principles? Would that make it less risky for a CEO to set a spending target for philanthropy? This is the kind of response I get:

"Yeah, it would help to have an agreement among all businesses—especially my competitors—that corporations will cough up at least the same percentage of profits for charity. Right now, trying to guess what that right level of giving should be is a nuisance. But understand that I don't want my company signing on to some giving target only to find out my competition isn't in the game."

The reaction brings us back to Chapter Two's "What's the right amount to give?" If CEOs are genuine about wanting a more prescriptive method of building a corporate contributions program, they should buy into the "ante up" approach. If the private sector as a whole were to agree that every business should budget at least 1 percent of its anticipated pretax net income for cash contributions purposes (using the Sabsevitz Ante-Up Formula), then there's the answer.

The rest is all mechanics.

Put together a senior management committee to craft a business-focused giving strategy. Assign a competent manager to staff the contributions function. Continue to let employees, shareholders, and others know that the company's conditional giving puts it in the same league as other businesses that have well-regarded comprehensive corporate citizenship programs.

Moving the ante-up model from a good idea to a widespread reality won't happen unless CEOs get on board. Making that leap means getting their attention. And that's not easy given the extraordinary demands on their time.

The CEO-Chairman *Split*

One of the first prospecting calls I made after launching my consulting business in the early 1980s was to PepsiCo's corporate headquarters in Purchase, New York. I was accompanied by my business partner at the time, the late Bill Bramstedt, who was a retired vice chairman of Caltex Oil (a joint venture of the then separate companies of Standard Oil of California and Texaco). Bill was a long-time acquaintance of Donald Kendall, PepsiCo's co-founder and, at the time, CEO of the food and beverage giant.

I recall sitting in Kendall's office overlooking the magnificent sculpture garden that to this day makes the PepsiCo campus one of the most spectacular corporate grounds in the world. The gardens, dotted with works by major artists including Rodin, Calder, and Moore, seemed to be the right backdrop for a man whose interests and concerns transcended carbonated soft drinks and Pepsi's line of Frito-Lay products.

The conversation with Kendall covered a lot of ground. But one topic made a lasting impression—the PepsiCo leader's contention that business leaders needed to play a much stronger role in the organizations and public agencies that sculpted our quality of life. Kendall wasn't just talk. He had a history of activism in all kinds of domestic and international nonprofits ranging from the National Alliance of Businessmen to the American Ballet Theatre. As many contributions as Kendall made outside PepsiCo, he said he wished he had the time and resources to do more. Then he pondered out loud about what would happen if corporations split the CEO and chairmanship responsibilities so company chairmen could devote a decent portion of their time to external affairs.

A lot has happened since that meeting so many years ago. The Donald M. Kendall Sculpture Garden has become more renowned than ever before. Kendall himself was inducted into the National Business Hall of Fame with the likes of Thomas Edison and Andrew Carnegie. He was also awarded the first Equal Justice Award by the NACCP Legal Defense and Educational Fund, which cited him for "his restless searching for fresh opportunity and a spaciousness of vision..." And Kendall's notion of dividing company leadership responsibilities between the CEO and chairman did a slow dance toward reality.

As of 2007, about 37 percent of the S&P 500 companies had adopted management models with two people running the show—a CEO and a separate chairman. Four years earlier only 21 percent of those companies had split their leadership roles between two people.

Most of the arguments for separating responsibilities at the top of a business revolve around the improvement of corporate governance. I would add another reason robbed from Chase Bank's David Rockefeller, who called on his CEO peers to "resume the role of what we used to call business statesmen." Regrettably, Rockefeller's words have largely been ignored and America is paying a hefty price for the loss of private sector statesmanship.

There are mixed opinions about whether cutting apart the CEO and chairman roles is a recipe for improving a company's internal operations. But it seems to be the right answer for freeing up top executive time to address *external* challenges that have an impact on the company's ability to do business. If companies were to agree that a corporate chairman commit one third of his or her time to nonprofit or public service initiatives, the United States would win big time. Following is just one example of how this executive talent might be leveraged.

GETTING SERIOUS ABOUT FIXING AMERICA'S SCHOOLS

The United States is in a quandary about how to fix its public elementary and secondary schools. As educators have lamented for years, American students fare poorly when lined up next to young people in other developed nations. International Student Assessment test scores, for instance, show fifteen-year-olds in this country lagging behind their teenage counterparts in sixteen other nations. Even more worrisome, an estimated 1.5 million young people in the United States drop out of school each year.

Overall, the country's pre-K through 12 education system—especially in economically depressed parts of our nation—is not performing adequately.

American businesses should be apoplectic about this situation. Schools are crucial to turning out capable workers and reasonably intelligent consumers. If schools fall short today, the forecast for businesses tomorrow is for very stormy conditions. Yet the business community's response to this challenge has been largely unimpressive.

This is not to say businesses have totally turned their backs on pre-college education. Trade associations such as the U.S. Chamber of Commerce and Business Roundtable are wrestling with the problem. And there is also a small group of industry captains pushing for changes in the way we educate our youth—people such as

- *Norman Augustine, the former head of Lockheed Martin*—wants the country to train more engineers and scientists.

- *Craig Barrett, Intel's retired CEO and board chairman* – worked with state governors and other business people to upgrade school standards through a program called Achieve.
- *Louis Gerstner, former head of IBM and RJR Nabisco* – thinks improving teacher performance is how American education can be transformed.
- *Sanford Weill, chairman emeritus of Citigroup* – founded the National Academy Foundation, which prepares students for working in the financial field and other professions.

And it's not difficult to find an assortment of company programs that take aim at the pre-college education field:

- *Time Warner Cable* – investing $100 million (over five years) to push the "STEM" (science, technology, engineering, and math) agenda in line with federal government priorities.
- *Discovery Communications* – $150 million for the "Be the Future" campaign.
- *Motorola* – an Innovation Generation program (another STEM initiative).
- *Verizon* – a free digital learning platform called "Thinkfinity" that brings high-quality education content to the classroom.

Perhaps the company with the longest and most striking track record in the education improvement field is IBM. Led by Stan Litow, a savvy educator who was deputy chancellor for operations and chief operating officer of New York City Public Schools, the company has made huge investments in school reform. Its long menu of grant-funded education programs ranges from an early childhood KidsSmart Learning Program to its high-school-focused Try Science program, carried out with the Association of Science-Technology Centers.

While these individuals and companies are notable in their efforts to improve American pre-college education, it will take many more business leaders to win the battle. So far, there is a paucity of high-end executives who are really invested in these efforts beyond showing up at a meeting or two, lending their name to a task force, or assigning a lower-level company representative as a study committee place holder.

If a group of company chairmen were to concentrate on education improvement by working in conjunction with local, state, or federal school officials and determined school reform advocates such as Bill Gates of the Gates Foundation, much could be accomplished. But it will take a meaningful investment of time, effort, and conditional grants to make this happen. A company chairman who agrees to attend a lunch meeting every quarter isn't the answer. A group of company chairmen willing to apply their organizational, analytical, and restructuring skills have the potential to make meaningful headway.

Consider how these executives might use a standard business approach to solving the pre-college education dilemma.

Problem: produce more high-quality "products" in the most cost-efficient manner possible.

Solution: start with an assessment of current production systems from raw goods (pre-kindergarten) to end product (high school grads). Leave production "lines" that meet acceptable standards intact (such as high-income suburbs with stable schools and wrap-around student support services). Production systems that don't meet output expectations are targeted for change (communities where schools turn out students with less-than-desired competencies or that have high dropout rates). Eliminate existing production methods (traditional K–12 method of educating children) and replace them with new systems geared to production needs (for example, incentive-based, school-to-work plans that engage businesses as full education partners; apprenticeship-based learning; and so on). Implement continuous improvement programs to ensure maximum cost-benefit outcomes.

Predictably, teacher unions would be in an uproar over any radical education shakeup. Rigid school administrators and government bureaucrats would balk. But by enlisting company executives who have won their stripes by jumping over these kinds of hurdles within their own businesses, innovative programs would have a much better chance of seeing the light of day.

Education isn't the only social issue critical to the long-term success of the nation's private sector. Business statesmen could be enormously influential change agents who could tackle issues ranging from homelessness to prison reform, energy conservation to obesity prevention. But such leadership won't surface if high-level executives aren't afforded adequate time and back-up business resources to address our country's most serious challenges. *Splitting apart the CEO and chairman responsibilities and carving out at least a third of the chairman's time for statesmanship work would be a major step in the right direction.*

The case for freeing up more high-caliber business talent was bolstered by a McKinsey & Company study conducted for the Committee Encouraging Corporate Philanthropy. The research concluded that businesses have an ability to "apply distinctive capabilities and resources to social issues that individuals, governments and independent-sector contributors cannot." How? By pressing business leaders to "seize opportunities for authentic engagement in society." That's a goal far more achievable if company chairmen had the wherewithal to focus on the "social issues" singled out in the McKinsey report.

Even when there is a split between the CEO and chairman functions, it doesn't guarantee a chairman will actually take on a larger statesman role. A discouraging finding from one recent study of fifteen hundred of the nation's biggest companies uncovered little evidence that stand-alone chairmen were answering David Rockefeller's call for executives to "sink their roots in their communities."

So no matter how a corporation's front office is configured, there's a long road to travel before a company chairman is likely to surface as a significant player in grappling with non-business problems. That leaves the corporate CEO (whether carrying the chairman's title or not) to work the helm when it comes to corporate giving.

As folded into the answer to this chapter's question, there are four actions a CEO can take to maximize the value of a company's contributions program.

Demand the Right Kind of "ROI"

Paying attention to corporate philanthropy isn't easy for many CEOs, given the crush of so many other business issues that bulldoze their way into a company's front office. Yet those CEOs who are able to put aside distractions and sharply focus on the *business* as well as the *social* advantages associated with conditional contributions frequently end up with high-grade programs. One case in point is GlaxoSmithKline.

USING SMART GIVING TO BOOST A COMPANY'S REPUTATION

Andrew Witty, GlaxoSmithKline's (GSK's) young CEO, made the kind of bold philanthropic moves that won him and his company considerable praise even among organizations and individuals usually quick to gore any pharmaceutical company in sight. Whether at Harvard or the Council on Foreign Relations, Witty hasn't missed an opportunity to outline his social responsibility strategies, which include

- Donating one-fifth of all profits made in poor countries toward building health systems
- Quadrupling the annual donation of GSK's drug albendazole, used to prevent lymphatic filariasis, which is more commonly known as elephantiasis
- Pricing a new malaria vaccine (if it passes clinical trials) at only 5 percent above cost for lower-income countries
- Loaning executives to poor nations to help in the treatment and prevention of diseases

GSK's contribution decisions have moved the second-largest pharmaceutical corporation in the world up the list of companies tracked by the Access to Medicine Index—a Netherlands-based service that rates drug companies on the basis of their commitments to underserved nations and individuals. What is GSK's Index standing? Number 1.

Witty's decision to capitalize on a strong contributions action plan has yielded other business benefits as well. GSK reports widespread support among employees. And Witty's passionate belief that a company can make a difference for people in the Third World while advancing its own P&L interests has attracted the kind of media attention that a broad-scale ad campaign could never buy.

Corporations that view a contribution as an expenditure that can and should yield a clearly defined return on investment are often the companies that ultimately squeeze the most value out of a donation. The ROI should not be measured just in social terms (how much bang for the buck a donation generates in improving a local community's quality of life) but also in business terms (how much value a donation generates for a company's reputation or increases consumer awareness).

The CEO's most important function is to demand that a system be developed, put in place, and constantly monitored to ensure this double-barreled ROI becomes the test for any contribution a business makes.

Say the Right Words

The CEO has to make it clear that conditional charitable grant making is important for the company. There should be no ambivalence or mumbling about this. If the CEO doesn't state emphatically that corporate philanthropy counts, then it probably will end up in the last seat on the business bus.

One of the main reasons I decided to join Johnson & Johnson was its CEO, Jim Burke—who stepped down about the time I took on my vice president role at the company. He was cut from the same cloth as other chief executives who had a national reputation for being out front in the social responsibility field—David Kearns at Xerox, John Filer at Aetna, and a few more. Burke was never more articulate than when it came to talking about a company's obligations to the world at large. Given his business upbringing, it was easy to understand why he was so passionate about the broad social role he felt a company should play. In the old days, J&J promoted executives on the basis of their business acumen *and* their involvement in local, state, or national affairs. The company's executive review process included being grilled on one's civic accomplishments as well as one's business achievements. Burke's rise to the top meant he had corporate social responsibility coursing through his veins.

Immensely helpful to Burke was the Johnson & Johnson Credo, which stated unequivocally that a core company responsibility was to be "a good citizen," defined as the supporter of good works and charities. J&J's CEO used the Credo to underscore the importance of corporate philanthropy and employee volunteerism. There wasn't an employee or retiree who didn't get the message. No question about it—corporate contributions meant something.

What Burke taught me was that *how* a CEO communicates a message can be as important as the message itself. Following is a short list of communication techniques that usually bear fruit.

Capitalize on Large Live Appearances

Some CEOs work a crowd better than others. However, even taking into account differences in presentation styles, nothing quite matches the communication effectiveness of a CEO who says something in real time. Large staff meetings (even if broadcast by video to remote locations) offer the boss an opportunity to spotlight philanthropy in a way that's difficult to do via any other kind of messaging. Think about what kind of employee reaction there would be to these words: "I want to take a minute or two to talk to you about the careful contribution of money and time you and I and our company should be making to our communities and nation. I cannot tell you how important this is to me...." This approach requires sincerity. A CEO who fakes it doesn't score points; quite the contrary. Done correctly and periodically, though, this is a powerful way to send a message while at the same time creating added respect for the corporation's chief executive.

Use the Printed and Electronic Word—Sparingly

Company employees, retirees, and shareholders are engulfed with too many letters, brochures, reports, and types of web-based information. Trying to get a few words through the clutter isn't easy. Nevertheless, there are times when even a paragraph or two dropped into the right printed piece or e-publication can make all the difference. Businesses that reference conditional corporate contributions in the company's annual report tend to be highly regarded in the philanthropy field. A couple of well-crafted paragraphs in what for most companies is their most important document can say more than a dozen other brochures that tout a company's philanthropy activities.

Let Praise Come from Others

One of the most effective ways a CEO can broadcast a company's philanthropic message is—not to say anything. Let someone else do the back-patting. A brief true story will illustrate how powerful this strategy can be.

HOW TRIBUTE CAN TRUMP TROUBLE

Years before its 1999 merger with Minneapolis-based Honeywell, the Allied-Signal Corporation operated a chromium production plant near the Chesapeake Bay not too far from Baltimore. Effluent from the plant leaked into the bay and created a PR nightmare for the company. A portion of the corporation's business was connected to defense contracting, and having a headline-grabbing problem occurring so close to Washington, D.C., turned out to be bad business. The event stirred up sour feelings among key Congressional leaders instrumental in the Defense Department budgeting process.

In addition to making sure no additional chromium made its way into the Chesapeake, Allied-Signal developed a national contributions initiative to prove it really wanted to be a comprehensive corporate citizen. It launched the Allied-Signal Program on Aging, with the Johns Hopkins School of Public Health as its partner. A blue ribbon selection panel picked innovative researchers working in the aging field, and the winners were brought to D.C., where they were celebrated at an event held annually at the Four Seasons Hotel in Georgetown. The awards dinner brought together an elite crowd of people with strong interests in aging—from old-time movie stars to Congressional staffers who did the backroom work for legislators engaged in aging policymaking. But most important, House members and Senators also turned up at the event.

At the awards dinner, the research winners (who received a substantial cash award and what became a cherished crystal trophy) were lauded. And so was Allied-Signal. From the president of Johns Hopkins to the most esteemed leaders in the aging field, praise was heaped on Allied-Signal for its vision and commitment. Congressional attitudes about the company softened, and Allied-Signal's government contracting work moved forward.

The Allied-Signal CEO did little or no flag-waving at the annual awards dinner. He didn't have to. A roster of credible guests handled that chore and did so in a way that no chest-beating employee could even hope to do. The CEO's communication role was to assign such importance to the dinner that he showed up—no matter what. And then he acted as a statesman by focusing his remarks on America's responsibilities to its growing senior population.

Using conditional contributions, companies can fund programs that allow for credible outsiders to say good things about a corporation. When and where appropriate, the CEO should be on hand to accept the praise in a self-effacing manner that brings even more respect to a corporation.

Meet with Employee Volunteer Stand-Outs

Aside from staff personnel who are paid to manage a company's philanthropy, there are employees who "go the extra mile" by performing good deeds outside the corporation. These individuals are powerful ambassadors for the corporation, and the more they know the company truly appreciates their efforts, the more effective they are likely to be. Whether coordinating a walkathon, chairing an influential nonprofit board, or running the United Way campaign, these individuals put a face on whatever conditional grants a company makes. Time and again, I have been told by corporate contributions and employee volunteer managers that other than a bonus, the most meaningful way to recognize these stand-outs is to have the CEO invite them to the front office for an informal visit.

One CEO told me that he hosts a small breakfast meeting for four to six high-achieving employee volunteers once or twice a month. Part "thank you" events and part focus groups, the breakfasts are a valuable two-way communication channel for the CEO. The chief executive picks up unfiltered information about what's going on inside and outside the business while the invited guests get top office confirmation that their extra efforts are highly valued.

Build the Right Team

The previous chapter outlined who should be on the "A" team for putting together and directing a conditional corporate contributions program. The senior executives who get the starting positions for the team need to be designated by the CEO. This point cannot be stressed enough.

When Jim Burke built the J&J philanthropy program, he handpicked members of the corporate contributions committee. A senior vice president named John Heldrich was singled out as chairman (Heldrich would later become nationally recognized for designing a "holistic model" that infused corporate contributions into a plan aimed at revitalizing small cities). Then Burke said to the new committee (in absolutely no uncertain terms), "I expect you to take on this responsibility the way you would handle your most important business assignment. If there's a meeting, show up. If there are additional responsibilities that go along with serving on the contributions committee, find a way to handle them. This is important to me, the corporation and to your professional development."

This may sound a lot like a corporate version of the Selective Service draft. And in some respects, it was. But if the CEO doesn't designate the right team members and make it clear that this is an important rung on their career ladders, it is probably doomed to become one of those duties that gets pushed aside or treated frivolously.

The dozen members of the Johnson & Johnson contributions committee—all high-ranking executives—had an 80 percent attendance record at meetings held throughout the year. They took part in an annual day-long offsite planning meeting, and each member shouldered individual responsibilities for parts of the contributions program. Would that have happened if the CEO hadn't sent out a message that was loud and unambiguous? Very unlikely.

Pick the Right Manager

Other than the CEO, few company employees have as much direct interaction with the public as the manager charged with overseeing the corporate contributions program or company foundation. For many nonprofit organizations and community leaders, the contributions manager is the alter ego of the CEO. The next chapter focuses on the kind of attributes a company should consider when selecting an employee to head the contributions office. Whoever is picked needs to have a comfortable and mutually respectful relationship with the CEO as well as the administrator and secretaries in the front office.

In most large corporations, the contributions manager and CEO will forge a dotted-line link, which means the two offices will communicate back and forth without the contributions manager's boss getting involved. I have worked with a few companies where this dotted-line arrangement makes the manager's boss *very* uncomfortable. A California biotech corporation is a good example. The company has a competent contributions director in place with an anxious and somewhat insecure vice president as her supervisor. The director and CEO bypass the vice president when discussing how to handle a sensitive donation request or make a decision about showing up at a charity dinner. The VP demands full disclosure about anything and everything discussed with the CEO. If something goes unreported, the director gets reminded of the slip-up at her next performance review meeting.

So, picking the right manager also means orienting the manager's boss as to how and why it is okay for the contributions head to have one-on-one time with the CEO.

The Four-Plus-Two-Step Plan

If a CEO wants his or her business to be a truly *comprehensive* corporate citizen, two more steps have to be taken:

1. *Support the ante-up concept.* Adopt the principle of budgeting the company's cash contributions at 1 percent of expected pretax earnings for the year by using the Sabsevitz Ante-Up Formula. If that's too difficult to do immediately, announce plans for moving toward that goal. Back up the right talk with the right amount of money earmarked for *conditional* grant making.
2. *Don't hide behind illusory smokescreens.* There are lots of ways to at least try to fool the public into thinking that a company is doing more than it really is in the corporate responsibility

field. Producing slick reports and spending big bucks on TV commercials that flag wave one or two company projects are a couple of typical tactics. For some companies, groups such as the Committee Encouraging Corporate Philanthropy (see Introduction) offer camouflage because membership in the organization gives the impression that companies have been "encouraged" sufficiently enough to fund their contributions programs so that they're at least as generous as the average business donor. Giving a few businesses that lag behind in their philanthropy this kind of cover was surely never the intent of the organization's founders—quite the contrary. Member companies that have contributions programs far ahead of the pack are more reflective of the leader-level businesses Paul Newman and other founders had hoped to inspire.

CEOs who practice the four-plus-two plan aren't, to steal Rosabeth Moss Kanter's phrase in her book *Supercorp*, "soft-hearted do-gooders." As Kanter reminds us, effective business leaders "push the limits of their market dominance and pricing power, compete aggressively and lobby governments for favorable treatment." But CEOs who understand the importance of comprehensive corporate citizenship do something else. They point their resources and business intelligence at social challenges that fall within their sphere of interest and understanding. They recognize that smart giving can and does translate into good business.

IN SUMMARY

Question 4: What's the right role for the CEO?

Answer: To carry out four functions: (a) demand the strongest possible business and social ROI from all contributions; (b) say the right words at the right time about program goals and purposes; (c) build the right executive team to develop, oversee, and evaluate the contributions process; and (d) pick a competent manager to provide day-to-day administration of the contributions program.

5

Who Should Administer Company Donations?

Want a job as a full-time corporate contributions manager? You probably have a better shot at being a major league baseball player or a professional ballet dancer. Of the million-plus companies and sole proprietorships in the United States, fewer than five hundred are estimated to have full-time employees who administer corporate contributions programs.

Corporate giving in the United States is largely a part-time management affair shouldered by thousands of workers whose primary responsibilities have nothing to do with philanthropy. But regardless of whether a company has twenty people working full time in a contributions department (yes, there are companies with staffs that large) or is a small business that expects the human resources secretary to keep a watchful eye on contributions, the next question in our baker's dozen list is important:

Question 5: Who should administer company donations?

Answer: A person (or team) who knows a company's mission and business objectives; is an effective external and internal representative for the company; is detailed oriented; and is sensitive to how company resources can be used to address social needs and opportunities.

Absent from the answer are terms such as *philanthropically motivated* and *socially conscious*. The assumption is that most people are prone to wanting to do good and act responsibly. Having these qualities alone won't make a contributions manager or administrator as effective as she or he should be. Remember, businesses are not charitable institutions. So it makes sense that those charged with overseeing a company's contributions should view themselves primarily as *business* people and not philanthropists. Their role is to extract the greatest possible business and social value from the donation of cash, product, or employee time.

Picking a World-Class Manager

Whether full time or part time, competent contributions managers exhibit common characteristics. In my involvement with hundreds of these people over the years, I have found that the "best of class" have similar qualities regardless of the number of hours a week they devote to handling contribution responsibilities. Following is an abbreviated list.

Business Savvy

Managers who stand out in the contributions field are those who know their corporations inside and out. They are aware of what their companies make or what services they sell and can speak intelligently about business opportunities and challenges. This sounds rudimentary, but it amazes me that there are managers running large corporate giving programs who give you a blank look when questions are asked about how much a business earns or the range of products or services the corporation offers. At the very least, contributions managers should do the following:

- *Read the company's annual report.* Even better, *study* the annual report from the CEO's introductory message to the audited financials.
- *Read and understand media and analyst stories or reports.* It's an excellent way to absorb outside impressions about the company.

- *Memorize the company's mission statement.* What are the fundamental underpinnings of the business, and how does the contributions program fit in with the mission?

I have met contributions managers who didn't know where to find their company's P&L statement. Others had no knowledge of their corporation's most important current and future markets. Publicly traded companies make this information totally transparent, and when people outside the business know more about a corporation than a contributions manager, something's wrong.

An Eye for Details

In many respects, corporate contributions management is a high-volume job. Small businesses are not immune from wave after wave of charitable requests. Larger companies (especially direct-to-consumer firms) typically get inundated with appeals. Managing the flow and keeping close watch on what funds are dispensed requires a nose for details. It takes only one errant donation or one callous rejection letter to stain the good work the contributions office may be carrying out.

This doesn't mean the chief contributions manager—whether a lone wolf or a department head with several direct reports—should be a do-it-yourselfer who spends days and nights making QuickBook entries for every donation that goes out the company door. Rather, the manager should have the knowhow to use the finance, data processing, and monitoring resources (in-house technology or outside vendors) necessary to keep things in order.

Public Appeal

When the insurance giant WellPoint asked me for help in its search for a new company foundation president, I suggested the corporation close its collective eyes and picture a candidate standing in front of a large crowd of prospective customers and investors. How articulate and compelling would that candidate be when talking about not just the company's social responsibility interests but also the company itself? Would the candidate fit the image WellPoint wanted to portray outside the company?

The second question reeked of superficiality. But I wasn't advocating that the insurance company hire a Brad Pitt or Angelina Jolie look-alike. Rather, I was proposing that the foundation president should come across as an executive whose demeanor matches the title. For many, many people and organizations, the contributions chief puts a face on the company, and first impressions being what they are, the face should be one that is (as much as possible) a reflection of what the corporation stands for on many fronts.

Another important point—particularly true for large companies—is that effective contributions managers commit to showing up at the right place and at the right time. For some individuals, this requirement can be an occupational deal-breaker. It means night work and travel. So if a manager doesn't have a flexible calendar or isn't a people person, then the company's contributions program isn't being leveraged the way it should.

In-House Focus

While handling the company's donation checkbook, a corporate contributions manager will never be short of fundraising "friends," invitations to meetings, and free cocktails or dinners. The larger the company's philanthropy payout is, the more these forces come into play. Such temptations constantly tug at the manager's calendar, and it's easy for some individuals to get so swept up in the outside world that they become strangers to those inside the company.

As noted, it is important to show up at those external functions and events that are necessary to the company. But it is equally important not to become so seduced by outside activities that a manager pulls back from key players *inside* the company. Contributions executives who are at the company conference table when it comes to making important business decisions tend to—as the late Rodney Dangerfield put it—*get no respect*. The more respect the manager has internally, the more effective he or she is in advancing the objectives of the contributions program.

Some philanthropy managers are legendary for time spent at special events, professional meetings, grantee site visits, and board meetings. Corporate representation is an important part of a contributions manager's job—but it's easy to go overboard. Working with decision makers inside the company is also crucial. Striking the right balance is a sign of a highly effective contributions manager.

What Size Staff?

In my earlier book *Corporate Social Investing,* I included a chart that outlined minimum staffing recommendations based on a company's annual contributions pay-out. Many years later, I still find those numbers to be on target (Table 5.1).

Businesses that allocate less than $5 million a year in gifts and grants can get away with administering those transactions

Table 5.1. Staffing Recommendations.

Annual Contributions Payout (in millions)	Personnel Numbers		
	Exempt	Nonexempt	Part Time
Under $5	0	0	0–3
$5–$10	1	1	1
$10–$15	2	1	2
$15–$20	2	2	1
$20–$25	3	2	2
$25–$30	3	2	2
$30–$35	4	3	2
$35–$40	5	4	2
$40–$45	6	4	3
$45–$50	6	4	3
$50–$75	7	5	3
$75–$100	8	6	4
$100>	9+	7+	5+

Source: Curt Weeden, *Corporate Social Investing* (San Francisco: Berrett-Koehler, 1998).

by doling out duties to staff who have other primary work responsibilities. Typically, smaller corporations look to personnel in human resources or finance to take on this added task.

According to a review of IRS statistics, about 10 percent—or 32,000—of the country's 319,000 "C corporations" (which include most of the largest businesses in the nation) file annual tax returns showing taxable income of $5 million or more. Subtracting the five hundred companies with full-time administrative staffs overseeing contributions activities, that leaves over 31,000 relatively large companies relying on either full-time equivalents or a mix of part-timers to run their respective shows.

As for the nearly one million "S corporations," which tend to register pretax earnings lower than those recorded by C corporations, full-time help is rare. The same is true for 700,000 partnerships that the IRS has on its books.

If a company doesn't have full-time help to handle contributions, does that mean the firm is less philanthropically inclined? A study of over one thousand small businesses sponsored by Advanta Bank and *The Chronicle of Philanthropy* helped answer that question. The study focused on companies with under five hundred employees (most were far smaller, though, with twenty or fewer workers). Annual revenues typically ranged from $100,000 to $250,000. The findings were fascinating. *Over two-thirds of the companies said they made cash donations (the median range was $500 and $2,000 per company); 41 percent contributed different types of services; 39 percent contributed products.*

Even more interesting are the results of an American Express survey of 750 slightly larger companies with annual revenues of up to $1 million. On average, these businesses claim they give *6 percent of their profits to charity.* Remember, the IRS data show that for all companies, the average level of corporate giving is at or around 1 percent of pretax net income.

There are explanations why very small companies record much higher levels of giving than larger businesses. Owners of small companies classified as "S" corporations can use their businesses as funding avenues for their personal charitable giving. Since S corporation profits and losses are ultimately factored into a personal tax return, an owner might choose to use the business to handle most or all contributions while not bothering to deduct any or few donations from her or his 1040 personal return.

So size clearly does have an impact on how a corporation manages its contributions activities. Here are a few notes for companies that have full-time contributions management employees—and those that don't.

For Companies with Full-Time Staff

Eighty-five of the five hundred businesses that *do* have full-time staffs are clearly big hitters in the corporate contributions world. This small cluster of companies reports cash and product contributions that in aggregate account for more than half the nation's total reported corporate donations.

Managers heading up contributions programs at larger corporations not only have different titles (vice president—community relations; president—company foundation; director of corporate contributions; and so on) but also have different levels of authority and influence within their businesses. And the variance in compensation and benefits is an eye opener. Some contributions program chiefs earn five-figure salaries and are not bonus eligible. Others are handsomely rewarded. Take, for instance, Ralph Boyd Jr., who was executive vice president of community relations for the embattled Freddie Mac and who also served as chairman of the Freddie Mac Foundation. In 2004, he earned $375,000, was paid a $500,000 cash bonus, and received $549,000 in restricted stock as added long-term compensation.

There is no standard career path that leads to the top spot in a company's contributions office. Some corporations carefully and deliberately search inside and outside the private sector for the best talent available to run their philanthropy and community relations activities. But there are also companies that use the office to solve personnel problems. Here are some examples:

- Parking a lesser performing executive (often someone who is a few years from retirement) in what the corporation considers to be a relatively innocuous job until the employment cord can be cut.
- Showcasing an African American, Hispanic, or Asian employee to give the company the appearance of being a

diverse organization at higher levels of management even
if that doesn't happen to be the case.
- Giving a lower-ranking female manager an impressive
  external title (such as vice president or even president of
  the company foundation) to suggest the company affords
  women an opportunity to pierce its glass ceiling.

Sometimes a company gets lucky and selects a contributions
manager for all the wrong reasons but discovers the individual has
all the right skill sets to get the job done. In other cases, a poor
choice ends up reinforcing preconceived ideas among many in
a company that the contributions job is more about tokenism or
cronyism than about effective grants management.

For Companies with Part-Time or No Staff

Very small businesses tend to have a looser definition of charitable
giving than larger corporations. Sponsorship of a local sports team
might be factored into what a small company considers charitable
giving, whereas a larger corporation would be advised (strongly) to
exclude that expenditure as part of its donations total. Even more
common are small companies that underestimate their annual
charitable support.

For example, my brother-in-law co-owns two jewelry stores.
He's known for a big heart and an open wallet. Some of the
donations he makes to community groups are logged for what
they are—charitable gifts. But he's a soft touch for "walk ins"
who nab a cash donation or an inventory item for a charity auction.
These relatively small commitments add up. But they don't always
get folded into what a company labels as company contributions.

For very small companies, it is the owner or small group of
senior executives who nearly always make donation decisions. A
contributions committee or company foundation board are rar-
ities among corporations that employ relatively few workers and
have revenues under $1 million (or even under $5 million, for that
matter). With contribution decisions usually made by the boss,
it is the front office secretary, administrative assistant, or company bookkeeper who often becomes the corporate philanthropy
manager of sorts. These executive-level support staffers can be
very competent gatekeepers who keep a small company's giving

focused and disciplined *if* the boss (a) allows them to act in that capacity and (b) is clear about giving priorities and exclusions.

Here are two tips for small and medium-sized businesses that I have found to be especially helpful.

Predetermined Giving Guidelines

Small to medium companies—particularly storefront businesses—are commonly overrun with requests from local organizations looking for support. Short of posting a *No Solicitations* sign on the front window, how do these businesses ward off unwanted appeals without creating a negative ripple effect that has an impact on their community or (even worse) customers? Answer: use written guidelines for giving.

A simple one-page statement can be as much of a godsend to a smaller or medium-sized company as printed guidelines for giving can be to a multibillion-dollar international corporation. Instead of trying to turn down a walk-in solicitor with whatever excuse of the day can be pulled out of the air, hand the fundraiser a sheet of paper that says

- We wish we could offer financial help to all the important programs and activities in our community.
- But because there are so many needs and because our resources are limited, we have found it necessary to focus our charitable giving.
- Our company gives generously to the United Way (or some similar "umbrella" charitable organization) as a means of assisting our community at large.
- In addition, we make a limited number of contributions for 501c3 organizations working to protect our waterways [or substitute whatever other narrowly defined interest area is a high priority for the company].
- Unfortunately, we are unable to provide products or financial assistance for auctions, sporting events, walkathons, dinners, and other special events.
- For organizations that do carry out programs that meet our guidelines, please provide us with a brief, written request (our usual response time is six to eight weeks).

Having this kind of written statement close at hand so it can be produced on the spot when the company is approached for a donation gives the business an *objective* rather than *subjective* means of reacting to a solicitation. A rejection is easier to handle if it isn't interpreted as being personal. This is an easy-to-produce resource that can make life much easier for smaller businesses—particularly those that are consistently solicited for charitable donations.

The Right Accountant

There are tax professionals who only take a rearview mirror approach to a company's income and expenses. Then there are tax professionals who not only review past financials but also guide and advise companies about steps they could take *now* to capitalize on tax code allowances. For very small companies that don't have a chief financial officer on board, having the services of a more proactive accountant who looks ahead and not just behind can be very advantageous.

Tax laws dealing with the charitable giving field are dynamic and often are affected by unanticipated events. A good example was the "Katrina Emergency Tax Relief Act" passed after the devastating hurricane ravaged the Gulf Coast in 2005. The law allowed larger businesses (usually C corporations) as well as smaller or medium-sized companies (usually S corporations) to claim an enhanced deduction for donations of food inventory and certain types of books but only for a limited period of time. When the deadline for taking advantage of these special tax benefits approached, another law was passed (Pension Protection Act) that extended the food inventory provision for an additional year.

Learning about changes in the tax code after the fact or not being advised about the tax implications of different charitable giving options before the close of a fiscal year are hallmarks of a less helpful accountant. A small business that gets counsel throughout the year from a well-informed tax professional is bound to be ahead of the game.

Lawyers and Grant Making

If a helpful accountant is an asset to a company's corporate contributions program, an obliging lawyer can prove to be equally or even more important. With grant making increasingly subject to legal review (especially among regulated businesses such as pharmaceutical and energy companies), lawyers are more entwined with contribution decision making than ever before. I can name more lawyers who are now in full-time corporate contributions management positions than at any time since I began consulting with businesses thirty years ago.

Corporate lawyers are trained to guard a company's interests on the outside and prevent employees from doing harm on the inside. That's important. But not all attorneys perform their duties the same way. They range from helpful problem solvers to anal retentive problem perpetuators. Lawyers who carry out their protectionist duties in a way that turns them into obstructionists can spell trouble for a business. At the other end of the spectrum are lawyers whose motto is, "If we can't do it one way, we'll figure out another way."

The difference between these legal philosophies was never more apparent than when I was called to consult with a deliberately unnamed New Jersey equipment manufacturer and, not long after, Bausch + Lomb, the optical care company.

TALE OF TWO COMPANIES: LEGAL ENCUMBRANCE; LEGAL ENCOURAGEMENT

The unnamed New Jersey corporation has a domestic and European workforce of eleven thousand employees and sales that top $2.5 billion. It has a solid profit to earnings ratio and operates with profit margins above its industry average. Primarily because of its relatively mundane product lines, the company isn't the most exciting corporation in America. But still, its management is competent albeit conservative.

The Garden State equipment firm runs its contributions program as part of its human resources department, with an experienced contributions manager handling day-to-day administrative duties. Hovering on all sides of the HR department are agents from the law department. Like many other companies, the business is deeply concerned about "fraud and abuse avoidance." The goal is to prevent sales employees and others from using inappropriate incentives (including the promise of charitable donations) to induce customers to purchase a company product—or to reward the customer for buying a product after the sale has been made.

There is no question that the equipment company's law department, including specialists in regulatory compliance, is needed to ensure that employees understand where the line is drawn between acceptable and unacceptable practices. However, it's not just about explaining "what can and can't be done." It's also about how flexible the law department is in helping employees—including those working in the contributions field—find ways to accomplish a business objective that is within lawful boundaries.

The legal and compliance personnel at the equipment company were so intertwined with the contributions review and approval process that nearly every proposed contribution action had to be blessed by the law department. In short, lawyers had de facto control of the contributions planning and maintenance process.

The result?

A complicated, bureaucratized policy manual on contributions (drafted by the legal department) that crushed the company's ability to maximize the value of its philanthropy program.

Bausch + Lomb, based in Rochester, New York, was acquired by the private equity firm Warburg Pincus in 2007. It also has revenues in excess of $2.5 billion and its employee headcount numbers around eleven thousand as well. Like the unnamed New Jersey corporation, Bausch + Lomb works diligently to avoid violating any anti-kickback laws and is committed to staying inside ethical parameters set down by trade groups such as the Pharmaceutical Manufacturers Association, Advanced Medical Technology Association, European Federation of Pharmaceutical Industries and Associations, and so on. With all these rules, regulations, and guidelines in play, both firms understood the need to have lawyers on the field. At the equipment corporation, I didn't see that as a plus. But at Bausch + Lomb, it proved advantageous because the legal team was more attuned to finding ways to turn a good idea into reality than coming up with reasons not to move forward.

When I was invited to participate in a half-day meeting to help plan Bausch + Lomb's contributions program, the general counsel and top compliance lawyers were in the room. There was no intimidation or idea stifling by the legal staff. In fact, some of the more innovative recommendations that bubbled to the surface during the meeting came from the lawyers. The attitude the legal folks brought to the meeting was, "Come up with a list of great philanthropic and community relations ideas first and let us worry about how to fashion them so they will stand any compliance tests down the road."

Here's the moral of this brief story—there is a necessary role for lawyers in the overall conduct of a corporate contributions program. The trick is to engage counsel in a way that keeps a contributions program manager out of jail without stomping on the innovation and energy that can be the difference between a powerful conditional contributions effort and a scattershot exercise in dispensing handouts.

Finding the Right Home for a Contributions Program

Although lawyers are more deeply engaged in the contributions process than they were a decade or two ago, it is not a common practice to have grant making administered out of the legal department. The Association of Corporate Contributions Professionals recently researched a cross-section of the largest private sector donors and found that only about 8 percent of the companies surveyed had philanthropy programs plugged into their law departments. Most companies (60 percent) have the function situated in their communications or PR departments. In some companies, contributions activities are managed out of human resources, finance, government affairs, or even the CEO's office.

A question constantly fired at me is, "Where *should* our contributions program be housed?" My response is usually, "'Where' is less important than 'who'." Assuming a company has a well-defined conditional grant-making plan in place and a competent day-to-day administrator on board, the contributions function should be able to operate effectively from within almost any corporate department. What can make an enormous difference to a contributions program is finding a high-ranking departmental executive who *wants* the function and can *advocate* to other senior executives on its behalf.

IN SUMMARY

Question 5: Who should administer a company's contributions program?

Answer: An individual (or team) who (a) knows a company's mission and business objectives; (b) can serve as an effective external and internal representative for the company; (c) is detailed oriented; and (d) is sensitive to how company resources can be used to address social needs and opportunities.

6

Does a Company Need a Foundation?

Until the pharmaceutical giant Pfizer set up shop in a hamlet near the southeast coast of England, the bucolic town of Sandwich was best known as the birthplace of the culinary invention that changed the contents of lunchboxes around the world. Its reputation took a different turn when a small group of chemists working in Pfizer's massive Sandwich research laboratory made a discovery worth billions of dollars.

Company scientists were studying a synthesized compound called Sildenafil, hoping it would blossom into a blockbuster treatment for hypertension and other heart problems. But high expectations gave way to disappointment after clinical trials showed the drug had no significant impact on patients with angina. Then researchers noticed a rather obvious side effect. Sildenafil triggered penile erections. Pfizer wasted no time in patenting the drug as a medication for erectile dysfunction. In 1998, the U.S. Food and Drug Administration gave the company the okay to market the drug under the brand name Viagra. A year later, the drug was a billion-dollar winner, and TV and print advertising would never be the same again.

In 1999, Pfizer went on a drug-selling tear. Viagra along with six other Rx products each contributed $1 billion or more to the company's top line. Flush with cash, Pfizer decided the time was right to make one of the largest corporate donations of all time. It paid $300 million to a single nonprofit. The lucky recipient? Pfizer's own company foundation.

This is when corporate philanthropy skeptics gasp. *A company can take a charitable deduction when it makes a gift to its own foundation?* Correct. Just like any individual can move money into his or her own individual or family foundation for charitable purposes.

Does this explain, then, why two-thousand-plus U.S. corporations have set up foundations? In a few instances, yes—but for the vast majority of businesses that have foundations, there are other reasons. Which leads to the next question in our baker's dozen list:

Question 6: Does a company need a foundation?

Answer: No—but company foundations are useful (albeit not necessary) for certain business reasons including record-keeping simplification, awarding certain international donations, bringing more focused attention to a company's philanthropy, and serving as a catch basin for appreciated assets.

Having a foundation for the sake of having a foundation is too often the underlying motivation for creating a company foundation. It's the old *if a lot of other businesses have a foundation, we should have one too* mentality. Frankly, many of the businesses that have established foundations would be hard pressed to explain the value of these funding mechanisms.

The most oft-cited reason companies give for setting up a foundation is to ensure a steady flow of contributions even if a company's earnings go south. The theory is that by building up foundation assets, the company will create a financial "holding tank" that can be drawn down during the dark days of a profit decline in order to maintain a somewhat even distribution of grants. This is an interesting theory, but one that doesn't stand up to reality. A large percentage of corporations don't have any significant savings at all in their company foundations (Table 6.1).

While the "holding tank" approach has been embraced by a few businesses, most companies with foundations use them as "pass-throughs" or placeholders. Pass-throughs get an infusion of

Table 6.1. Twenty-Five Large Asset-Based Company Foundations (2008–2009).

Company Foundation	Foundation Assets (millions)
Alcoa Foundation	$392
The Merck Company Foundation	334
Wells Fargo Foundation	315
Verizon Foundation	258
Fidelity Foundation	252
The Pfizer Foundation	210
Abbott Fund	208
SunTrust Foundation	199
The Capital Group Co's Charitable Foundation	199
The Wachovia Wells Fargo Foundation	175
WellPoint Foundation	165
Newman's Own Foundation	160
BP Foundation	147
The USAA Foundation	142
IBM Foundation	137
General Motors Foundation	136
Motorola Foundation	131
Freddie Mac Foundation	129
MetLife Foundation	114
Nationwide Foundation	113
Medtronic Foundation	112
AT&T Foundation	112
Georgia Power Foundation	111
The Cargill Foundation	109
Alabama Power Foundation	102

Source: Large Asset-Based Company Foundations, Copyright © 2010 The Foundation Center. Used by permission.

cash from a company at the beginning of the fiscal year and drain the cash by the close of the year. Placeholders are foundations that are kept on the books as largely inactive funding vehicles that could be used at a later time.

If a company doesn't plan on using a foundation as a "holding tank," is it worth the time and limited amount of money to put a foundation in place? Some corporations answer, "Yes." Following are four other often-heard reasons businesses cite for setting up a foundation.

1. *Record-keeping simplification.* When a business makes a direct contribution (meaning that the donation is paid directly from the company and not via its foundation), it is supposed to obtain written verification for each charitable contribution of $250 or more it awards. However, when a company foundation makes a donation of $250 or more, written verification isn't required. How much of a time saver is this for a business? As it turns out, not a lot for many companies for two reasons:

A. Verification is usually not that much of a burdensome task for companies without foundations. The IRS seems satisfied if a company makes a legitimate attempt to collect verification information by sending a simple request letter, postcard, or email to the grantee and then keeping a copy of that communication on file. Most of the time, a nonprofit will respond, but if that doesn't happen, the company's effort to acquire the information demonstrates its attempt to comply with the regulation. So the verification process isn't as onerous as some make it out to be.
B. Companies that do have a foundation often chase nonprofits for grant verification even though the step isn't necessary. Go figure.

Overall, I have not run into too many companies where foundations have actually simplified the record-keeping process. On the contrary; company foundations tend to add complexity to the grant-making process, especially if the corporation uses its foundation to pay for a portion of dinners and special events (a bad idea, as will be explained later) or for other purposes.

2. *International donations.* A company can use its foundation to directly fund organizations and programs outside the United

States. However, this is not a commonplace practice among U.S. corporations, mainly because of a provision called "expenditure responsibility"—a term that deserves more explanation.

Suppose a business based in the United States wants to make a cash donation to a university in Malaysia. The university doesn't have a nonprofit (501c3) tax status in the United States, which means if the company makes a direct payment to the college, it won't be able to write off the transaction as a charitable tax deduction. It can, however, make a donation to the university through its company foundation. But to do so, the foundation has to assume responsibility for the expenditure. According to the IRS, that responsibility must include (a) checking to make sure the grant is spent only for the purpose for which it is made; (b) getting a complete report from the grantee about how the funds are spent; and (c) making a full report to the IRS.

This is a lot of work.

A much easier option for the company is to find a 501c3 nonprofit in the United States that is set up to direct funds to Malaysia. The company routes its gift either directly or through its foundation to the U.S. organization. This "channeling" comes with a price. The corporation loses some of the control it otherwise would have had if it had used its own foundation to move the grant money to the Malaysian university. And the intermediary nonprofit may skim some of the donation to offset its handling expenses. However, the advantage of not having to process the expenditure responsibility paperwork required by the IRS usually outweighs any control concerns a company has. Besides, many of the internationally focused nonprofits are so accommodating to corporate donors that any preferences a business has for how funds should be used are rarely pushed aside.

3. *Management attention.* If a corporation without a foundation has a lackluster or poorly thought-out grant-making program, a company foundation can bring at least *some* added senior management focus to the program. Because a foundation requires its board to meet periodically, it is a means of getting executives to focus on contribution issues, albeit for a moment in time.

When businesses have a strong contributions committee actively engaged in setting directions for the company's grant making, a foundation may not be that advantageous. It could even prove to be a distraction. But in cases when it is difficult to muster much if any executive attention to a company's philanthropy, a foundation may be a way to start moving the business in the right direction.

4. *Asset "catch basin."* If a company has land, stock, or other property that has appreciated in value, there are benefits that accrue to the company if the property is "gifted" to the company foundation. The corporation circles around any capital gains tax and can be rewarded with a notable tax write-off. This kind of transaction doesn't happen often, but when it does, the numbers can be big.

Of all the business reasons for establishing a foundation, reason number 4 tops the list. Many of the companies with the largest foundation asset pools have used this "catch basin" provision to infuse funds into their foundations.

Foundation Pros and Cons

Some corporations have a clear understanding of why they have a foundation. For others, it boils down to nothing more than, "We think it's a good idea." Maintaining a foundation just to have it around isn't the best decision a company can make. In fact, a few corporations have actually closed down their foundations just to avoid any unintended rule violations. (There has been a small decrease in the number of company foundations since 2005.)

A lackadaisical attitude about how a company foundation is used can lead a company into rough waters. Here's a scenario of what can go wrong if a corporation isn't watchful about how it administers its foundation.

FALLING INTO SELF-DEALING QUICKSAND

Chuck Gilfant and his wife are being directed to their Lincoln Center box seats for an evening performance of the New York City Chorale (a fictitious 501c3 cultural organization). Widget Worldwide's CEO and spouse are using free tickets sent to them by the Chorale in recognition of the company foundation's generous annual donation.

"Got some good news," Widget's chief financial officer says to his boss. The CFO and his wife are sharing the box with the Gilfants.

"What is it?"

"Our tax people tell me that we can get our company foundation to reimburse us for the head count we're carrying in the contributions department."

Gilfant looks interested but not ecstatic. There wasn't a lot of manpower in the philanthropy section, but then again, every penny counts. "You're telling me some of the money we gave to the foundation as a charitable gift can be used to pay for personnel costs?"

"That's the deal."

"What about other overhead expenses like telephone or copying? Is there a way we could get any rent payment?"

The CFO shakes his head. "The only costs we can offset are for full-time and part-time employees who do work for the foundation," he explains. "If staff is fooling around with something other than foundation programming, we're not supposed to charge the foundation for that time. But from what I hear, the IRS isn't too concerned about how closely we watch the clock."

The CFO stops talking when his Blackberry begins to vibrate. Three minutes to curtain time gives him an opportunity to take a call before the "turn off all phones and beepers" announcement.

"Uh, we have a small problem," the CFO says to Gilfant after disconnecting.

Widget's CEO slumps in his seat and waits for the bad news.

"Apparently, we're self-dealing," the CFO acknowledges.

"What?"

"Seems that we shouldn't have taken these free tickets," the CFO explains.

"What the hell are you talking about?"

"The foundation isn't permitted to give an economic benefit to anyone who's on the board like we are unless we're here to do some sort of due diligence on the Chorale," says the CFO. "It's self-dealing. So we'll need to reimburse the foundation for the cost of the tickets. Out of our own pockets, I mean."

Gilfant grimaces as the symphony conductor walks center stage to loud applause from the audience. The CFO clicks off his Blackberry, and the orchestra opens with the first movement of Beethoven's *Pathétique*.

The tale points out that the rules of the road for a company foundation are not always understood and there are times when a corporation would be better off funding certain organizations via donations from the company and not its foundation. Had Chuck Gilfant's firm made a direct donation to the New York City Chorale and not used its foundation to cover the cost, Widget's CEO wouldn't be writing a personal check for two tickets to an event he wasn't crazy about attending in the first place.

Company foundations have their place—in certain circumstances. But running a corporate contributions program strictly through a foundation definitely has its limitations. Conditional grant making linked closely with business objectives is sometimes more difficult to orchestrate through a foundation. Companies looking to extract the greatest possible value from a donation are usually better off making a direct grant (outside of the company foundation). Why? Because *quid pro quo* restrictions that apply to any charitable donation are likely to be more narrowly defined when a gift is processed through a foundation.

When a corporation funds a nonprofit program or activity directly and not through its company foundation, it can classify its support as an ordinary business expense and not a charitable gift if too much return value is generated for the business (and if the nonprofit accepting the donation is willing to risk having the donation classified as unrelated business income).

Also, keep in mind that a foundation is a much easier target for an outside audit than a company's direct contributions payments. A corporation's philanthropy program is frequently a target for an internal audit because it is an excellent training ground for an in-house audit team. If and when a company is subjected to a full or partial external audit, the non-foundation contributions program is usually not high on the list of business activities to get scrutinized.

The "PAP" Impact

For one industry sector, a different kind of company foundation has become popular in recent years. A number of large pharmaceutical businesses have set up *operating foundations* to distribute medications through what are commonly called "patient assistance programs" (PAPs). Operating foundations are defined by the IRS as entities which devote most of their resources to the "active conduct of exempt activities." Rather than fund nonprofit recipient organizations that then use foundation support to carry out programs, an operating foundation administers—or operates—its own programming.

For pharmaceutical firms, these operating foundations have become hugely important. Businesses can donate quantities of drugs to their own operating foundations and take advantage of a very advantageous supplemental tax benefit (see next chapter). The drugs are then dispensed to pharmacies and treatment centers for use by patients who must validate they do not have the means to purchase the medications. While company operating foundations technically take ownership of the drugs donated to them, such ownership is largely a paper transaction. Operating foundations don't have their own warehouses or shipping systems. The donated drugs are handled much the same way as a company's other commercial products.

In addition to tax advantages (operating foundations don't have to pay a tax on undistributed income and they provide the company donor a more liberal deduction based on its adjusted gross income), pharm companies also reap another benefit from these foundations: control. Without moving product donations through a nonprofit intermediary, businesses are better able to ensure drugs get to end users on time and that they are being used to help people who are truly in need of assistance.

The explosive growth of pharm company operating foundations is evident in the ranking of all foundations in the United States. Of the top fifty foundations in the country (based on annual payouts in 2008–2009), eleven were operating foundations set up by pharmaceutical businesses to handle their patient assistance programs (Table 6.2). According to the Foundation Center, the Bill and Melinda Gates Foundation topped the list of all foundations, but several pharmaceutical company foundations were not far behind.

Not surprisingly, the impact of these largely product-heavy operating foundations has not gone unnoticed by private foundations that rely on cash to fund their grant programs. I have heard muttering in some corners about how company PAPs have shanghaied the foundation field by using (or what some contend is

Table 6.2. Pharmaceutical Company Foundations in the U.S. Top Fifty.

Company Foundation	Rank Among Top Fifty Foundations
AstraZeneca Foundation	3
GlaxoSmithKline Patient Access Program Foundation	5
Abbott Patient Assistance Foundation	8
Sanofi-Aventis Patient Assistance Foundation	9
Johnson & Johnson Patient Assistance Foundation	14
Lilly Cares Foundation	19
Genentech Access to Care Foundation	18
The Bristol-Myers Squibb Patient Assistance Foundation	20
Wyeth Pharmaceutical Assistance Foundation	31
Merck Patient Assistance Program, Inc.	32

Source: "Top 100 U.S. Foundations by Total Giving." Copyright © 2010 The Foundation Center. Used by permission.

abusing) operating foundations to move product that should be handled via other ordinary business channels. Whether a valid criticism or cheap shot, the reality is that company operating foundations are here to stay unless the U.S. Department of the Treasury changes the rules.

Dos and Don'ts

So, whether a company is considering launching a foundation (which is not that difficult to do) or asking itself whether or not to maintain a foundation, consider these points:

- *Do* have a foundation if it provides your company significant tax advantages. If a company can shift appreciated assets into its foundation and get rewarded with a substantial write-off, then the foundation has real value. Yes, a business could donate those same appreciated assets to some other nonprofit organization and get the same tax benefit. However, if there is a large amount of money involved, it probably makes sense to pour the dollars into a company foundation to develop an asset base (think endowment) rather than make a huge money dump into the nonprofit field one year with no capacity to continue that level of funding in the future.

- *Don't* incorporate a foundation or maintain a foundation without a clear understanding of how, when, and why your company will use the foundation. Whether the company foundation has assets or if it relies on an annual infusion of money (pass-through funding) by the corporation, a business needs to specify exactly what the foundation should be used for. The critical question is, What's the business objective for having this philanthropic entity sitting in its midst? If there are no compelling responses to that question, think again about whether a foundation is right for your corporation.

- *Do* set up a foundation if the company can't get its corporate contributions act together. I admit this is a shaky reason at best. But the hope and expectation is that at the very least, a foundation will force a company to list its charitable giving purposes and require foundation officers to connect once in a while. With luck, the foundation will spark the development of a much more comprehensive corporate contributions program.

- *Don't* use a foundation as the *only* conduit for funding the company's contributions activities. A corporation should also budget for grants that can be made directly from the business—not paid out via the foundation. What percentage of a total contributions program should be funneled through a foundation? That depends on the size of the company and its annual contributions payout. But as a general rule, *at least* one third of a corporation's grant making should be made directly from the business—not from the foundation. High-impact conditional grants, dinners, special events, and most other "branded" donations generally should not be foundation expenditures.

- *Do* use foundation funds to pay for approved administrative costs. Tax laws require the foundation to pay out at least 5 percent of assets during its fiscal year (if that doesn't happen, the foundation is subject to penalty). In addition to whatever grants are paid by the foundation, "reasonable and necessary administrative expenses" can also be counted for purposes of meeting that minimum. A company foundation can reimburse the company for salaries, benefits, consulting fees, travel expenses, training costs, and a few other expenses (ask your company's tax office or outside counsel for specifics).

- *Don't* count the money your company puts into its own foundation as part of its Sabsevitz Ante-Up Formula calculation (Chapter Two). To truly be a "comprehensive corporate citizen," a company should budget contributions to nonprofits other than its own foundation equal to 1 percent of its anticipated current year pretax net income. Any donation a company makes to its own foundation will show up as a charitable deduction on its tax return—so technically a business could make a case for including this commitment as part of its "ante up" payout. But this is the kind of money-shifting that is contrary to what a comprehensive corporate citizen should be doing.

- *Do* join the Council on Foundations if your company has a foundation. Annual membership fees in this organization are based on a company foundation's assets, and grants can be paid by the foundation and counted as part of its administrative costs. The Council offers companies a long list of benefits, and at the top is legal and tax advice the organization can provide. The rules and regulations having an impact on all foundations fluctuate and are likely to undergo even more radical changes in the years ahead. Use the Council to make sure your company is standing on firm ground. Having the Council's "Good Housekeeping Seal of Approval" input will help your company avoid a misdirection of foundation donations and can be very helpful should the foundation undergo an outside audit.

- *Don't* allow the company foundation to morph into an independent or quasi-independent foundation that is too disconnected to the corporation. There will be those in the foundation world who will argue this point vehemently. But a foundation that bears the company name should reflect the interests and goals of the business. It also should be directed by company executives. Enlisting noncorporate people to serve on the company foundation's board of directors is—in my view—a bad decision.

Quiz: Should We Have a Foundation?

Corporations don't *have* to have a foundation in order to run an effective contributions program. In some cases, foundations can be more trouble than they're worth. However, there are plenty of situations in which the vexing provisions of the tax code are minor considerations when cast against the benefits that can come from having a company foundation. To determine if a foundation is right for your company—or if an existing company foundation is worth keeping—take a quick quiz.

Is there a business reason for a company foundation? If there is a clear, evident purpose for the foundation, then it should be in the corporate philanthropy game plan (assuming the business reasons are significant enough).

What is the cost benefit of having a foundation? To answer the question, the company needs to list *all* the expenses associated with maintaining a foundation, including expenses incurred in filing the annual 990-PF (the yearly "tax return" for a private foundation). If the foundation is used rarely or not at all as a grant-making tool (which is the case for some businesses), then a company should ask itself if shoveling out administrative fees makes sense.

Is the foundation used to offset reasonable and appropriate administrative costs? Whenever a business that has a foundation uses me as a consultant to work specifically on contributions matters, I recommend that all or part of my fee be paid by the foundation. It is surprising how many companies tell me they do not use their foundations to offset these or other kinds of allowable expenses. Most continuing education expenses for staff, including meetings, conferences, and workshops conducted by the Association of Corporate Contributions Professionals, Conference Board, Council on Foundations, U.S. Chamber of Commerce, Committee Encouraging Corporate Philanthropy, and so on, most likely can be charged to the foundation.

If the company has a foundation, does it also pay out contributions directly from the corporation? Some funding commitments including certain major conditional grants should *not* be made via the foundation. To maximize the value of a company contributions program, don't restrict grant making just to the foundation.

Is the foundation being used as a smokescreen to make the company look more socially responsible than it really is? One CEO told me his company set up a foundation because "it makes us look and sound more charitable." He left out the rest of the sentence: "... than we actually are." A company foundation that's essentially a cover-up for a corporation's stinginess is indefensible. Company foundations—when they make business sense—should be folded into an overall comprehensive corporate citizenship strategy.

IN SUMMARY

Question: 6: Does a company need a foundation?

Answer: No—but a foundation can be useful if there are business reasons that warrant setting up such a foundation, including (a) record-keeping simplification; (b) awarding certain international donations; (c) bringing more focused attention to a company's philanthropy; and (d) serving as a catch basin for appreciated assets.

Should a Company Donate Products or Services?

When the annual donations of 105 companies were recently tallied by *The Chronicle of Philanthropy*, the total came to $12.1 billion. But here's the kicker—*only about one-third of that amount was cash!* What dominated the giving picture?

Product donations.

While it would be inaccurate to conclude that product giving is king for every business, the fact that as a group, the nation's leading corporate contributors donated $2 worth of product for every $1 in cash is an eye opener. The ratio of cash-to-product giving is even more extreme among businesses with super-large philanthropy programs. In Chapter Two, I mentioned that thirty-eight mega-corporations were giving below the 1 percent of pretax net income level—and that if these firms hiked their annual donations to that 1 percent level, another $2.6 billion would be pumped into the nonprofit arena. And here's the rest of that story.

Of the $8.9 billion donated by these thirty-eight companies, only $1.9 billion was cash. The fair market dollar value of donated products accounted for the remainder of the total. Put another way, *only 21 percent of the contributions publicly reported by these thirty-eight companies was cash.*

With product donations playing such a significant role in the corporate philanthropy field, the next of our baker's dozen questions is particularly important.

Question 7: Should a company donate products or services?

Answer: Companies with product-giving potential should capitalize on the business and social benefits of product-giving opportunities wherever possible. Product, land, and equipment donations should be reported at fair market value for contributions purposes. The estimated value of services (including employee volunteer time) should not be factored into publicly reported contributions totals—but should be reported as separate social responsibility commitments. Ante up 1 percent of a company's estimated current year pretax net income (following the Sabsevitz Ante-Up Formula) for cash contributions to be allocated in addition to product donations.

Product-Giving Tax Incentives

There are compelling reasons why the popularity of product giving has soared over the past decade. Without question, the tax advantage of donating product in lieu of cash is number one on the list. Let's pay another visit to Widget Worldwide, the manufacturing corporation we first met in Chapter One, to get a better understanding of how tax incentives have sparked such a strong interest in product contributions.

WIDGET'S PRODUCT-INSTEAD-OF-CASH STRATEGY

Widget Worldwide makes—not surprisingly—widgets. Each widget costs $5 to make and then is sold on the open market for $20.

The company is well known to ABC, a U.S.-based international aid and relief organization. ABC's president happens to belong to the same country club as Chuck Gilfant, Widget's CEO. After a lot of prodding, Gilfant relents to an ABC request for a meeting to explore "mutual interests."

"We know Widget is interested in moving into China," the ABC president says once the meeting gets under way. Gilfant doesn't look surprised. Neither does the Widget VP with philanthropy and community relations responsibilities who has been asked to join the meeting. The company's plans to expand to China are an open secret.

"We think we can help give you the kind of name identity that could be useful to your business development," the ABC executive rolls on. "If Widget could support us with a $100,000 grant, ABC will direct it toward economic development projects that will make the government extremely happy."

Gilfant turns to his VP, who has been fully prepped for the meeting and the ABC request. "Could we swing that big a cash grant this year?" the CEO asks.

The VP tries to make his anguished expression look unrehearsed. "I don't think so, Chuck. Not with what the economy is doing to us."

Gilfant fakes a disappointed look. The ABC president came into the meeting assuming his organization would get *something* from Widget. Now even a token donation is looking iffy.

"But maybe we could—" the VP muses.

Gilfant raises his eyebrows. "What?" he asks, knowing exactly what his VP will say in response.

"We could donate product," the VP says softly. "I'd have to check our inventory, but there's a possibility—"

The ABC president perks up. "China could use widgets as part of its vocational training programs for the country's poorest citizens," he says enthusiastically. "And since you're not marketing there, at least for now, donating the product won't cut into your sales. It'll be a great way to introduce your line and score points with the Chinese trade office."

"How many widgets are we talking about?" Gilfant turns back to his VP.

"If we stretched, we might be able to come up with $100,000 worth of our main line. At $20 apiece, that's five thousand units."

It was the same main product line that would be phased out next year and replaced with new and improved widgets.

"If you do this," the ABC executive says, "it will give a lot of people in China the kind of hands-on training that will make them more employable in a much shorter amount of time."

"Which could give us a labor pool we can tap into if we decide to move any of our manufacturing to China," Gilfant notes.

ABC's president nods. "Exactly. And I can guarantee you those state-owned enterprises and ministry officials who could make or break your business in China are going to think Widget International walks on water."

Gilfant and his VP trade glances. "Sounds good to me," says Chuck.

"One more thing," the ABC president adds and then puts a cherry on top of the deal. "Our organization has a freight subsidy arrangement with the federal government. Getting a shipment of widgets to China won't be that expensive. This will be a win-win for everyone!"

ABC's president is right—it *is* a win-win deal.

Widget makes a product donation to ABC that's worth $100,000 according to the fair market value of the contributed goods. ABC adds $100,000 to its revenue line because that is what the organization would have had to spend if it went to the open market and purchased the product. Widget Worldwide gets credit for making a $100,000 donation, but the actual cost of the product contribution is only $25,000.

But, as the TV hawksters are quick to add—*there's more!*

By tapping into an old tax provision that gives companies an added deduction for certain kinds of donations, Widget gets to increase its tax write-off to two times cost. Widget gets a $50,000 deduction for a $25,000 donation of a product that would be obsolete next year. Factoring in the avoidance of an inventory carrying charge and the value of getting the Widget name introduced to commerce officials in China, the donation turns out to be a fantastic deal for Widget.

But wait! *There's even more!!*

If Widget elects to publicly disclose its gift to ABC, what number does it report? The $25,000 it cost to make the donated widgets? Never (few bits of information are so carefully guarded by a company than what it actually costs to make a product). What about the $50,000 tax deduction? No (companies file an 1120 annual return each year to the IRS that includes a total for charitable contributions—but the dollar value of a specific non-cash donation is not made public by the IRS and rarely divulged by the company). The $100,000 fair market value of the donated widgets? Absolutely. And why not? It is the same number ABC added to its revenue line.

To nail down the maximum tax benefit forthcoming from the donation to ABC, Widget needs to get a statement from the nonprofit organization that says the contributed product will be used "exclusively" for assisting the "ill, needy, or infants" (if Widget sold software, computer peripheral equipment, or optical cable supplies and donated that material for certain educational purposes, it could get the same kind of supplemental tax benefit). ABC complies because the widgets will be part of a program aimed at educating impoverished Chinese citizens. Should the IRS discover the widgets aren't actually being used for the stated purpose, it will be ABC that will come under fire. The letter sent to Widget should be enough to keep the IRS away from its doors.

Any business that makes product and understands the tax advantages associated with donating its goods is drawn to this increasingly popular way of fueling its corporate contributions program. So it comes as no shock to discover that product donations have emerged as a preferred kind of corporate philanthropy for many businesses (especially manufacturing firms) in recent years (Table 7.1).

Table 7.1. Top Corporate Donors, 2009.

	Total Giving (Cash and Products, in Millions)	Product as a Percentage of Total Giving
Pfizer	$2,356	97.4
Oracle	$2,104	99.6
Merck	$921	93.8
Johnson & Johnson	$640	74.4
Abbott Laboratories	$583	90.0
Microsoft	$516	78.1
Comcast	$407	90.2
Eli Lilly	$402	82.5
Walmart	$378	11.2
Bristol-Myers Squibb	$284	82.3

Source: The Chronicle of Philanthropy, August 2010.

The "Leave Behind" Impression Benefit

Beyond the extraordinary advantage of getting a stepped-up tax benefit, a product donation has the capacity to do even more for a company. Years ago, the communications and public relations agency Hill & Knowlton teamed up with the research firm Yankelovich Partners to probe public opinion about corporate giving. The results were fascinating. The general public, it seems, isn't all that impressed with a company that cuts a large check to a charity. But what *does* impress the average citizen are those businesses that donate product, services, or both. What accounts for this mind-set? Recall is part of the answer. Consider the following two scenarios.

TWO DONATION SCENARIOS

Situation A

Printed on an inside page of a local newspaper is a "grip and grin" photo of a business executive and a nonprofit CEO. In front of the pair is a cardboard-mounted, blown-up company check made out to the charity for $10,000. The caption below the picture explains that the business presented the unrestricted contribution during the nonprofit's annual lunch.

Situation B

Over a five-year period, Kellogg's Company donates $125 million worth of Rice Krispies, Special K, Pop-Tarts, Eggos, and a host of other company-produced food products to Feeding America (some might remember the organization by its former name, America's Second Harvest). The brands regularly show up in food banks and other poverty-focused charities that get periodic public attention via print and TV or radio references. Like product placements on TV shows and movies, the brands get imprinted in the public's collective mind.

Situation A is here and gone in a nanosecond. The check is handed over to the nonprofit and the cash gets melded into other funds collected by the charity. Days, weeks, or months later, the public (except those directly connected to the organization that received the gift) is unlikely to have any recollection whatsoever of the company's generous commitment to the charity.

Situation B creates a different mental impression. Those boxes of cereal that were a backdrop to a TV news report on hunger in America and those cartons of Kellogg's products being airlifted to victims of the Haiti earthquake are stuck in the public's head.

Researchers at Rensselaer Polytechnic Institute and the California Institute of Technology found that our brains react strongly "when visual exposure occurs without conscious recognition." This helps explain why product placements (what Hollywood sometimes calls "product integration") in movies and television programs work—sometimes far better than the "conscious recognition" that's given to paid ads. Seeing but not paying particular attention to an Apple computer while watching the TV show *House* leaves a mark because, so say researchers, the impression triggers "our non-conscious mechanism for optimal preferences."

While the study didn't examine our mental reaction to product donations, the science is probably the same. There's a good chance that many of us experience a subconscious reaction while watching the Salvation Army offload Pillsbury Poppin' Fresh baked goods in the aftermath of a tornado.

Over the years, I have seen carefully positioned product contributions do more for a company than ad campaigns that carried a much higher price tag. So even if there were no tax incentives for giving products away, a strong case could be made for using product contributions to activate the public's "non-conscious mechanism" in a way that's beneficial to a company.

Of course product donations aren't the only way a business can create a "leave behind" impression. Certain types of "branded" employee volunteer activities can accomplish the same objective. Just keep in mind that while the value of certain product donations can be folded into a company's charitable deductions, the IRS does not allow businesses to deduct the value of volunteer time. Even so, branded volunteerism can deliver other important benefits. Here are a couple of examples:

- At the Motorola Corporation, over eight thousand
  employees annually engage in a Global Day of Service.

The workers get a half day off to volunteer in different projects around the world (forty-two countries). Most company workers wear a distinctive t-shirt bearing the Motorola name and logo. From Spain to Singapore, employees become walking billboards for the corporation and stir up a public impression that sticks.

- The food service company ARAMARK runs a program called Building Community that engages workers across all business lines to assist community centers in providing job training, food, and health care for underserved families. During the year, these branded employee activities get a lot of media attention (over 170 media placements in one recent year), which puts a bright spotlight on the ARAMARK name.

Product donations and certain kinds of employee volunteer efforts can do a lot to boost brand awareness or for businesses. And not just for consumer companies interested in garnering general public interest in their goods or services. Corporations can also have an impact on very specific groups or audiences with product contributions that generate a powerful "leave behind" impression.

For example, when the medical technology company BD partnered with the International Council of Nurses to donate twelve thousand syringes to vaccinate health care workers in Swaziland, it scored points with nursing professionals, who are very important BD product users.

Finding Products to Donate

Companies sometimes take products from their current inventory and donate them to NGOs. But where product giving can make a major economic difference to a corporation is when a business checks out other pipelines for donation candidates.

Slow-Moving Inventory

To get a maximum stepped-up tax benefit, a donated product has to be "on the shelf" or available for sale at the time the donation is made. This establishes the fair market value of the product based on a price set by a "willing seller and willing buyer." For any donated goods that are no longer offered for sale (and therefore don't have an evident fair market value), the added tax incentive can't be claimed.

Usually, production and marketing executives are well aware of those products destined to oblivion well before they are taken off the shelf. Assuming these products meet quality standards, such slow-moving items should be considered donation candidates before they are removed from the marketplace. A fifteen-minute coffee break with the right tax, marketing, and line managers will reveal whether a product donation makes financial sense.

Procter & Gamble's water purification powder called PuR is a great example of a product that had trouble getting traction as a commercial offering but ended up putting a sheen on the company's reputation. P&G acquired the company that made PuR in 1995 (a $265 million acquisition) with the hope that the purification sachets would turn into a strong revenue stream. That didn't happen. But rather than dump the line, P&G began donating sachets. Following the 2004 Asian tsunami, the company provided a billion glasses of safe water for disaster victims.

Today, the Children's Safe Drinking Water initiative stands as one of P&G's most recognized corporate philanthropy commitments.

Useable Returned Goods

This option is a bit trickier. While I was at J&J, one of our affiliate companies that made Tylenol (and still does) had a large shipment of the pain reliever returned because the label was applied upside down. Everything else was fine. The container was sealed, the tablets were in no way compromised and the product had a full shelf life.

Trying to remove the bad label and run the bottles through another labeling cycle was just too expensive. The product couldn't be sold commercially if the bad label had to be pasted over. But we came up with a different idea. What about affixing a different label to the bottle that would turn the product into a specialized donation—one that met the United Nations' need for "paracetamol" (another name for the Tylenol analgesic), which had an established market value outside the United States (albeit much lower than the price for Tylenol)? The special label was produced and pasted on the containers. The product was donated via the United States Committee for UNICEF and made available to a number of countries where safe pain relievers are in constant short supply.

When considering a returned product as a contribution candidate, think safety, quality, and company reputation first—financial advantage second. If the product is in any way compromised other than cosmetically, then it should not be given away. It makes no sense to stretch for a tax benefit only to risk having the contributed product create a public relations nightmare for the corporation.

"Produce to Give" Option

Although I have preached this idea to many businesses, few have actually implemented a plan to manufacture product for the express purpose of giving it away. It's a more sophisticated concept, and it requires the cooperation and involvement of many players inside a company.

The objective of produce to give is to keep a production line going for a few extra minutes, hours, or (rarely) days in order to churn out extra product strictly for donation purposes. The expense of manufacturing this additional product is usually minimal (ingredients and some related cost of goods), since labor and G&A charges are often shouldered by the products that are destined for the commercial marketplace.

Of the companies that do practice produce to give, no business does it better than Merck, the huge pharmaceutical corporation. The company was one of my first consulting clients, and I still remember meeting with J. Lloyd Huck, who was Merck's president at the time. We sat in his office housed in an unimposing building in Metuchen, New Jersey—a gritty industrial town not far from Newark (Merck moved its headquarters to White-house Station, New Jersey, in the early 1990s). After talking about Penn State, which was Huck's alma mater and his passion, we reviewed a number of cash-giving strategies for the company. Then Huck mused about how his corporation could and should think more creatively about how to make product that could be given away.

Three CEOs later, Merck stands out as a master at making products that meet the needs of selected nonprofit organizations. The corporation sends a product list to six NGOs through its "Annual Allotment Program," which is part of a larger medical outreach initiative. The half-dozen nonprofits then check off which products they could use along with the quantities desired. Merck references these "wish lists" to produce product for contribution purposes but only if the company has manufacturing capacity to do so. There are no guarantees, but most of the time, NGOs get their free pharmaceuticals and Merck's status as a philanthropy frontrunner gets a major boost.

Consider how imposing these reasons are for a company to make a product gift—significant tax advantages, a "leave behind" impression that is more lasting than most cash donations, a way to get added benefit from slow-moving inventory or returned goods that might otherwise be destined for the scrapheap. No wonder product giving has become so popular.

Product-Giving Resentment

Ah, but not everyone is a fan of product contributions. One reason why is what is perceived by some to be a mammoth "generosity gap" between product-giving companies and businesses that have little or no product to donate.

In 2008, a Conference Board survey showed that pharmaceutical companies had a median giving level more than *eight times higher* than the median for all 197 corporations included in its survey population. No surprise that the fair market dollar value of product is what accounted for this enormous difference in giving. I talked about that survey over a lunch with Andrew Pleppler, who at the time had responsibility for managing the Bank of America Foundation. Pleppler's a long-time friend and has a well-deserved reputation as one of the country's savviest corporate grant makers.

"You doled out over $200 million in 2007," I said, glancing at a year-old report I had dug out of my files.

"That's right," Pleppler said with an understandable amount of pride. The bank had not yet felt the effects of the financial industry implosion.

"Yeah, but Pfizer gave a billion in '07," I said. "That's five times what the bank donated."

Pleppler pointed his fork at me. "They're counting more than dollars and you know it. So stop sticking it to me or I'm not buying lunch."

He was right, of course. Pfizer and dozens of other companies that make high-margin products put cash and the fair market value of product in the same sack when reporting philanthropy totals to the public. The only "product" BofA has to offer is—more cash. The result? Mr. and Mrs. Main Street America—who don't know and don't particularly care how a company totals its giving—regard Pfizer as a much more generous corporate citizen than Bank of America, even though the giant pharmaceutical company's *cash* giving was actually *$130 million less* than the bank's contributions in 2007.

Insurance, banking, and even some low-margin manufacturers have complained about what they consider to be corporate philanthropy inequities. After all, why shouldn't they get an added tax benefit for sending cash to the ill, needy, and infants? Why is it that just product donations get the benefit? And what about businesses such as law firms, consulting companies, architects, auditors and others that make contributions of time, which is, in effect, their "product"? Tax laws not only hold back added tax benefits for these kinds of pro bono services—they exclude volunteer time for *any* kind of charitable tax deduction.

It's understandable why companies that have no product to give or those that sell products that have a very low mark-up between cost and fair market value (which includes most retailers) get upset. However, the unhappy businesses that occasionally call for a repeal of tax incentives given to product-giving corporations are pushing for the wrong solution to what they see as a problem. A better answer is to keep product-giving incentives in place, advocate for similar inducements that would apply to the donation of cash to certain "high need" areas, and revamp the way corporate donations are reported.

What also might make these non-product-giving companies feel better is a commitment on the part of product-donating businesses to use the Sabsevitz Ante-Up Formula to muster 1 percent of their expected current year pretax earnings for cash giving in addition to their product-giving efforts.

A Self-Administered Product-Giving Checkup

A simple response to this chapter's baker's dozen question is—it behooves a company to take advantage of product-giving incentives but only if product can be donated in accord with our conditional grant-making principles. To figure out if a company should be in the product-giving arena—or if it should be prospecting for more products to donate, answer these next ten questions.

1. *Does your company have inventory that could become product donations?* It's amazing how many companies have products that are candidates for donation purposes but are never contributed. There are a lot of reasons why this doesn't happen. Too much work to hunt for such opportunities. Managers who don't want to bring any more attention than necessary to products they mistakenly produced or mishandled. A lack of understanding about the product contributions process, particularly among those at the loading dock.

A corporation should lift whatever stones are necessary to see if it has inventory that could be donated—and what the financial impact of donating would be compared to alternatives (disposal, discounted sales, and so on). Even if the tax benefits are negligible, the inventory should be evaluated as a marketing, sales, or reputation-enhancement resource.

If an inventory evaluation reveals there are certain products that could be contributed, then a business should find a way to make that happen *if* other conditions (below) can be met.

Put yourself in a shareholder's shoes. If a product could be donated so as to generate a financial benefit to the business *and* improve the quality of life for an individual or community, wouldn't you expect the company to make the donation? As fiduciaries for the shareholders (owners) of a business, those charged with overseeing a corporation's contribution activities are doing the company a disservice if product-giving options are not identified, evaluated, and (when appropriate) exercised.

2. *Will products being considered for donation meet safety and quality standards?* For dated products such as pharmaceuticals, regulations require that items must be donated well in advance of shelf-life expiration. Remembering that it sometimes takes months

for a product to move from its point of origin to its final destination, it is important to make sure time doesn't compromise the integrity of the donation—this is especially true for a drug or food item.

The safety and quality of a donated product has to take precedence over all other considerations. If not, the product may be subject to a recall (donated products are subject to recall, and companies have to make a good faith effort to recover those items). Even if there is no recall, an unsafe or poor-quality product donation has the potential of sparking a nightmarish public relations problem.

It's simple: *don't give any product away that your company wouldn't bring to the commercial marketplace.* If there's any doubt about safety or quality, bite the bullet and send the product to the dump.

3. *Are there likely to be any negative PR ramifications to a product gift?* Even safe and high-quality donations can stir up problems. Contributing books printed in English to a country where citizens only read French is begging for an exposé in *Time* magazine. Donating copying machines to a location where no service representatives can maintain the equipment is a bad move.

An experienced nonprofit organization carefully picked to receive donated product can be enormously helpful in keeping a well-intentioned corporation out of trouble.

4. *Can you be sure your product donation won't erode your commercial market?* Giving away product to customers who otherwise have the capacity to purchase the product isn't a way to win friends in the sales and marketing departments of your company. There are occasions when crossing this line is acceptable—in the wake of a major disaster, for instance. And in some cases, using donated product to "seed" a market in advance of sales is a good strategy (caution has to be used as to how far a company can go with this "in lieu of sampling" tactic). But in general, directing donated goods away from locations where the same product is available for sale usually stands up as good advice.

There is also the "gray market" concern. If products are donated to an unscrupulous or inexperienced nonprofit organization, there is a chance these goods will be sold for pennies on the dollar to fringe marketers who will then return them to stores at a lower price than what the donor corporation charges. The gray market problem showed up on my doorstep while I was a Johnson & Johnson employee. Cases of Johnson's Baby Powder that had been donated to an organization seeking help for infants in poverty-stricken parts of Latin America somehow made their way to the shelves of small stores in Miami and other parts of South Florida. Lesson learned? To ensure that donations don't compete with sales, pick the right nonprofit partner(s).

5. *Can you identify a trustworthy and effective nonprofit as a product-giving recipient?* There is a plentiful supply of charities willing to accept products from corporations. And for good reason. Remember that nonprofits get to record the fair market value of product gifts as revenue. One sizeable contribution of product can make an organization's "top line" look very impressive. And since certain funders (for example, large private foundations, the U.S. government, and some individuals) are more inclined to pay attention to organizations that have a healthy revenue stream, it is understandable why nonprofits have an interest in non-cash donations. But wanting product donations doesn't necessarily equate to an ability to handle those contributions in the best way possible.

I have worked with businesses that open the door to any nonprofit interested in accepting a product donation. This is a risky deal for a corporation and totally unacceptable if the product being donated is subject to recall. A better policy is to limit product donations to a small group of carefully vetted organizations that can contribute product in locations and to end users that are acceptable to the donor corporation. Forging a solid working relationship with six to ten experienced nonprofits is usually sufficient for any corporation—even a mega-sized business.

When sorting through product-giving nonprofit partner options, it helps to categorize organizations into two piles: those that have a strong capacity to manage product donations within the United States, and those that have product-giving capabilities outside the country.

Gifts In Kind International—the Virginia-based organization that is one of the largest NGOs in the country—and Feeding America (formerly America's Second Harvest) are probably the two most called-upon nonprofits when it comes to donating product for domestic delivery. IBM uses Gifts In Kind to channel new technology and refurbished equipment donations to grassroots organizations in the United States. Numerous companies partner with Feeding America, which provides liability protection for donor businesses as well as free pickup of product contributions. There are scores of other nonprofits that have proven themselves as effective stewards of product donations. Any charity that models its product donation policies and standards after those adopted by Gifts In Kind and Feeding America is probably worth considering as a recipient of a company's product contributions.

For product donations going outside the United States, extra care is needed. Moving goods beyond the nation's borders is not for the inexperienced nonprofit organization. There are tariff considerations, shipping problems, and cultural concerns that can come into play when donating product to certain countries and regions. For example, Johnson & Johnson donated several containers of medical supplies that were shipped by ocean freight to Indonesia. Port managers refused to offload the goods until a "fee" was paid in local currency. This large, unexpected expense wasn't in the company's philanthropy budget and also alien to the corporation's stand on under-the-table payoffs of any kind. It took protracted negotiations to get the goods off the ship and en route to Indonesian hospitals and clinics.

Some U.S.-based nonprofits have a "drop and run" reputation in regard to overseas product giving. These organizations can usually get product into an international location quickly but don't have an on-the-ground presence to manage product usage over the long haul. In the wake of catastrophic disasters, drop-and-run groups can be effective. But if a company is looking for a more sustained involvement in a specified international location, nonprofit organizations that have people and facilities in place are probably better choices.

Based on a review of over 150 companies, the following list includes those U.S.-based nonprofits (or international organizations which have a U.S. office that qualifies donors to receive donation tax benefits) that large corporations most frequently use for international product-giving purposes. The list is not intended as an endorsement and doesn't include other nonprofits that have strong connections to one or a small number of specific countries.

Popular Product-Donation NGO Recipients

- AmeriCares
- International Committee of the Red Cross
- U.S. Fund for UNICEF
- World Vision
- Catholic Medical Mission Board
- Heart to Heart International
- Doctors Without Borders
- Project HOPE
- MAP International
- Direct Relief International
- CARE
- Brother's Brother Foundation
- Interchurch Medical Assistance
- Gifts In Kind International
- Direct Relief
- International Rescue Committee
- Save the Children
- UNAIDS/Global Coalition for Women & AIDS

Note that some of these groups have religious affiliations. Although most corporations distance their charitable giving from religious organizations, exceptions are commonly made when religiously affiliated nonprofits agree that product (and, in some cases, cash) donations will not be used to advance their sacramental or theological interests.

Whether a product donation is destined to stay inside the United States or is to be sent overseas, the nonprofit selected to handle the contribution is crucial. Hence, use a small cluster of dependable and closely monitored charities as your product-giving partners.

Finally, companies are advised to do a periodic "pulse check" of the nonprofit community to determine if there should be any additions or deletions to their lists of preferred nonprofit partners. Circumstances and conditions change both within the nonprofit world and within locations where products are donated. For example, sending contributed goods to China via a private voluntary organization that has fallen out of favor with the government may not be your company's best move. Check the Association of Corporate Contributions Professionals (ACCP) for developments on this front. For pharmaceutical and medical device companies, stay in touch with the Partnership for Quality Medical Donations (PQMD).

6. *Have you taken into account all shipping costs—"hidden" and others?* More than one business has worked out a product contribution with a nonprofit organization only to learn after the fact that the *company* is expected to pay the shipping bill (which can be significant, especially for donations bound for places outside the United States). It is best to get a clear understanding of which party bears the burden of these expenses *before* sealing a product-giving deal.

A good question to ask any nonprofit being considered as a product donation recipient is, Do you have access to government subsidies for shipping contributed goods and materials? Surprisingly, a lot of nonprofits do. Uncle Sam offers different kinds of shipping help to nonprofits, such as assistance offered via the Denton Program, a commodities transportation arrangement that allows the Department of Defense to use extra space on U.S. military cargo aircraft to transport humanitarian assistance materials. Along with ocean freight transportation options, this allows a nonprofit to cancel out what could be very substantial shipping costs.

There are plenty of occasions when a company *should* pay for some or all of the shipping expenses related to a product donation. Expecting the recipient nonprofit to swallow these costs can, at times, be unreasonable—especially given the benefits the corporation may be reaping as a result of the donation. A nonprofit can't sell any of the donated products in order to offset shipping and handling expenses. So if it doesn't have access to free or deeply discounted shipping services, the charity has to dig into its own coffers. Many corporations with ongoing product-giving programs understand this and make annual cash contributions to partner nonprofits to help defray these costs.

7. *Do you thoroughly understand the stepped-up tax incentive for product donations?* Particularly among medium-sized and smaller businesses, there is still a lack of awareness about product-giving tax incentives. Even tax professionals in the know will sometimes

ignore the benefits that accrue from product donations often claiming the added deductions are "small potatoes" compared to other tax-avoidance options.

Whoever is carrying the contributions administration ball inside a business should remind finance and tax people that there are also costs associated with throwing product out—and then remind them there are business and ethical advantages to donating goods, which, by the way, reduce a company's tax obligations.

Tax professionals are far more inclined to pay attention to this argument if a non-tax manager knows a little about section 170(e)(3) of the seventeen-thousand-page federal tax code. This section outlines rules for contributions of inventory and other property. Here are the key points that businesses (other than S corporations) should firmly grasp:

Product Donation Tax Rules

- A qualified product donation generates a tax deduction based on the cost of the product *plus* an added deduction equal to 50 percent of the difference between the product's cost and its fair market value—*but* not to exceed twice cost. So if a product costs $1 to make and sells at a fair market price of $8, a company can deduct the $1 cost as a charitable donation plus 50 percent of the difference between $1 and $8—*but* not to go beyond twice cost. Hence, while 50 percent of the $7 difference between cost and fair market value cited in this example would give a company an additional $3.50 tax deduction, the law says: *sorry*. The company's deduction is restricted to twice cost—in this case, $1 for the cost of the product and an additional $1 for the tax deduction "step up"—a total $2 charitable tax deduction.
- To qualify for the step up, the nonprofit organization accepting the product donation has to agree it will be used "solely for the care of the ill, the needy, or infants." In 1997, the law was expanded to allow companies to get the step up for the donation of computer equipment used for educational purposes in elementary or high schools. Two often-asked questions are (a) What's the

government's definition of "infant"? Answer: "An infant is a minor child as determined by the laws of the jurisdiction in which the child resides" and (b) What's the definition of "needy"? Answer: "A person who lacks the necessities of life as a result of poverty or temporary distress."

- Products accepted by recipients as charitable gifts cannot be exchanged for money, other property, or services. Some nonprofits (and even some companies) are under the misimpression that a product contribution can be held for a time and then sold as a means of generating cash. Not so.
- The recipient is required to provide the company with a written document which states that the contributed product will be used in accordance with all IRS provisions.
- In cases when a donated product is subject to FDA regulation, the product has to satisfy all FDA rules for at least 180 days after the donation has been made. This is a sensible provision because it gives a nonprofit six months to get a dated product donation to its end point before expiration.

A little knowledge about section 170(e)(3) will go a long way in getting companies to consider product-giving opportunities more seriously.

8. *Are you publicly reporting product donations at fair market value?* Don't bother looking for a government or regulatory mandate that says, "Companies shall report product at fair market value." Nothing like that exists. As a result, some businesses report product contributions at wholesale value and others at tax value, and some seem to pick a number out of the air. Although the trend is to use fair market value for public reporting purposes, there are plenty of businesses that handle their reporting differently.

Even nonprofits aren't totally consistent in the way they log the value of product donations. One might think every charity would take a product's fair market value and plug that dollar amount into their revenue totals. Not always. California-based Direct Relief International, for instance, says that although accounting standards require reporting product at fair market value, "we continue to use the wholesale prices published by independent, third-party sources for valuation whenever possible." The humanitarian organization acknowledges that "a strong incentive exists to use higher valuation sources such as retail prices." But Direct Relief International holds to a more conservative approach because, it says, it's a way to "instill public confidence and give the most accurate, easy-to-understand basis for our financial reporting."

While Direct Relief International's intentions are admirable, its reporting policy adds more confusion to an already confused state of affairs.

Some businesses rely on outside valuations to peg average wholesale prices, which are then used for public reporting purposes (Thomson Healthcare's *Redbook* is an example of a resource that lists wholesale prices for pharmaceuticals). But other companies shun this practice. As a consequence, the public has no way of knowing what the overall value is of the ever-growing flow of product donations made to nonprofit organizations.

Here's a recommendation to both sides of the product-giving aisle: *publicly report the fair market value of any and all donated products.* Period. No exceptions.

If businesses and nonprofits adhere to this accounting principle, the corporate philanthropy picture will become a bit less fuzzy.

9. *Are tax, production, and marketing managers engaged in product-giving planning?* Making the product-giving process a team effort usually results in a bigger payoff for the company and for those who ultimately benefit from product gifts. In nearly every manufacturing company where I have been invited to consult, employees (sometimes reluctantly) acknowledge there are pockets of product that could be converted to donations. But the steps necessary to give the product to an approved nonprofit organization are either not understood or considered too much of a hassle. To many in a corporation, it's a lot easier to dump goods than to route them to a charity. And because the product value doesn't represent a big dollar number, at least in relative terms, the finance and tax people don't get worked up about a lost giving opportunity.

Attitudes change when all relevant players are seated around the same table. If production, marketing, and tax or finance people are given an opportunity to plan a strategy that fully capitalizes on product donations, they become owners of the process. When that happens, prepare for a notable increase in the number of pallets of product earmarked for a charitable organization instead of a landfill.

Coordinating the process and making sure all the key people stay in the product-giving loop is the corporate contributions manager's job. Constant reminders of how product donations are moving the company's P&L needle in the right direction and are helping to carry out the corporation's social responsibility will keep the momentum going.

10. *Are product donations vulnerable to any unethical business practices?* In 1999, the World Health Organization (WHO) issued a disturbing report. Using surveys of drug donations made to locations such as Bosnia, Albania, Rwanda, Somalia, Honduras, and other developing nations, WHO reported that as many as 60 percent of drugs found in some countries were "inappropriate." A large number of these substandard or useless drugs appeared to have been donated by retailers, drug stores, physicians, and other individuals—not by manufacturers. However, some apparently were supplied by pharmaceutical producers.

As WHO points out, unwanted drug donations can create untold problems. Not only are some no longer efficacious, others simply don't have any relevance to the health care problems affecting the country where they end up. "Once in the country, they clog up already overloaded distribution systems and become difficult to dispose of," WHO states.

It is totally inappropriate to use product-giving channels as dumping grounds, whether for drugs or any other donated items. Companies should establish standards and practices that prevent the misuse of products in this manner and hold corporate contributions managers accountable for upholding these provisions. Pharmaceutical companies and nonprofits that accept donations from these businesses should follow WHO's guidelines for "good drug donations." All corporations need to treat product donation channels with as much care and oversight as they do when sending goods to commercial customers.

Use this ten-point "check up" to assess if or how your company should have a product-giving program. If the decision is "we should," then benchmark a few businesses that have well-established product-donation systems in place. If you are looking for a good example of product-giving policies and standards, visit GlaxoSmithKline on the Web at http://www.gsk.com/policies/GSK-on-product-donations.pdf. The company has one of the most comprehensive and well-thought-out statements on product giving I have seen.

Equipment, Land, and Building Donations

Although not as commonplace as product donations, noncash contributions can include land, buildings, and equipment. These are often mega-dollar transactions that provide businesses with many of the same benefits as product donations. However, because of the usual size of these gifts and other conditions that have to be folded into the terms and conditions linked to the donation, it is best to rely heavily on the company's tax and legal experts.

To make the point about the magnitude of some of these land and building gifts, consider one of the most talked-about contributions back in the mid-1980s. RJR Nabisco made an unsolicited offer to Wake Forest University—take our company's worldwide headquarters as a gift. The corporation was leaving its Raleigh, North Carolina, location and heading for Atlanta. The property (land and buildings) was appraised at around $40 million—the largest donation in the university's history. Any strings attached, the university asked? The only thing not included in the donation of the ten-acre site, the company CEO said, was his wife's picture.

Real estate issues, property appraisals, and an array of other concerns put building and land contributions into a different non-cash-giving category. Even equipment donations that require depreciation evaluation need to be handled slightly differently from the donation of products that a company makes or sells.

Product Giving and the Ante-Up Factor

Now comes this chapter's toughest challenge—an attempt to convince product donor corporations to agree to the following:

Comprehensive corporate citizenship means companies that make product donations will also agree to make conditional *cash* grants equal to 1 percent of anticipated current-year pretax profits, which can be calculated using the Sabsevitz Ante-Up Formula.

The statement raises the obvious question: Why shouldn't corporations be permitted to use product to meet their "ante-up" requirements? There are three good reasons.

1. *NGOs' need for cash.* As mentioned, product donations can only go so far in meeting the overall needs of the nonprofit world. Many organizations provide services that don't require significant product gifts—and even those that do make the point that product donations don't pay the bills that go into running an organization. As one nonprofit president told me, "We can't meet payroll or cover our phone bills with cans of tuna fish and boxes of diapers; we can't tutor a migrant child with donated aspirin and carbonated beverages." The hard fact is that cash is still king for virtually all nonprofit organizations.

2. *Difference between cash and product donations.* Let's face it—product gifts generate such advantages for a company (or at least *should* yield those benefits if the product donations are managed properly) that they get oh-so-close to the *quid quo pro* borderline. Technically, product donations are as legitimate a philanthropic commitment as cash. While cash donations need to be in line with the overall interests and vision of a corporation, product contributions are by their very nature resources that have a special impact on a company's P&L. They can be used to take care of business in many ways—brand reinforcement, reputation enhancement, elimination of disposal fees, added tax deductions, and so on. Cash belongs in one philanthropy column; product in another. When putting together a budget for the cash column, a product-giving company should "ante up" like every other business.

3. *The fairness issue.* This is the hot button that financial, insurance, and other non-product-producing companies are prone to push. The ideal corporate philanthropy picture would have *all* companies budgeting 1 percent of their expected current-year pretax net income as a cash starting point for their overall contributions program. Product-giving companies could then supplement the cash base with the fair market value of product donations. That will put them in a position to say to banks, insurance companies, and others, "Listen, we've paid our ante up in

cash and are doing even more by donating product." That would end most of the complaints coming from the non-product-giving business sectors.

Donation of Time and Services

This chapter has dwelled on product giving and its extraordinary impact on modern-day corporate philanthropy. But what about the donation of services?

Because the tax code doesn't allow a company to take a charitable deduction for many types of services a business might extend to a nonprofit organization, these commitments are not as carefully tracked or monitored. Free office space, use of telephone banks for phonathons, copying and printing assistance, use of administrative staff to do fundraising mailings, pro bono accounting help—these are not unusual ways for companies to help nonprofits. The monetary value of these types of support won't be found on a nonprofit's revenue line but do represent important and sometimes sizeable cost offsets.

Most companies confess that any extensive contribution of services usually is tied to a high-ranking corporate executive who has a special interest in a specific nonprofit (in other words, he or she is on the board). If donated services are limited (for example, use of meeting rooms and free coffee and Danish), the costs are so low and commonly bundled with other ordinary business expenses, they usually slip under the radar. However, there are situations when these non-cash, non-product contributions have a high monetary value.

One of my consulting clients allowed a nonprofit working on children's health to use a corporate-owned office suite rent free. After a turnover in the company's front office, the new administration had far less interest in giving up valuable space for an organization that had little connection to the business. The corporation quickly discovered, though, that it is far easier to open a door than to close it. The separation took a lot of time, and in spite of the company's years of hospitality, the organization left the building with a sack full of hard feelings.

Given the experiences of many companies, consider these two suggestions. First, don't give free room and board to a nonprofit.

While there are some (very few) exceptions to this rule, a business would be better served by making a grant to an organization to help defray living expenses elsewhere. Second, whenever a company provides free service of any kind, be clear that it should be considered a one-time deal. If the service is continued, great. If not, the organization was fully informed ahead of time. Regardless of what a nonprofit might say, every service commitment a business makes breeds hope and expectations for continuity. Make it absolutely clear on the front end that donated services are temporary.

IN SUMMARY

Question 7: Should a company donate products or services?

Answer: For those companies with product-giving potential, seek out and make product donations if such donations are in accord with our conditional grant-making principles. Publicly report product at fair market value as part of a company's overall giving total. Account for services and employee time separate from cash/product giving. Using the Sabsevitz Ante-Up Formula, budget 1 percent of estimated current year pretax net income for cash contributions in addition to whatever product-giving commitments are made for the year.

8

How Much Should a Company Donate for Dinners and Events?

Elton John headlined the 2008 Breast Cancer Research Foundation's "Hottest Pink Party" in New York City. The event drew twelve hundred big hitters and a battery of celebrities to Manhattan's Waldorf-Astoria. Sponsor donations by Conde Nast, Hearst, Time Inc., Wrangler, and other businesses poured in, and when the night was over, the foundation tallied the results. The dinner raked in $5 million.

In Richland, Washington, organizers of one of thousands of charity golf tournaments held annually throughout the United States called on local businesses to sponsor an eighteen-hole scramble—a money raiser for the local Children's Hospital and Regional Medical Center. Companies put together foursomes (never difficult to do) and cut checks ranging from $3,000 to $10,000 for the event.

Anything out of the ordinary? Hardly. Dinners, golf outings, walkathons, and an array of other special fundraising events abound. They are time-tested methods NGOs use to tap the company cash register, and in most (not all) instances, they work. The sheer number of these event requests can drive a corporate contributions manager batty, which is why the next question has made its way to our baker's dozen list:

Question 8: How much should a company donate for dinners and events?

> **Answer:** Budget a dollar amount or percentage of total giving for special events based on (a) company size; (b) location; and (c) class of industry—and then stick with the budget. Fund events directly from the corporation—not a company foundation if there is one—and support only events that are in sync with conditional grant-making principles.

Too many companies lack discipline when it comes to special event funding. Businesses frequently find it more difficult to say "no" to a dinner request than to a straight-up appeal for a cash or product donation. The result? A lot of money for food, beverages, table and chair rentals, musicians—and, oh yes, charity.

Cause Marketing Forum estimated corporate sponsorship spending on festivals and fairs at $781 million during 2010. Add another $841 million for arts organization sponsorships. Together, these sponsorship totals equal the $1.6 billion companies spent in 2010 on cause marketing (more on this quasi-sponsorship category later).

What can a corporation do to tighten the reins on special event support and make such spending more beneficial to a company? Over the years, I have put together the "10-Tip Guide for Funding Special Events," which I ask businesses to consider when determining how to cope with the flood of special event appeals.

THE 10-TIP GUIDE FOR FUNDING SPECIAL EVENTS

1. Accept the Fact that Some Dinner and Event Support Is Going to Happen.

Very few corporations can avoid supporting at least a few charity events. Businesses that claim they won't fund any dinner or event are on a fool's errand. Corporate contributions managers who think they can deflect every event request that flies over the company transom are unrealistic. It also doesn't make sense to state publicly that the company will not fund *any* special events and then relent when the local Boys & Girls Club convinces you to take a table at its monthly corporate recognition lunch. Hypocrisy isn't pretty, and it can put a stain on other good works the company carries out. If the business rules out supporting certain kinds of events (such as golf and tennis outings), then hold the line. No exceptions. But set policies that are realistic, keeping in mind that except in rare cases, some event sponsorship is going to happen. To state emphatically that a company doesn't support charity dinners, for instance, borders on lunacy. I have yet to run into a company that hasn't been tapped for a dinner sponsorship.

2. Create an Annual Special Events Budget and Stick to It.

As disciplined as companies may be about keeping the lid on other kinds of gifts and grants, too many corporations treat dinners and other nonprofit-sponsored activities differently. Requests get decided on an appeal-by-appeal basis, and while there may be a presumed cap on event spending for the year, that cap is often blown into oblivion with other line items in a contributions budget raided to pay for excess event spending. If the company has a fixed funding plan for events, all hands should agree early in the fiscal year that other parts of the contributions budget will not be raided for any unplanned special activities. If an unexpected dinner or event is deemed to warrant company support, then it is up to senior management to either increase the contributions budget or charge the cost of the function to some other budget line item.

3. Support Only Those Special Event Requests That Have Business Relevance.

So how does funding a $10,000 Race for the Cure relate to the business? Ask the employees who push for company support or the nonprofit organization running the event to come up with the answer(s). It is amazing how many business benefits can accrue from a walkathon—it can be a morale builder, departmental team-building opportunity, part of a brand promotion campaign (t-shirts, hats), and the list goes on. The goal is to identify the business advantages before an event is held and then look for ways to measure the benefits once the event is over. Many times an NGO can recommend and then deliver many more ways an event can be useful to a company than can corporate contributions managers.

4. You Want the Table? Then You Fill the Table.

Typically, a special event request is linked to someone inside the business, often an individual working at a senior management level. To make life easier for the corporate contributions staff, the rule should be that if the company supports the event financially, it is up to the employee connected to the nonprofit to recruit company representatives to fill a table or participate in the sponsored activity. When an event involves the CEO or chairman, the rules are obviously different. But otherwise, there should be a policy in place that makes it absolutely clear about whose job it is to round up attendees for a charity event (in many cases, not an easy task, especially for black-tie dinners laced with speechmaking). By the way, filling a table is different from recruiting employees for a golf outing. It's amazing how many upper-level executives can find time for a charity golf tournament but not for a "formal dress required" dinner.

5. Limit Any Nonprofit to No More Than One Event Per Year.

Special events can be so lucrative for some charitable organizations that they schedule four to six functions (sometimes more) each year. And there are plenty of companies that pay to show up at all or most of these events. A better (and less costly) policy is to tell such organizations, "We can only pay for one special event a year—is this the one you want us to consider or is there something down the road more important to you—and us?"

6. For Each Company-Assigned Nonprofit Board Member, Budget for One Special Event.

When a corporation tells an executive it would be a "good idea" if she or he were to serve on a designated nonprofit board, then the business should anticipate that the executive eventually will come forward with a request to support a dinner or some other fundraising event. Assuming the request has business relevance, it should be approved. It is awkward and unfair for the corporation to "volunteer" an employee to a nonprofit board and not come through with support for one special event. Let's be clear: we're only talking about managers who are assigned to nonprofits to represent the company. This obligation doesn't apply to employees (senior executives or otherwise) who are on a nonprofit board by their own volition.

7. Keep All Dinner and Event Spending Out of the Company's Foundation.

For all the reasons covered in Chapter Six, pay for special events directly from the corporation and not via the company foundation.

8. Use the ``in Lieu of'' Option When and Where Appropriate.

Suppose Widget Worldwide concluded it would be too difficult to recruit ten employees and spouses to fill a table at the American Heart Association's Be My Valentine banquet. But also suppose Widget determined that getting its name on the table sponsor list at the banquet would be a good way to reinforce its connections to other customers attending the dinner. Chuck Gilfant's corporation should consider an "in lieu of" option. It says to the Heart Association, "Listen, if we buy a table for $5,000 and send ten people to the banquet, you're going to be handing over at least 20 percent of that check to the Hyatt Hotel for food and beverages that our people will eat and drink. So instead of your netting $4,000 from Widget, we want you to have the full $5,000 for your organization's work. We'll turn the table back to you and keep our people home. We need you to agree, though, that Widget still gets a prominent listing as a sponsor."

9. Think Twice About Auctions, Silent Auctions, Door Prizes, and Other Give-aways.

The actual cost of funding a special event can skyrocket if a company gives in to all the "add ons." Sometimes it makes sense to provide product as a free premium for participants. For example, I ran a meeting at which I persuaded Starbucks to donate coffee mugs stuffed with company-branded products. To this day, many attendees continue to use the mugs, which are a constant reminder of the corporation's connection to the meeting. Other businesses paid big bucks for other non-branded give-aways at the same event–computer memory sticks, books, and so on. Ask anyone who attended that meeting if they recall which company provided the cash used to buy these attendee gifts. The recall won't come close to memories of Starbucks. The takeaway is this: "add ons" make sense if they bring more value (such as lingering name recognition) to a company. But if there isn't any apparent advantage, then don't go beyond the table, event, or sponsorship payment.

10. Don't Abuse–or Be Abused by–the ``Chit System.''

In locations where there is a concentrated population of companies, there's often an understanding that "if I scratch yours, there'll come a time when you're going to be scratching mine." If your CEO is inviting my CEO to buy a table at a dinner where your company is being "honored," that table sponsorship comes with an IOU. This point is worth keeping top of mind when a nonprofit asks your CEO to sign a few letters ("We'll write the letters, so there won't be much work involved at all....") that are sent to other company leaders asking them to sponsor an event table. Every business that responds positively then has a "you owe me" slip in its own special events file. When I was at Johnson & Johnson, a friend who ran a corporate philanthropy program arm twisted the company into picking up a $25,000 sponsorship for a New Jersey Performing Arts Center dinner in Newark. For many business-based reasons, we went along with the request. A few months later, it was payback time. I drafted a letter which my CEO sent to my friend's CEO asking that his company buy a table in support of a Robert Wood Johnson University Medical Center bash in J&J's home town, New Brunswick. It didn't take long for a $25,000 donation to arrive in the mail. While this kind of reciprocity will be forever a part of corporate philanthropy, such "event swapping" should be kept under control as much as possible.

Hopefully, the "10-Tip Guide" will prove helpful in sorting out which special event requests are worthy of support and which should be turned away. There are a few other suggestions that also come in handy when weighing whether to say "yes" or "no" to an event appeal.

The Event Request Sorting Process

There are companies that make a valiant attempt to control the flow of event requests. Sony USA, for example, says "no" to testimonial dinners. Covidien (the health care products and pharmaceutical company) doesn't support galas and tables if the payment is the only source of company support for an organization. But most businesses are soft on special event requests, which is why our "10-Tip Guide" can be so useful. However, even the ten tips won't always shake out event requests that should be funded and others that should not. That's when using a final screen with a tighter mesh can prove helpful. Try putting requests into one of three categories and then evaluate them accordingly.

1. *Already-funded organizations.* For NGOs that are about to get a non-event cash or product donation from a company, consider presenting them with a "lump-sum" funding strategy. Tell the nonprofit the corporation will commit a total dollar amount to the organization for the year that will cover all direct grants and special events. Ask the NGO to come forward with a proposal that takes into account this funding stipulation. Surprise! The company may be invited to the nonprofit's dinner or golf event— *no charge.*

2. *Non-grant-supported nonprofits.* There are occasions when a nonprofit is not on the list of NGOs to get a direct company grant or company foundation donation. However, the corporation decides that sponsoring one of the NGO's special events would be to its advantage (meaning that the event will yield business and social value).

When making such a commitment, a corporation will do itself a favor by clearly informing the nonprofit that (a) this is a commitment the organization shouldn't count on each year; (b) it is not a segue to a "regular" charitable donation; and (c) the company will not entertain requests for any other special events over the next twelve months (remember that some nonprofits thrive on numerous events conducted throughout the year: the Spring into Spring Ball, Summer Garden Festival, Fall Tennis and Golf Challenge, Winterfest, and so on).

3. *"We want to honor you" events.* This time-honored strategy of seducing a company to buy its way into an event usually works like a charm.

> Congratulations—your business is the corporate philanthropist of
> the year.

Not only does the "honor" mean your business is expected to
fill a few expensive tables, the organization probably wants your
CEO to put his or her name on a large pile of solicitation letters
addressed to other senior executives who will feel obligated to take
a table or two. It should not come as a shock to discover that these
events have little to do with a company's stature as a corporate
citizen—it is mainly about the ability of the company to attract a
lot of money to an event. Yes, there are exceptions. But very few.

Don't let the company ego get in the way of making sound
decisions when it comes to reacting to these thinly disguised
appeals. There are times when it makes more sense to politely
tell an NGO that while the corporation appreciates the invitation,
it does not want to be singled out for its philanthropy when so
many other businesses in the community are equally as engaged
in supporting important local programs and activities.

The Disqualified Persons Minefield

Chapter Six already made the point that company foundations
should not be called upon to fund special events. Let's dig deeper
for an explanation as to why this isn't a good idea.

Tax accounting principles connected to dinners and events are
about as interesting as mothballs. Still, it helps to have a cursory
understanding of why some enterprising auditor could have a
field day with a business that didn't handle its charitable-giving
record-keeping properly.

Let's return to Chuck Gilfant's Widget Worldwide Corporation
as a means of bringing more clarity to this not-so-scintillating topic.

Widget is talked into paying $500 per seat for a table of ten
($5,000 total) at the Kennedy Center's Annual Spring Gala. The
public relations office that administers the company's contributions program finds five executives along with their spouses to
attend the event. The Kennedy Center sends Widget an invoice
for $5,000, including a statement that says, "In accordance with
IRS requirements, the Association has determined your corporation may elect to take a charitable income tax deduction of $400
per ticket or $4,000 . . . ."

So why did Widget receive this kind of notice, and why the limitation on what the company can declare as a donation?

Tax rules dating back to 1993 require charities to tell a donor how much money is being siphoned off a special event payment to offset expenses that give attendees a "tangible economic benefit" (a.k.a. meal plus entertainment). Once upon a time, businesses could have taken the full $5,000 as a deduction to the banquet—but no longer. Using the statement from the Kennedy Center, Widget can fold $4,000 into its overall charitable deductions listed on line 19 of its annual tax return.

If Chuck Gilfant should ask the contributions manager to use company foundation funds to pay the full $5,000, the tax department would hopefully intervene and shout, "Don't go there!". As pointed out in Chapter Six, foundations come with a lot of potholes that are not easy to dodge. Two of the biggest are called "self dealing" and "disqualified persons."

The tax code says it's an act of self-dealing if disqualified persons receive tangible economic benefits flowing from foundation grants. Who are disqualified persons? Using our mini-case study, anyone connected to Widget Worldwide who could reap a tangible benefit from the company foundation's purchase of a dinner table. While there is no specific IRS guidance as to whether *all* employees of the company are disqualified persons or if only certain executives fall in this category (such as company foundation board members, corporate officers, and so on—again, see Chapter Six), the best advice is to consider *all* employees as disqualified persons.

Adhering to this line of reasoning, any Widget employee who attends the Kennedy Center benefit would be a disqualified person.

A case could be made for sending certain Widget employees to the banquet as a means of monitoring how the company's direct grants made to the Kennedy Center are being used. The IRS says a disqualified person(s) can accept benefits (in this case tickets) so long as they are "reasonable and necessary" in carrying out the exempt purposes of the foundation. The five people handpicked to show up at the banquet will be doing zero monitoring. So will their spouses. And even if they were monitoring, is it worth raising a red flag that could wave in a foundation audit? Definitely not.

So please—skip the company foundation when it comes to special events.

How Much Should We Spend?

Still left unaddressed is a determination about the most appropriate level of support for events. As our answer to this chapter's question notes, a company's size, its industry (direct-to-consumer? business-to-business?), and its location are all factors that influence a corporation's decision about how much it should spend to support special events. Most companies accept the fact that these variables make it impossible for a one-size-fits-all formula to work for every business. Even so, they want some general guidance on deciding what's reasonable—and what isn't—when it comes to event funding.

Here's a *very* broad suggestion about budgeting for events that is more applicable to businesses with annual contribution allocations that exceed $5 million than to others:

> For every $20 in cash gifts and grants donated by the company, its foundation, or both, budget $1 for special events.

This 20:1 rule is a good starting point for larger businesses, which should then tweak the ratio on the basis of their own unique circumstances. For smaller firms, the ratio is likely to be different. For companies typically paying out under $5 million a year in donations, dinners and events may represent 20 percent (even more for very small businesses) of overall support for nonprofits.

Factor in these other considerations—a company's location and industry classification. They *do* matter when it comes to event spending. Here are some examples.

The farm-equipment manufacturer Deere & Company has its headquarters in Moline, Illinois. Its revenue line is about the same size as that of the accounting firm Deloitte Touche Tohmatsu, which has its U.S. headquarters in Manhattan. And while each business has a number of small satellite offices in different parts of the country and abroad, special event solicitations are heaviest in and around their headquarters locations. Guidestar, the nonprofit tracking service, lists 567 charitable organizations in Moline. New York City has 6,042. Want to bet which company has a larger special events budget? Sometimes it's about where a business has its deepest roots.

International Paper is the world's largest forest products company. Most of its sales are business-to-business, which means it has limited exposure to the Main Street consumer. JCPenney generates the same amount of revenue as International Paper—except it has over a thousand stores in the United States and Puerto Rico, which means the corporation is consistently and literally in the consumer's face. Businesses dependent on retail sales are far more vulnerable to special event solicitations (as well as other kinds of appeals) than back office or "b-to-b" companies.

No matter how much is spent on special events, each payment should be as "conditional" as any other commitment a company makes to a nonprofit organization. A corporation should be able to answer unequivocally why a special event payment is in some way important to the business. If that's not possible or if the reason is too much of a stretch, then the corporation has done an injustice to its owners.

Reporting Events as Contributions

The following recommendation is where the tax world and I will most surely part company:

> For public reporting purposes, add in the full payment made to a nonprofit for an event as part of the company's total corporate contributions spending.

Tax purists will denounce this idea because it doesn't accurately reflect what the company is taking as a charitable deduction. My retort: corporations rarely if ever report a contributions number that lines up with what a business declares as a charitable deduction (for more, see Chapter Twelve). Double back to the $5,000 table Widget sponsored at the Kennedy Center gala. There's no good reason why Widget shouldn't tell the world it was a $5,000 sponsor. That's the amount the Kennedy Center will show on its books. And even though some Widget employees may have received "tangible economic benefits" at the Spring Gala, they wouldn't be attending the event if it weren't for the charitable intent of the company.

Just as it has now become common practice for corporations (rightfully) to report the fair market value of product donations (see Chapter Seven) even though the company deducts a much lower dollar amount as a tax deduction, there should be no soul searching over publicly reporting total ticket, table, and sponsorship payouts as part of a corporation's overall conditional contributions commitment.

Event Fundraising Is Here to Stay

When the philanthropy watchdog group Charity Navigator produced a report that claimed charity-sponsored special events were costing $1.33 for every $1 raised, nonprofits said, "baloney!" The reaction came as no surprise. The spaghetti dinner, butterfly ball, and race for (fill in the blank) do make money for most nonprofits. Turns out the way income and expenses are reported for these special events belies an easy analysis, which led some to charge Charity Navigator's report as being misleading.

The sharp reaction to Charity Navigator's research wasn't surprising. Many NGOs rely on special events to "make their numbers." If special events didn't work, the number of charity dinners, walkathons, and golf outings would have dipped long ago.

Company contributions managers tell me constantly that special events are thorns under the saddle. Paying the unplanned-for sponsorship bills and finding employees to show up for a dry-chicken-and-bad-wine benefit can be aggravating. Still, figuring out how best to cope with these fundraising functions is important. Special events are not going away.

IN SUMMARY

Question 8: How much should a company donate for dinners and events?

Answer: Budget a dollar amount or percentage of total giving for special events based on (a) company size; (b) location; and (c) class of industry—and then stick with the budget. Fund events only if they align with conditional grant-making principles. Do not use the company foundation to fund special events.

9

Should a Company Fund the United Way, or Are There Better Alternatives?

Like ipecac syrup, focus groups can bring up things in a most unpleasant way. I found that out—several times, in fact—when asking small groups of corporate contributions managers to talk about the United Way.

"We're expected to get 100 percent of our employees to give, and if someone balks, there's hell to pay," a West Coast manufacturing executive said at one such meeting a few years back.

"What kind of hell are you talking about?" I asked.

"The kind that shows up on your annual performance appraisal."

Over a seven-year period, I moderated dozens of these hour-long quasi-focus groups, most of which touched on the United Way and other "umbrella" fundraising organizations (nonprofits set up to raise money for multiple charities or causes). Many of the discussions were folded into three-day management education workshops open to corporate contributions and community relations professionals. "Managing the United Way Campaign" never failed to elevate the blood pressure among managers asked to comment about "worksite giving campaigns." Here are some of the more frequently made comments about the United Way:

- "Inefficient and overpaid staff"
- "Takes away money that should be going directly to other nonprofits"
- "Supports organizations we (our company) shouldn't be funding"
- "An unnecessary middleman"
- "Too prone to corruption and favoritism"
- "A relic that should be replaced by new desktop giving options"
- "Pushed by CEOs who are part of an old-boy network"
- "Scandal-ridden and unregulated organization"
- "Funds groups like the Boy Scouts that discriminate on the basis of religion and sexual preference"
- "Uses guilt, coercion, and humiliation to arm twist donations from employees"

These discussion groups generally included United Way supporters who were often outnumbered by detractors. The organization's proponents tried reminding anyone willing to listen that local United Ways have a large degree of autonomy and that just because one is poorly run doesn't mean that every community-based United Way is deficient. Those comments prompted rebuttals, most of which sounded much like this actual statement made by a contributions manager: "Look, the problem isn't just about what United Way does with the money it collects but the tactics it uses to force employees to give. At my company, each department is expected to be 100 percent committed to the United Way. Management has a way of letting everyone know if you're in or not. Secretaries publicly tell the department if someone's pledge form is missing. A United Way giving thermometer constantly reminds everybody they better be doing their 'fair share,' which usually means giving more than they did last year. And there have been times where people who donate over a certain amount are allowed privileges not given to others who can't or won't give to the United Way. This is out-and-out coercion!"

There are only two other organizations that come close to raising the same number of hackles as the United Way—the American Red Cross and the Boy Scouts of America (more about these organizations later). If put to a vote as to which of these nonprofits is the biggest thorn in a contributions manager's side, the United Way would certainly take the blue ribbon.

So against this backdrop, here's the next question drawn from our baker's dozen list:

Question 9: Should a company fund the United Way, or are there better alternatives?

> **Answer:** Companies should support the United Way—but conditionally. Alternative or additive worksite giving campaigns should be given careful consideration using the same assessment criteria a company applies to its United Way contributions decision making. Support should be dependent on (a) a company's senior management involvement; (b) assurance that the United Way's practices are consistent with a company's nondiscrimination policies; and (c) acceptable United Way management performance and reasonable operating expenses. Company support of the United Way will vary depending on the overall size of a firm's annual cash giving (typically ranging from 5 percent to 25 percent of total cash donation).

With a hefty number of contributions managers voicing animosity about the United Way, some will be surprised by the answer to this question. But there are sound reasons for the response. Before making a case for United Way support, here is a bit of background.

United Way Realities and Misconceptions

I've spent a lot of time trying to figure out what it is about the United Way that generates such strong reactions among company contributions managers. The prime reason seems to be a pervasive attitude that the United Way operates like a kind of charitable IRS that requires employees to fork over a certain amount of money for the common good—or else. Whether justified or not, that's a rap that hangs over the United Way like a dark cloud.

What I've also discovered is how little most people (including corporate contributions managers) actually know about the United Way movement. I suspect that even if all the facts were put on the table, plenty of individuals would still continue to have trouble with the organization. Nevertheless, here's information about the United Way that occasionally gets distorted—even by paid philanthropy professionals.

A National Network

The United Way is not one large, integrated organization. Instead, it is "a national network of nearly 1,800 local organizations..." Local groups set themselves up as 501c3 operations and are given rights to use the United Way name if they comply with certain conditions and standards. Here are some of the requirements:

- Establishing a code of ethics for volunteers and staff including a provision for full disclosure of fundraising practices and other activities
- Subjecting the local chapter's books to an annual audit by an independent CPA
- Undergoing a self-assessment of programming and financial management every three years
- Paying the United Way of America a fee in accordance with a "membership investment formula"

In recent years, the United Way of America (the national headquarters is in Alexandria, Virginia) has made a concerted effort to enact and enforce standards aimed at keeping all its affiliates in line. This is not an easy job. At a United Way leadership conference several years ago, I was asked for my definition of the movement. My answer: "United Way is a confederation of loose cannons." Today the organization and its locals are a bit less "loose," but the media are there to remind us that the United Way is not tight enough to prevent a transgression here or there.

Added to the occasional present-day misconduct or mismanagement by local United Way officials, the organization is haunted

by the kind of *really* bad behavior that made for large and sometimes lurid headlines. No one has yet to put as deep a scar on
the United Way as William Aramony. The twenty-two-year veteran head of the United Way of America went from king of all
nonprofits in the 1970s and 1980s to inmate at a federal prison
camp in North Carolina. He was convicted in 1995 on twenty-
five counts, including mail fraud, wire fraud, and filing false tax
returns. But what made the story into a tabloid sensation was how
Aramony allegedly used some of the $1.2 million looted from his
organization to pay for a number of outrageous sex-capades.

Although the Aramony scandal happened a long time ago, it
still resonates even among corporate contributions managers who
weren't out of high school when the United Way chief was carted
off to jail.

Still a Popular Charitable Choice

In spite of its past and present problems, the combined collections
of all United Ways in the country make the organization by far
and away the largest nonprofit in the United States (according
to rankings published by *The Chronicle of Philanthropy*). United
Way revenues took a hit following the 2007 recession, but the
organization is still a force. It takes in between $3.8 and $4 billion
each year and is a crucial financial lifeline to many community-
based nonprofit organizations.

And where does that money come from? The United Way still
depends on worksite campaigns and corporate gifts for about half
its annual revenue. Years ago, worksite fundraising drives played an
even more dominant role in generating United Way funds. Today,
leadership gifts, endowments, and foundation donations have
picked up the slack as workplace support has edged downward.

Continued Corporate Support

It would be misreading trend data to conclude that Corporate America is stampeding away from the United Way. It
isn't—although there's no denying that business employees
are less involved with the organization than in the past. The
Consulting Network, a consulting and research group, reported

that United Way lost nearly 19 percent of its workforce donor base in just three years. Even so, plenty of companies are still solidly connected to the organization. To underscore that point, consider corporations the United Way labels "National Corporate Leaders." These large businesses—around 130 of them—account for $1 billion in donations to the organization each year.

Corporations headquartered in America's midsection are the most faithful United Way supporters, according to my unscientific focus group research. I have talked with company CEOs in the nation's heartland who view the United Way as a reflection of the way America was and should be again. Making a United Way pledge is a statement that you're in line with the nation's core values. That's not a view shared by every business or every employee. Still, there are places in the United States where the private sector holds the United Way in very high esteem.

Not Usually a High-Cost Operation

The accusation that United Way is a kind of overpaid monetary tick that attaches itself to the underbelly of those nonprofits that actually do all the work in a community is overstated. Yes, the United Way costs money—its administrative expenses average around 13 percent of the funds it raises. But soliciting, processing, and reporting contributions are steps that incur costs. If a local United Way is hovering around 13 percent in overall administrative costs, that's not bad (some local United Ways tout administrative expenses under 10 percent). If a United Way is peeling off 25 percent or more to meet its operating expenses, then it's time to ask questions.

I have heard the loudest complaints about United Way's overhead from local nonprofits that *get* support from the United Way more so than from charities that don't receive assistance. Some of the organizations that collect United Way dollars aren't pleased with how much the "middleman" charges for raising and distributing donations. Others complain they are hamstrung in their efforts to raise more money from companies that give to the United Way. The main reason why? Many corporations won't give added assistance to nonprofits that are getting United Way funds.

Companies should be attentive to United Way criticisms but also need to carefully evaluate those concerns. Community nonprofits receiving United Way financial help can always unshackle themselves from the organization if they feel they can raise more money on their own. Most of these nonprofits come to the conclusion that even after carving out 13 percent of dollars collected, United Way provides a valuable revenue stream.

Working on Continuous Improvement

Finally, the national United Way office is pushing for major changes in the organization's mission. Specifically, United Way of America wants its affiliates to give the highest priority to achieving these three goals by 2018:

- Cut in half high-school dropout rates
- Cut in half the number of families with working parents who don't earn enough to cover basic expenses
- Increase by one-third the number of Americans who are healthy

While these are admirable targets, the national office acknowledges that only one in five locals have bought into this ambitious plan. The organization hopes most of its affiliates will eventually come on board—but concedes that 15 percent to 20 percent of them may never agree to the change.

These are important realities about the United Way that often get misconstrued. But even with accurate information in hand, there are corporate contributions managers who remain anti–United Way. Why?

Major Corporate Giving Concerns About United Way

There appear to be two major charges levied against the United Way by corporate contributions managers who have problems with the organization.

Ineffective Use of Corporate (not Employee) Donations

Most company gifts to the United Way remain at the local affiliate level and are usually folded into a general pool. Unlike many employee donations, they aren't "donor designated" for any particular program or project. This unrestricted support gives community-based United Way board members and staffers great discretion in how to leverage the corporation's donations. Some company contributions managers are highly critical of the process local United Way organizations use to distribute these funds. There are anecdotes aplenty about how alleged favoritism and backscratching determine where United Way dollars get dispensed. This concern can *really* be pumped up when unhappy nonprofits that get zero or minimal United Way assistance complain (usually loudly) to local businesses.

If companies lose confidence in a local United Way's capacity to prioritize a community's needs and address them accordingly, then corporate dollars are likely to dry up. The way to prevent that from happening is to bring business leaders at the highest level possible into the policymaking ranks of the United Way. And in many parts of the country, United Way has done this to a fare-thee-well—sometimes much to the vexation of the corporation contributions manager who feels backed into a corner by this approach. If an executive high up the corporate ladder wants a check cut for the United Way, it shall be done even if the contributions professional feels differently.

No other nonprofit in America has been so successful in recruiting senior business executives as board members as the United Way. According to my conversations with corporate contributions managers and even some United Way personnel, this ability to penetrate so many company front offices is a prime reason why the organization continues to be relatively well funded and influential.

Arm Twisting Employees to Give Their Own Donations

I regret not jotting down every "give—or else..." story I have been told about what some employees consider to be unacceptable United Way worksite campaign tactics. Frankly, many of these tales seem to be more perception than reality. But in the fundraising world, perception rules. So, the stories abound.

Corporate contributions managers grumble the most when upper management gets infected by an over-the-top "participation complex." Typically, this condition sets in when a company CEO is named this year's United Way chairman or vice chairman, or is appointed to some other exalted board role. Not wanting to be embarrassed, the CEO lets his direct reports know the corporation needs to make a strong showing on two fronts: (a) dollars raised and (b) the number of employees participating in the campaign by giving at least *something* to the United Way. The trickle-down effect starts and the word gets circulated that there's not a lot of distance between job security and a United Way gift or pledge.

Again, most of these perceptions are off base and are frequently fueled by those who have a predetermined dislike for United Way. Still, real or perceived accusations that managers are too heavy handed when it comes to worksite campaigns may have something to do with the nationwide fall-off in employee giving to the United Way. While the organization could once count on donations from nearly half the workers in the country, the percentage of worksite donors has dropped to around one-third.

Even with these two negatives looming large, United Way continues to lead the way when it comes to employee worksite giving campaigns. In a survey of one hundred large businesses, the Association of Corporate Contributions Professionals found that 46 percent of the companies conduct an annual fund drive exclusively for United Way—no money is collected for any other nonprofit. For those companies that include a laundry list of charitable organizations as part of a worksite campaign, the United Way still is a "menu pick" and does attract some employee support.

The Case for United Way

The following explains why I conditionally endorse the United Way as an organization that should be on the list of corporate contributions recipients.

The Best Alternative

Some United Way detractors contend the organization has outlived its usefulness. The claim is that the United Way movement is a throwback to the old World War II "Red Feather" days when several nonprofit groups joined together to unite their fundraising efforts. During the 1940s, donors were encouraged to put feathers in their caps to signal their generosity. Times have changed but the United Way has not kept up, critics charge.

There is some merit to this argument. Times *have* changed. And with that change has come a surge of nonprofit organizations, many of which duplicate services and are poorly administered. Sorting through which of these many nonprofit groups are worthy of support is—in many respects—far more demanding a job than it was years ago. So is the difficult task of prioritizing the challenges a community faces.

The "conditional yes" to this question? There are cities and regions in the United States where the United Way has not performed adequately. If there are other "federated drives" active in a community that are obviously more effective than the United Way (for example, America's Charities, Earth Share, Community Health Charities, and so on), then companies should look for funding alternatives. But of the eighteen hundred United Way locations throughout the country, most are reasonably functional. They do a good to excellent job of pinpointing the most pressing issues facing a community and then use that perspective to determine how best to address those needs by allocating United Way dollars.

If a corporation is genuinely sincere about addressing the most pressing needs of those towns and cities where it has interests, then channeling contribution dollars through the United Way usually makes the most sense.

Ability to Prioritize and Meet Community Needs

Here's what frustrates me about company complaints aimed at local United Ways. Too often, business people moan about how inadequate the organization is even though there's at least one company representative (usually a mid to high-level executive) who sits on the United Way board of directors or is a member of the corporate liaison committee. Whoever wears the company hat when attending board meetings should push for decisions that are in line with corporate concerns.

All too frequently, a company's United Way board representative is someone who drew the short straw and got stuck with the job. If the corporate representative ends up lying low and doing as little as possible, that's an injustice to the United Way and to the business. Think about this analogy. The financier Carl Icahn buys a stake in a company and tries as hard as he can to get a seat on that company's board. Why? So he can influence critical decisions about the company's future. Businesses should view the United Way in a similar way. If a company is going to pour money into the organization, it has a fiduciary responsibility to have an articulate, knowledgeable, and effective activist at the board table.

If this latter model is in place, then the United Way isn't "those guys"—it's "us." If an employee or retiree has a beef about actions taken by the United Way, the complaint should be passed along to the company's board representative or liaison. In short, a condition for saying "yes" to funding the United Way is that the right company executive gets assigned to the organization's board to ensure the corporation's social investment gets tended to in the best way possible.

Addressing the "Most in Need" Challenge

A lot of employees won't like the following recommendation:

> Businesses should conduct organized worksite giving campaigns that go beyond computer-based solicitations.

There is a trend afoot that substitutes the computer for old-fashion face-to-face worksite fundraising. Having been subjected to worksite campaigns in which management pushes and prods workers to support the United Way, I can understand the appeal of exchanging the intrusion and hoopla of a fund drive for a more private and passive means of making a personal charitable decision. In the privacy of my work cubicle, I can click (or not click) my donor choices without being hassled or intimidated. But there's a problem with this trend. Without the on-site campaign with all its clatter and pushiness, employee donation decisions go in a different direction. And that's not necessarily in the best interest of the company—not to mention a community.

For sure, there have been United Way (and other federated drive) campaigns that have intimidated and embarrassed workers.

That's unfortunate. There should be fundraising standards in place that prevent that from happening. However, a campaign that energetically calls on employees to shoulder their "fair share" when addressing serious community issues isn't crossing the line. Without this kind of encouragement (call it pressure, if you want), a lot of nonprofits that have an impact on a community's quality of life won't get adequate support. Here is an explanation why.

Fundraising is far from an exact science, and we don't know all that much about the psychology of giving. But statistics do give us clues about the charitable choices individuals make. What we know is that people tend to assign the highest philanthropic priority to those organizations, causes, and programs that *personally* affect them and their families the most. Viewed this way, "charity" is actually quite self-serving. You make a gift to the National Parkinson Foundation because a relative is afflicted with the disease. You receive a solicitation from United Cerebral Palsy but since no one you know has that particular malady, the fundraising letter is dumped. You support your college with an annual contribution and get recognized on a donor list that impresses your old classmates. A private college that has no alumni affiliation with you or your family wants to create a scholarship fund for children of Iraq and Afghanistan war veterans. You say "no."

This selection process is especially evident when it comes to religious institutions. Nonprofit organizations that get most richly rewarded by individual contributions have spiritual roots. Over a third of all the billions of dollars in donations made each year go to religious groups and causes. Weekly, monthly, or annual gifts made to your church, synagogue, or mosque can legitimately be written off as charitable tax deductions—even though in most cases, a large percentage of the donated money goes to offset the operating and capital costs of an organization that yields benefits to you (a place to worship, religious classes, fellowship gatherings, and so on). Granted, many religious groups carry out humanitarian activities as well. But funds spent on such purposes generally only add up to a small percentage of the total collected.

Taking into account both religious and secular donations, Americans who file itemized tax returns and take a charitable tax deduction are clearly generous (donations equal around 2.6 percent of their adjusted gross income). However, as the Center of Philanthropy at Indiana University and Google found in a 2007 survey, their philanthropy often bypasses causes and programs that address very serious social needs (only 8 percent of donated dollars were directed toward "basic needs"). Homelessness. Health-care access for the poor. After-school programs for children in single parent households. Hunger. Underserved elderly. The list goes on. If nonprofits that deal with these challenges get any broad-scale individual support at all, it's generally loose change. Unless, of course, people make an unrestricted United Way donation or a contribution to a similar organization that addresses these needs. Sure, there are exceptions. There are altruistic donors who give first to those causes that help the poor and underserved. But these people are not in America's philanthropic mainstream.

Apply these realities to the worksite. Without an organized campaign that puts at least a little pressure on employees to donate to a general pool used to support causes workers would otherwise circumvent, money won't go there.

There is too much at stake to boil down a worksite giving program so employees are simply asked to check their computer screens and click on a nonprofit or two they might want to support. Those who choose to give at all will, in most cases, pick causes and organizations that are personally relevant. Unless there is an organized effort to educate employees on the importance of donating to other nonprofits that deal with significant local problems or are protecting the community's quality of life, most donations won't flow to these organizations. An occasional email asking employees to "give generously" isn't a substitute for a campaign that confronts prospective donors with the flesh-and-blood consequences of giving or not giving to charitable programs an individual would probably circumvent.

I know endorsing this in-your-face type of fundraising will irritate some. Many of those who will protest the loudest, though, actually have very soft hearts. Some of my libertarian friends who consider themselves over-taxed also resent being over-solicited by nonprofit organizations. If you are running a phonathon for Easter Seals or doing a solicitation mailing for Meals on Wheels, these get-your-hand-out-of-my-pocket types are the last people you want to approach—unless you bring them nose-to-nose with a crippled child or an elderly shut-in who couldn't survive without a daily delivery of food. Then these seemingly uncharitable individuals turn amazingly generous. But that only occurs if fundraising loses its abstractness and is translated into human terms. Which is what happens when a company conducts an effective worksite campaign.

Two Conditions

Let's get back to my conditional endorsement of United Way. The conditional "yes" has to be applied to two distinctly different ways companies are asked to support the United Way.

Business Donations to the United Way

A local United Way (or in some communities, a different and more effective federated campaign organization) can provide the right kind of conduit for funding those activities and programs important to a company's plant or office location. When considered in this light, United Ways are part of the conditional grant-making strategy that should be the platform for any corporation's philanthropy program. If a company seeks to recruit and retain the best employees (what company doesn't?), then it has to be concerned about the quality of life in and around its worksite(s). If a United Way is on top of its game, it will be playing a major role in keeping that quality as high as possible—supporting programs that reduce crime, providing youth services, expanding job training opportunities, and so on. Rarely is a company in a position to address these matters as a do-it-yourself undertaking. Businesses can't undertake the kind of needs analysis that a competent United Way organization should be able to carry out. Nor can a company do a better job than a competent United Way of monitoring and evaluating effectiveness of community programming.

If a corporation buys this argument, then the next logical question is, What size investment should we be making to our communities of interest via the United Way? And—should that investment be tied, in some way, to the level of giving on the part of our employees and retirees?

There is no hard and fast rule as to how much of a company's annual giving should be set aside for United Way organizations. Usually the level of funding is determined by three factors: (a) the overall size of a corporation's contributions program (most often reflective of a company's P&L); (b) the number of sites and personnel a company has; and (c) how active a company's management (particularly the CEO) is in the United Way movement.

A business that has a relatively small giving program (under $1 million a year) might allocate 25 percent or more of its cash giving to United Ways in those locations where it has a presence. However, for businesses with large philanthropy programs, donations often hover between 5 percent and 7 percent of cash giving (less for businesses with monster-sized contributions programs—for example, ExxonMobil allocates only 3 percent of its annual contributions for worksite giving support).

Some companies use their employee headcount as a way to calculate their United Way support; for example, they might contribute $100 per employee. Other companies reserve a larger percentage of United Way giving for their headquarters locations and apportion donations to satellite offices based on revenues or earnings.

As a rule, the more office and manufacturing sites a company has, the higher the total giving will be to United Way, as compared to corporations that have one location or are present in very few communities. Also, when a top executive takes on a United Way leadership role at either the local or national level, company donations tend to spike as long as the executive holds that elevated United Way position. Many senior executives assert that their United Way leadership is so high profile it does more for a company's reputation among key stakeholders than any other non-business commitment they can make. Under the condition that an executive can extract that kind of value from a modest bump up in a company's donation to United Way, the argument is sound. Compare the cost, for example, to a reputation enhancement ad the company might place in a Friday edition of *USA Today*. At the time of writing, the cost for a one-time, color advertisement is $450,000.

There's a caveat to the recommendation that companies include the United Way in its conditional grants portfolio, and it's called—Boy Scouts of America. In the 1990s, the United Way got caught up in a nasty dispute between the Boy Scouts and groups that argued the youth organization (the largest in the nation) discriminates against homosexuals. The U.S. Supreme Court issued a ruling in 2000 that gave the Boy Scouts the right to decide who can—or can't—join its ranks. The decision reaffirmed the Scouts' position that avowed homosexuals should not be registered as members or leaders of the organization (atheists and agnostics are also excluded). Several companies discontinued their direct support of the Boy Scouts, declaring they couldn't support an organization that ran counter to their own nondiscrimination policies. The problem spilled over to the United Way since it was a funding source for many Scout programs around the nation.

When some United Ways balked at continuing support for Boy Scouts, the scouting organization adopted a position statement that called on United Way chapters to keep funding its youth programs around the country:

> In our pluralistic society, the strength of local United Ways has been their ability to bring together and support a mosaic of community needs. These needs are best met through a comprehensive mix of agencies, many of which serve exclusive constituencies.

Not all corporations were swayed by this argument, and some struggled with how they could keep funding the United Way if the Boy Scouts were included on the list of recipients. As a way around the problem, some companies funneled money via the United Way to a scouting program called "Learning Through Life." The venture is a subsidiary of the Scouts aimed at helping public school students build self-confidence in social skills and is open to all—no discrimination based on religious views or sexual preference. Other United Ways stopped funding Boy Scouts out of general revenues but gave donors (companies as well as employees) the option of "donor designating" contributions that could be passed through the United Way and sent directly to local Scout groups.

Few corporate contributions issues proved more contentious than the Boy Scouts funding dilemma and its spillover to United Way support. There are a lot of strong Boy Scout advocates scattered through the ranks of the private sector. Some stood behind the Scout's decision regarding homosexuals. Equally as vocal were employees who insisted corporations needed to uphold nondiscrimination policies when making grant decisions. Caught in the middle were corporate contributions managers and, in some cases, the United Way.

It is very difficult for a company to hide from the Boy Scout issue when considering United Way support. A contribution has to be conditional on the basis of a corporation's own nondiscrimination policies and how a business interprets those policies in regard to its dealings with outside organizations. Although this problem is not as "hot" as it was in the early 2000s, it remains a burr under the saddle for many a corporate giving manager.

Worksite Giving Campaigns

Take away or drastically cut back employee giving at the workplace and the United Way would be in deep trouble. If the organization had to trade off getting a grant from a company for gaining access to its workforce for solicitation purposes, my guess is that employee access would be the choice. That's how important employee giving is to United Way's financial health.

On the surface, the employee worksite campaign may seem to have a dotted-line (at best) linkage to a corporation's charitable giving. Actually, there are two strong connections. First, as mentioned earlier, some companies match employee and retiree donations to United Way, which makes the worksite campaign very relevant since it ends up as a line item on the corporate giving budget. And second, a recent study by the Association of Corporate Contributions Professionals found that 23 percent of these annual campaigns are run out of the contributions office; 25 percent administered by a company's community relations department. Given how much time campaign management can take, the process can have a *huge* impact on a contribution department's operations. The more hours devoted to a campaign, the fewer hours available to deal with other aspects of a company's contributions activities.

Here are a few recommendations for handling an employee worksite fund drive:

- *Allow it to happen.* As noted, exposing employees (and retirees, where possible) to local needs is important.
- *Rotate leadership.* Any manager who has been responsible for a full-fledged worksite campaign knows how it can eat hours and even resources (supplies, meeting space, and so on). If the campaign responsibility is moved around to

different departments each year, the workload becomes less onerous. There is an added benefit to this approach. Various business units get a closer look at the United Way or other federated campaign organizations. Shared ownership is nearly always a good idea.

- *Provide administrative backup.* I have found the best practice for running a worksite campaign is to have corporate contributions personnel provide backup to the department handling the annual campaign. "Backup" is not synonymous with doing 95 percent of the work. It means helping with employee donation processing, resolving any issues with the United Way or other fundraising actors, and providing continuity or history from one campaign to another.

- *Cap the matching.* If a company does have a policy of matching employee and retiree donations to United Way or other federated campaign groups, the total should have a firm end point. "Our company will match employee donations 1:1 up to $500,000 . . . ." or a similar position enables the company to budget its total obligation without breaking the bank and yet still hold out a generous enough matching incentive that can be used to encourage employees to make their own donations.

Look for Added-Value Options

United Way has a place in a corporation's conditional grant-making program if (a) the company has a high-level and active representative on the local United Way board; (b) the local United Way is not at odds with the company's nondiscrimination policies and practices; (c) United Way overhead and management competency are not in question; and (d) company funding is kept to a reasonable percentage that is based on the overall size of a contributions program.

Finally, in weighing how best to support United Way, companies should check for any added-value funding options. For example, the Walmart Foundation brought together the United Way and two other nonprofits (One Economy Corporation and the National Disability Institute) to reach out to low-income individuals who qualified for free tax-filing assistance at ninety-one of its store sites. The $4 million project was a good way to alert the general public (a.k.a. prospective customers) that Walmart in conjunction with H&R Block, Liberty, Colbert/Ball, and others offered in-store tax preparation services.

Postscript

Here is an endnote about the people who work for federated campaigns.

Raising money for an assortment of nonprofits is different from soliciting funds for a single organization that has a sharply focused mission. If they are to be truly effective, people who work for United Way and similar "umbrella" fundraising groups need to take a broad view of the nonprofit world and perceive the importance of many different organizations. It's a difficult job and it takes genuine compassion bundled together with dogged determination to be successful. I have met a lot of people in the past who have both these qualities plugged into their DNA. But two individuals stand out.

Compassion

Don Sodo, the retired CEO and president of America's Charities (as mentioned, another worksite giving organization that competes with United Way), has a Robin Hood quality so powerful it can magically remove the contents of your wallet. Sodo isn't a communist or a socialist. He isn't a champion for the even distribution of all wealth. Quite the contrary; Don applied good old capitalistic methods when running his nonprofit organization. But he *is* a believer in the "there but for the grace of God go I" factor, which he uses to jackhammer your conscience.

Five minutes with Don Sodo and the most hardened detractor of an organized worksite giving campaign will be writing a check.

Why?

Because Sodo and many others like him are genuinely compassionate human beings who believe in their mission—to collect charitable donations from individuals and do everything in their power to make a difference to people most in need of that charity.

Chutzpa

Betty Beene was the top national United Way executive until January 2000. Beene stirred up antagonism among some local affiliates when she proposed strengthening the role of the national United Way office by centralizing pledge processing and developing direct ties with large businesses. The pushback to her ideas came to a boil, and Beene left her post a year earlier than planned. While critics carped about Beene's plan to revamp the United Way, no one complained about her hustle. And for good reason.

A year before she stepped down from her CEO role, Beene scheduled a visit to Johnson & Johnson. The company chief executive at the time was Ralph Larsen—a big United Way supporter and even bigger cheerleader for Beene. When the always-prompt Beene didn't show up for the 11 A.M. meeting, Ralph and I began to worry. Forty minutes later, she limped into the office with bruises on her face and hands. She apologized profusely for being late and explained she had been hit by a meat truck. While driving from Manhattan to New Jersey, the truck slammed into Beene near the Holland Tunnel. Disregarding her totally wrecked car and her injuries, Beene hobbled to the closest auto rental location she could find and made a bloody drive to J&J's headquarters. She pitched an appeal for an additional grant to the United Way that day. We said, "yes." How could we possibly turn her down?

When compassion gets coupled with grit, fundraising takes on a dynamic that makes it tough for a company to say "so sorry."

IN SUMMARY

Question 9: Should a company fund the United Way, or are there better alternatives?

Answer: Companies should support the United Way—but conditionally. Alternative or additive worksite giving campaigns should be given careful consideration using the same assessment criteria as applied to company giving to the United Way. Support should be conditional on the basis of senior executive involvement in the organization, nondiscrimination policies that are not in conflict with the company, and acceptable management performance and operating expenses. Funding should be a reasonable percentage of total cash contributions spending (5 percent to 25 percent is a typical range but levels will vary widely based on the overall size of a company's cash-giving program).

10

How Should a Company Respond to a Disaster?

After the 9/11 terrorist attack in 2001, many companies talked about setting up emergency bank accounts as set-asides for disaster response. None, to my knowledge, ever did so—at least not for the long term. Instead, mega-disasters—whether they occur inside or outside the United States—remain events that require unscheduled management attention and unbudgeted resources. Which is why an answer to the next question in our baker's dozen list can be so perplexing:

Question 10: How should a company respond to a disaster?

Answer: Prepare a general "top drawer" disaster response strategy to be used for future domestic or international catastrophes. Coordinate with human resources on employee and retiree assistance policies. Select and screen NGO disaster-response partners ahead of any calamity. Look for ways to make an early disaster commitment but explore options for "banking" such support to be used for longer-term relief and rebuilding efforts. Establish a framework for any special employee matching-gift initiative the company may elect to offer following a disaster.

Emotions run high after a major crisis. They can point a business in a direction that may not be the most beneficial either for the company or for those most affected by the disaster. Getting ahead of the storm (literally in some cases) is a good idea for businesses—even small companies. Here are a few road signs to follow:

1. *Develop a top-drawer disaster plan.* Putting together a pre-crisis, "What if a disaster hits?" plan is well worth the effort. Once such a plan is crafted, businesses should stick it in a top drawer where it is readily accessible. The plan doesn't have to be complicated but it should be inclusive. It should have a link to the latest summary of tax provisions that affect employees and their families who are disaster victims.

The plan should be specific about worksite giving initiatives—for example, "in response to significant disasters, as determined by senior management, our company will match employee donations on a dollar-for-dollar basis up to $500 per employee if contributions are directed to the following nonprofit organizations (list)."

To the extent possible, a plan should also include some means of deciding how much money or product will be allocated by a company in response to a disaster. A few corporations have developed a quantitative evaluation system that can be used to gauge the level of disaster support. One uses a scoring system that rates specific "decision factors" from 9 (highest priority) to 1 (lowest) (Exhibit 10.1).

Scores in each category are assigned different weights and then the adjusted scores are totaled. On the basis of the results, the corporation makes disaster funding decisions ranging from $0 to $1 million. Using this kind of evaluation matrix may be too much of a "deep dive" for some corporations. But a simple checklist similar to the "decision factors" noted in the exhibit will add important substance to a top-drawer disaster response plan.

2. *Work with HR on a coordinated employee and retiree support plan.* If employees or retirees are affected by a disaster, businesses often make a concerted effort to provide direct help (for example, no-interest loans, temporary housing, special medical services, advice on how to capitalize on tax breaks given to disaster victims, and so on). While HR generally makes the call on most of

Exhibit 10.1. Disaster Response Assessment Tool.

Decision Factors	Rank (9 = high to 1 = low)								
	9	8	7	6	5	4	3	2	1
Top Category—A									
Company presence in an affected area	☐	☐	☐	☐	☐	☐	☐	☐	☐
Catastrophic damage	☐	☐	☐	☐	☐	☐	☐	☐	☐
Infrastructure damage	☐	☐	☐	☐	☐	☐	☐	☐	☐
Support needed by government and relief groups	☐	☐	☐	☐	☐	☐	☐	☐	☐
Intermediate Category—B									
Loss of lives	☐	☐	☐	☐	☐	☐	☐	☐	☐
Immediate needs of survivors	☐	☐	☐	☐	☐	☐	☐	☐	☐
Lowest Category—C									
Company equipment applications	☐	☐	☐	☐	☐	☐	☐	☐	☐
Health and safety issues	☐	☐	☐	☐	☐	☐	☐	☐	☐
Security concerns	☐	☐	☐	☐	☐	☐	☐	☐	☐
Total Score: _____									
Weighted Score (Total) _____									

these decisions, there are ways to use nonprofit programs and organizations to shoulder at least some of the assistance.

Again, *prior* to any disaster, having contributions and HR examine and agree upon employee and retiree response options makes more sense than waiting until a crisis happens.

3. *Pick the right nonprofit partner.* The right partner should be of particular concern to businesses that donate products following a disaster. In many cases, the nonprofit organization that receives a product contribution also carries a billboard that bears the corporation's name. How many media clips have made it to the evening network news showing a nonprofit team working in a disaster zone with crates of supplies in the background stenciled with names such as Eli Lilly, Walmart, or Dell? As mom used to say, "You're known by the company you keep." A wise corporation will use due diligence to ensure those NGOs on its

"preferred list" of disaster relief partners bring something positive to the corporate name.

One suggestion is that nonprofits on a company's preferred recipient list should get a retainer. Businesses should provide them with a small annual cash contribution to help them offset costs incurred when corporations conduct periodic checkups on a nonprofit's ability to respond effectively to a disaster. How much? A $5,000 unrestricted donation seems reasonable in most cases.

4. *Don't rob Peter to pay Paul.* After 9/11, I was asked to make a presentation on corporate philanthropy strategies to a New Jersey company that will remain unnamed. The business was one of many that sent a cash contribution (in this case, $1 million) to the special fund set up to assist 9/11 victims and their families. The allocation was made before the end of 2001. Then the company CEO told the corporate contributions manager to cut $1 million out of the 2002 contributions budget to pay for the 9/11 gift. A cluster of schools, arts groups, and hospitals ended up financing the company's disaster relief largess.

So here's what should be the rule of thumb: don't practice this kind of trade-off. In the best of worlds, companies would build up a reserve and have it available for disaster relief. But that hasn't happened. Consequently, it's all about finding money as soon as a mega-disaster makes headlines. Since these are unbudgeted expenses, corporations should agree they are supplemental to the predetermined contributions budget. In other words, they should be additive to the Sabsevitz Ante-Up Formula spelled out in Chapter Two.

Especially when companies are splashing around in rough economic waters, it is tempting to pull money from one pocket and jam it into another. That's the wrong tactic. Disasters are outliers to a corporation's "predictable" giving program. They should be treated accordingly.

5. *Consider the three "R's."* Charitably inclined businesses, like people, react swiftly after a major disaster occurs. That's when needs are most evident and usually are visually presented in such a powerful way that it's difficult *not* to be responsive. For corporations, a speedy reaction can produce added benefits. Companies that donate early have a better chance of being singled out in print and TV roundup stories about corporate contributions.

Using self-generated stories, companies can also communicate their fast action to employees and other stakeholders. Pressing needs plus opportunities for reputation-enhancing exposure motivate companies to move hastily after a catastrophe occurs. The usual way of reacting is to send money, product, or both to organizations battling to save lives and rescue victims.

There's nothing wrong with that except—it's only one of the three disaster response "R's." Funds pour in for *recovery* activities because they are the most publicized and most immediately needed. A few weeks or months later, longer-term *relief* requirements (such as temporary housing, interim school programs, health care access, and so on) become clearer although not as widely communicated. After these issues are addressed, *rebuilding* emerges as a protracted and usually costly hurdle.

New Orleans is a living example of how the three R's so often play out. The surge of support that flowed into the city right after Hurricane Katrina tore through the city was monumental. But most of the money was earmarked for *recovery* with some assistance extended to meet *relief* needs. Very little corporate funding made it to the *rebuilding* stage. And therein rests the problem.

Rebuilding is frequently the most expensive, most time-consuming, and least alluring (from a donor perspective) part of the disaster response cycle. Ask any NGO that has had experience coordinating long-term disaster relief efforts. Raising money for a crisis following the initial recovery stage can be tough. Memories fade quickly, and other disasters pop up that lure emergency funding in different directions. Remember Hurricane Rita? It slammed the U.S. Gulf Coast only a few weeks after Katrina and siphoned away money businesses might have otherwise directed toward relief and rebuilding efforts in New Orleans.

Corporations can address these longer-term disaster response concerns by making an early but *conditional* donation or pledge following a crisis. Businesses have a need to get on a disaster response donor list quickly—so postponing a publicly disclosed commitment until the relief or rebuilding phase of the disaster cycle kicks in just won't work. However, there is no reason why a business can't negotiate an agreement with a nonprofit organization to accept a contribution at the front end of a crisis but hold back using the support until later in the disaster response process.

A few companies have enacted different strategies that have infused dollars into the latter stages of a disaster response initiative. Here are a couple of examples.

- *Aetna* matches employee gifts for disaster relief purposes on a year-round basis. Funds are provided to nonprofits the Aetna Foundation identifies as "best suited to provide short- and *long-term relief and reconstruction*" purposes. As an interesting side note, I have not run across any company that defines "disaster" in such a comprehensive way as Aetna—"[a disaster is] a flood, high water, wind-driven water, earthquake, volcanic eruption, drought, blizzard, pestilence, famine, fire, explosion, building collapse, transportation accident or other situation anywhere in the world that, for hundreds of victims, causes human suffering and generates basic human needs that cannot be alleviated without assistance."
- *Chevron* staged its assistance to Aceh Province in Indonesia, which was devastated by the 2004 tsunami. The corporation (which along with other oil companies has business interests in and around Sumatra where Aceh is located) helped fund emergency efforts immediately after the tidal wave's devastating impact. But Chevron then rolled out another $15 million to support reconstruction efforts through its Aceh Recovery program. In effect, the corporation managed its own stage-by-stage disaster response project.

These recommendations apply to any disaster regardless of where it occurs. But other crisis response steps taken by companies often depend on whether the event takes place on U.S. soil or elsewhere.

Domestic Disasters

A major crisis (natural or manmade) in the United States tends to trigger a different response mechanism than a catastrophe taking place in some distant location. I have worked with a number of companies on the heels of various domestic and international disasters. Three questions invariably pop up regardless of geography.

However, if the crisis has an impact on a U.S. location, these questions get *very* close attention:

- First, are there employees, retirees, or others close to the company who have been affected by the crisis? If so, before any other steps are taken, come up with a plan to help these individuals.
- Second, did the disaster take place at or near a location where the business has a presence? If so, the company's reaction will be more significant than if the disaster happened closer to home.
- Third, what are other companies—particularly benchmark businesses—doing? For many corporations, being too out front or lagging too far behind is a prescription for trouble. Companies will search for the middle, and if it's within the corporation's financial comfort range, that's where a business will end up.

Answering these questions will absolutely, positively bring the American Red Cross (ARC) into focus. The organization is always a front-line responder, and there's nothing like a calamity to bring pro and con views about ARC to the surface. When those views get aired, they usually touch on the national organization's recent history, which has been marked by one upheaval after another. Following is just one stormy chapter torn from ARC's recent past.

THE AMERICAN RED CROSS SAGA

"You're not going to believe this." Robert "Bo" Short was on the line. The vice president for strategic partner relations at the American Red Cross spoke in a whisper.

I didn't think any news coming out of ARC's main office would send me into a state of disbelief. The organization had been a soap opera for years. But Bo Short was right—for a moment, I didn't believe him.

"Everson's gone!" Short said. *"Finished!"*

"What?"

"I'm telling you, it's over." Short's voice remained low and intense. The news had just leaked out of ARC's front office, and this was one of the first calls the VP was making.

"What the hell happened?" I couldn't get my head around what Short was saying. Mark Everson was the fourth person since 9/11 to sit in the president's chair at one of the most venerable organizations in the country. He had been on the job for only six months.

"I'm not sure," Bo said. "But it doesn't sound good. Not when you hear things like *inappropriate relationship with a subordinate —*"

Short didn't need to paint the rest of the picture. What details I didn't immediately imagine were spelled out in the media over the next few days. ARC's board asked for Everson's resignation after learning about the CEO's relationship with an unnamed female employee.

"Everybody here's in shock," said Bo. As well they should have been. Although Everson was considered an "odd choice" by many inside and outside the organization (he was former commissioner of the Internal Revenue Service), his early administrative moves had won over those who had doubts about his leadership. His ouster was another deep gash on ARC's image, which had been damaged by earlier problems.

The seemingly constant turmoil at ARC's headquarters irked many contributions managers, and that irritation sometimes became explosive. One flare-up occurred when an interim ARC chief executive named Harold Decker (one of two Everson predecessors) accepted an invitation to talk to one hundred company representatives about his organization's programs and plans.

Decker had been handed the front-office job after the ARC fired Bernadine Healy, a tough-talking physician who had the misfortune of sitting in the Red Cross front office on September 11, 2001.

At the meeting, Decker tried explaining what ARC was doing with $600 million in post-9/11 donations collected during Healy's tenure. Half the money had been donated by businesses. Decker talked about a "Liberty Fund" the Red Cross had set up as a holding tank for the money that was to be used strictly for 9/11 victims, their families, and rescue workers. There was pressure on ARC from some quarters to put a portion of the 9/11 money into a general pool that would be reserved for future catastrophes including the possibility of more terrorist assaults. But the organization held fast and the contributions remained restricted to those directly affected by the September 11 tragedy.

Decker took a pounding over ARC's national call for blood donations after the Twin Towers collapsed and part of the Pentagon was still smoldering. With many deaths and only a limited number of casualties requiring transfusions, the need for blood turned out to be minimal. Yet the Red Cross kept pressing for more blood donors until it had a sizeable oversupply. With only a forty-two-day shelf life, some of the blood ultimately had to be dumped. Many of the contributions managers who also had responsibility for employee blood drives were furious.

It was Decker's calm demeanor and candidness that got him through the meeting. I remember thinking that ARC would be smart to cross out his "interim" title and make him the permanent CEO. But Decker said he wasn't interested.

"Why not?" several people wanted to know.

Pausing to choose his words carefully, Decker replied that dealing with disasters such as 9/11 was something he could handle. But working with ARC's fifty-member board of governors was a different kind of challenge. At the time, the board was dominated by thirty local Red Cross chapter representatives with a few government, academic, and business leaders thrown in. The contentious board-management struggle convinced Decker he didn't want a permanent seat in ARC's presidential suite.

But Rear Admiral Marsha Evans did.

Evans walked into a storm—literally. She took over from Decker and was in ARC's pilothouse when Hurricane Katrina struck in August 2005. Less than five months after the storm ripped the Gulf Coast apart, Evans was finished. She left not long after a Congressional committee hammered the ARC for its ineffective response to the disaster.

Months before the hurricane, Evans appeared before the same group of hundred-plus companies Harold Decker had addressed earlier. Several corporate contributions managers blasted her for ARC's fundraising practices following a rash of wildfires in southern California. She took the volleys of complaints far more personally than Decker—at one point, coming close to tears. When asked about her relationship with the ARC board, her remarks were cautious, but it was easy to detect an underlying friction, which had to have contributed to Evans's decision to leave the organization.

After Evans resigned, ARC appointed another interim CEO – Jack McGuire, formerly the head of the Red Cross Biomedical Services. Jack had done a stint at Johnson & Johnson years earlier so I knew him by reputation. He had good linkages to the Food and Drug Administration, which was a plus for the Red Cross since the FDA had repeatedly criticized the organization for its handling of blood collections.

McGuire made two appearances before the corporate audience that had hosted Decker and Evans. The group had now swelled to over 150 company contributions and community relations managers. McGuire had an amazing gift of gab and was able to talk over and around issues that got stuck in the craw of earlier ARC chief executives. McGuire's glibness and his deep experience with ARC reportedly put him on the short list of candidates for ARC's permanent top job. But the Red Cross moved in a different direction and, instead, hired Mark Everson.

After Everson made a quick exit, ARC appointed still *another* interim CEO (the organization's general counsel) and *another* "permanent" chief executive – Gail McGovern, a Harvard Business School professor and former AT&T and Fidelity Investments executive.

The revolving front office door at the ARC coupled with the strained relations between its board and management have made companies wary about the organization. Nevertheless, there is yet to be an NGO that pulls in more money, food, clothing, and other materials after a major crisis than the ARC. Because it has such an extraordinary prominence in the domestic disaster relief field and because it is congressionally blessed, it gets heavily funded but also gets constantly scrutinized for its performance. And if things don't go smoothly, as was the case in the aftermath of Katrina, companies don't hold back their displeasure. Here are a few examples:

- "Truckloads of ice were sent to the wrong staging
  area .... they were never told where to go .... stayed until
  the ice melted ... ridiculous ...."

- "We had prepared food for more than a thousand people but we couldn't get through on the phone to anyone who knew what we should do . . . ."
- "We had tens of thousands of dollars worth of supplies ready to be shipped but we were put in line behind some old lady who wanted to FedEx a quilt . . . ."

These complaints may sound like exaggerations but they were reinforced by a Government Accounting Office report which found "strained relationships" between FEMA and ARC that hampered relief efforts. Even more obvious to corporate contributions managers was how ARC fell short of the coordinated and effective disaster response carried out by the "Sallies"—the name sometimes given to Salvation Army workers and volunteers. During both 9/11 and Katrina, companies commented about how quickly the Sallies responded to each crisis and how efficiently they carried out their business.

So why not shift company donations to the Sallies instead of ARC?

In some cases, corporations already do give funding priority to the Salvation Army. Individual, corporate, and foundation gifts make up about a third of that organization's multibillion-dollar budget (depending on the year, the Sallies and ARC are not that dissimilar in revenues received). However, unlike the Red Cross, the Salvation Army does not view itself as a "first responder" to a crisis but rather a supporter of first responders. Many company representatives I have talked to regard this more a matter of semantics than practice since the Sallies are often seen on the front lines of a crisis before any other organization shows up. Regardless of how the organization is categorized, it is the Sallies' Christian affiliation that keeps some businesses on the funding sidelines. Even though the organization doesn't religiously discriminate when coming to the aid of disaster victims, the Salvation Army still has deep faith-based roots.

Businesses tend to walk a wavy and confusing line when it comes to supporting religious organizations that provide disaster relief. A company that might have trouble funding the Sallies in the United States may have no qualms about making a donation to the Catholic Medical Mission Board for disaster support overseas. A company could say no to the Salvation Army largely because of its desire to keep an arm's length from religious groups—but at the same time it will cut a check to Habitat for Humanity, which is another Christian-based nonprofit. The fact is that many religious organizations do have the capacity to provide help in the wake of a disaster, sometimes more rapidly and effectively than secular nonprofits. For that reason, it makes more sense for a company to build flexibility into its giving guidelines, much the way computer chip maker and hardware manufacturer Intel does:

> "[Intel does *not* support] sectarian or denominational religious organizations, such as churches, missionary groups or funds, whose activities primarily benefit members or adherents, unless funds are being sought for purposes that will benefit the broader community."

Many corporations such as Northrop Grumman take a harder line regarding religious groups—"as a rule, we don't fund religious organizations." This policy seems a bit too limiting. It should be made clear that in certain circumstances, faith-based groups are in the running for corporate funding.

While religious-based nongovernment organizations (NGOs) sometimes play a role in domestic disaster relief efforts, it's their international outreach that is especially notable. It isn't unusual for NGOs with religious affiliations to be first on the scene after a crisis hits a part of the world where other relief organizations would be suspect or not welcomed.

Businesses that have at least some "elasticity" in their international giving strategies won't rule out religious groups as conduits for aid and assistance in situations like this. Recognizing that international and domestic disaster response tactics can often differ, business standouts in this field don't attempt to build a one-NGO-for-all plan. Instead they earmark "preferred" nonprofits that can be called upon in the wake of a crisis in the United States. As for disasters that happen in other parts of the world, decision making follows a different course.

International Disasters

When does a corporation make the call to send assistance following a horrific catastrophe outside the United States? Is it a determination based on a body count? Number of people injured? Number of people left homeless? Number of employees, customers, or other stakeholders affected? Extensiveness of property damage? Ease of getting aid to victims? Number of other companies sending aid?

For most companies, all these questions end up on the table after a headline-making, large-scale crisis outside the United States. When there are employees or others with a connection to the company who have been affected by a disaster, a corporation's response will mirror its reaction to a domestic crisis (but possibly and probably working with different NGOs than might be called upon in the United States). However, when a monumental calamity occurs in a place where most companies have absolutely no business interests, executives struggle with whether a response is in order—and if so, how big a cash or product donation should be and where assistance should be directed.

Two classic case studies offer insight on how companies respond to a natural disaster in locations of little business relevance.

DISASTER CASE STUDIES

Case Study 1: Tsunami

The day after Christmas in 2004, an earthquake and tsunami ravaged parts of Indonesia, Sri Lanka, India, and a few other countries. Measured in lives lost, the event was the single worst tsunami in history—over 280,000 people killed and 1.1 million people displaced. The destruction was so extensive the United Nations estimated the relief operation would be the costliest in human history.

Unbeknownst to the private sector, the Southeast Asia catastrophe would be the first leg of a "disaster triple whammy" that would push the crisis response capabilities of many corporations to the limit. Only eight months after the tsunami struck Myanmar and other Asian locations, Hurricane Katrina would ruin huge stretches of America's Gulf Coast. Weeks later, Hurricane Rita—the most intense tropical cyclone ever observed in the Gulf of Mexico—would hit Louisiana and Texas at a cost of over $11 billion.

The week between Christmas and New Year's is typically a dormant period for U.S. businesses. But in 2004, company executives put aside their holiday gifts and picked up their Blackberries trying to figure out what the right humanitarian response should be after the tsunami washed over such a far-away and commercially insignificant location (except to a few oil corporations that were active in the region). Several businesses reacted swiftly with relatively modest donations. But it was Pfizer that ultimately set the high bar, donating $10 million in cash and another $25 million in medicines. Deutsche Bank and Coca-Cola followed with $13 million and $10 million donations, respectively. Those commitments sparked another forty-plus companies to come forward with cash donations of $1 million or more. And once those donations were announced, a slew of businesses followed with their own six-figure contributions.

Had the tsunami followed Hurricanes Katrina and Rita, it is unclear how corporations would have responded. Best guess is that the level of support would have been lower. "Donor fatigue" does factor into a company's disaster response decision making. However, given the enormity of the tsunami crisis, businesses would have been hard pressed not to give something. More than likely, a few companies would still have made very sizeable donations. Predictably, some would come to the conclusion that a large contribution if properly promoted could draw more public attention than a thirty-second Super Bowl commercial (the cost of a half-minute TV ad run during the 2005 Super Bowl, which was played only a couple of months after the tsunami, was $2.4 million).

Case Study 2: Haiti Earthquake

It was inconceivable that another natural disaster could rival the death and destruction caused by the Asian tsunami. But in January 2010, the unimaginable happened. An earthquake ravaged Haiti, leaving sections of the poorest country in the Western Hemisphere in ruins. Although there were few U.S. companies active in the country, the private sector was quick to respond to the crisis, with over three hundred corporations donating $122 million in cash and products within a month of the disaster.

What was particularly revealing about the response to the Haitian calamity was how so many businesses turned to the ARC as the primary recipient for their disaster contributions. Over 125 of the 300 companies that reported their donation decisions to the U.S. Chamber's Business Civic Leadership Center directed funding to the ARC. Ironically, some of these companies were among the most vocal critics of the Red Cross. Yet when a major disaster hit relatively close to home, the businesses elected to fund ARC as a first responder. Table 10.1 clearly makes that point.

Table 10.1. Corporate Support to NGOs Providing Haitian Relief Services.

NGO	Corporate Support*
American Red Cross	126
U.S. Fund for UNICEF	15
Doctors Without Borders	15
Save the Children	13
International Red Cross	12**
CARE	8
UN Friends of World Food Program	6
Clinton-Bush Haiti Fund	5
Project HOPE	5
Oxfam America	4
Direct Relief	3
MediShare	3
AmeriCares	2
Catholic Medical Mission Board	2
Salvation Army	2
Heart to Heart	2

(*continued*)

Table 10.1. (*continued*)

NGO	Corporate Support*
World Vision	2
Wyclef Jean's Yéle Haiti	2
American Refugee Committee	1
Animal Relief Coalition for Haiti	1
Change International	1
Concern Worldwide	1
Feed the Children	1
Florida Disaster Fund	1
Habitat for Humanity	1
International Medical Corps of America	1
International Rescue Committee	1
Jewish Renaissance Fund	1
Mercy Corps	1
Miami Global Institute for Community Health and Development	1
Operation Compassion	1
Pan American Development Foundation	1
Plan International	1
Share Our Strength	1
SOS Children's Village	1
Telecom Sans Frontieres	1
United Way Disaster Relief Fund	1

*Number of times NGOs were referenced as disaster response recipients by three hundred companies. Total does not sum to three hundred, since some companies did not specify which NGOs were provided cash or product assistance.

**Includes Red Cross or Red Feather organizations from outside the United States.

Source: Business Civic Leadership Center.

The tsunami and Haiti crises underscore the point that there is no absolute formula a corporation can use to judge if and when it should react to an international disaster that doesn't have some direct effect on its business. But answering a few questions will generally guide the company in the best possible direction.

Is it the right thing to do? Is the disaster so terrible in respect to loss of life, onset of disease, displacement of huge numbers of people, and so on that it warrants a response? If the magnitude of the event is so significant, it will usually prompt a CEO to sound the call: "We need to do *something!*" What that *something* is usually is left to a company's contributions administrator and those executives sitting on a corporate contributions committee or company foundation board.

Are there any predictable consequences if support is provided? Will the company be blasted by customer groups, investors, or others who feel the business didn't act fairly by reacting to one crisis while ignoring another of more consequence to special interests? The principle of an action causing a reaction has to be weighed by a company. The nub of a complaint would be that (a) there are plenty of lesser crises that have a bearing on people and places important to a company and (b) like taxes and death, other terrible calamities will occur in the future.

Sometimes the magnitude of a crisis in a far-off, business-irrelevant location will overwhelm these concerns. There are other occasions, though, when managers have to decide whether releasing humanitarian funds will win praise or draw fire.

Will employees be critical of the company if no support is rendered? Here's an interesting observation that is entirely unsupported by credible data—I haven't seen any appreciable increase in employee pride when a worker's company sends money or goods to help earthquake, tornado, or flood victims. The reaction seems to be, "Well, of course—what would you expect? It's the way our company operates."

But if a corporation is *not* included on a list of private sector donors responding to a highly publicized crisis, an employee "cringe factor" will sometimes set in. Working for a business perceived to be behaving badly can put a nick in employee morale. It's not so bad as lugging around a sandwich board that reads "Enron" or "Lehman Brothers," but worker allegiance and performance aren't bolstered when employees think their company is so socially irresponsible that it's an embarrassment.

Are there "safe" NGOs that should be enlisted as partners? There are plenty of NGOs in the disaster relief and assistance field. The time to figure out which are the best possible partners for a business isn't a few hours or days after a crisis but rather *before* a catastrophe strikes. Doing a thorough investigation of a nonprofit takes more than a phone call or a quick Internet search. A review of an organization's working relationships with other companies, its reputation in countries outside the United States, and its governance structure—these are all worth careful study. Even if an NGO does end up in a company's disaster response network, it should be put through a thorough exam every so often. NGOs aren't static entities—they change, and so does the relief and assistance environment.

Years ago, Johnson & Johnson had over twenty NGOs on its "preferred" list of organizations that could be called upon in case of an international crisis. It was simply too much to stay on top of that many nonprofits. The corporation eventually whittled the preferred list down to the following seven NGOs, on the basis of their global reach and their ability to distribute different types of donations:

- Project HOPE
- AmeriCares
- MAP International
- Catholic Medical Mission Board
- Direct Relief International
- International Aid
- Heart to Heart International

Because this small cluster of preferred nonprofits could be enlisted to handle product contributions—in some cases re-callable pharmaceuticals and medical devices—J&J was (and continues to be) rigorous in its monitoring of these organizations, including annual on-site inspections of their warehouses. The corporation also maintains a list of "specialty" NGOs that it accesses when unique distribution needs crop up. But it is the "big seven" that are used as distributors of J&J's international product donations for most ongoing aid purposes as well as disaster response.

J&J's preferred and specialty list won't necessarily be the same for other companies—particularly those not in the health care field. So the list of seven isn't a cut-and-paste recommendation for other businesses.

There's a reason why a meticulous assessment of an NGO is important. Over the years, I have seen good intentions spawn impressive amounts of disaster relief assistance that never made it to where donations were supposed to go. Some funds earmarked for Darfur refugees didn't filter through the layers of corrupt intermediaries. Some donated food supplies for flood victims in Central America were diverted to the black market.

Quality assurance in the disaster relief business is hard to come by unless a company has picked the right nonprofit to handle its cash or product donations. The odds of choosing an NGO that's best suited to work with a company are much more favorable if the corporation makes this kind of decision when the waters are calm and not when all hell is breaking loose.

Cash or Product?

Most businesses (and individuals) understand it's *cash* that non-profits need and value the most following a disaster. Monetary contributions give disaster organizations the flexibility to acquire materials and services that don't always get donated. But while nonprofits might prefer money, they often are at the receiving end of other kinds of contributions.

Disasters have a way of eliciting new and used product dona-tions from well-intentioned contributors. When those products are not relevant to a disaster or there are too many donations of a particular item, the system gets clogged. NGOs end up with truck-loads (literally) of second-hand clothing but not enough blankets; an over-supply of canned goods but a shortage of diapers; pallets of toothpaste but no toothbrushes; and so on.

As explained in Chapter Seven, corporations have an added incentive to give away product that is not fully depreciated when such donations are used to help the "ill or needy" or for a few other purposes. Because disasters almost always involve contributions to the needy, some companies may search out willing nonprofits to accept product donations that frankly may be peripheral to emergency or longer-term disaster response efforts.

But what if the process were to change?

What if a predetermined system were in place in which frontline nonprofits could tap into a network of businesses that produced specific goods vitally needed following most disasters? A network of companies that pledge to donate products (up to agreed-upon limits) if a major crisis happened?

This type of "on demand" strategy would provide NGOs with essential products and would still give companies their stepped-up tax benefits. Most important, disaster victims would be helped with the right kind of donated goods when they are most needed.

On a very limited basis, this kind of NGO-to-business outreach is already going on. In 2004, for instance, Miller Brewing stopped its beer production to produce bottled water for Florida residents blasted by Hurricane Charley. The disaster response was a classic example of corporation cooperation—the energy company Excel handled the water delivery, Owens-Corning Glass donated bottles, NorthStar Print Group contributed the labels, and Inland Paperboard and Packaging donated the cardboard containers. This impressive effort began with a "what we need" alert from disaster response coordinators.

An "on demand" system can't be concocted by NGOs on their own. Nor will it work if it is viewed as a program orchestrated exclusively by the federal government. However, FEMA might be the most appropriate facilitator for bringing together the right parties who can piece together a workable disaster command center. This is not an easy task but one that will be worth the effort given the payoff to those devastated by a natural or manmade disaster.

Pre-Disaster Planning

This chapter's underlying message is: when it comes to disasters, *plan ahead*. During the immediate aftermath of a major crisis, conditions are so chaotic that prudent decision making becomes difficult if not impossible. The calm before the storm is the time to develop a well-thought-out plan that can be appropriately mulled over and blessed by senior management.

The time to debate whether a company should or shouldn't assist the ARC isn't in the midst of a hurricane, earthquake, or terrorist attack. That issue should be addressed before the winds blow or an explosive device is detonated. My advice about how companies should deal with ARC? To some extent, I am in step with what one corporate contributions manager recently said after his peers ripped the ARC apart:

"Get over it."

For all its real or perceived shortfalls, ARC remains the first responder of choice for donors (whether they be people or businesses) following a disaster in the United States. And as the Haiti case study makes clear, the ARC can also be an extremely popular choice for routing aid to locations outside the United States. This reality is unlikely to change. Probably the best way to "get over it" is for corporations to do more to help fix whatever problems stand in the way of constructing the best possible partnerships between the organization and the private sector.

Yes, there are other high-quality nonprofit organizations that can respond rapidly and effectively to a disaster (see Exhibit 10.2). But the American Red Cross has been and continues to be in a special category since it was chartered by Congress as a "federal instrumentality" in 1900.

Exhibit 10.2. Organizations Providing Disaster Relief Services (partial list).

Action by Churches Together*	American Rescue Team International
ActionAid International	
Adventist Community Services*	Amnesty International
Adventist Development & Relief Agency International*	AMURT
	Baptist World Aid*
African Medical & Research Foundation	Brethren Disaster Ministries*
	Brother's Brother Foundation
AmeriCares	CAFOD
American Jewish World Service	CARE
American Radio Relay League	Cartre Centre (Emory University)
American Red Cross	Catholic Charities*

(continued)

Exhibit 10.2. (*continued*)

Catholic Fund for Overseas Development*

Catholic Medical Mission Board*

Catholic Relief Services*

Children's Disaster Services

Children's Hunger Fund

Christian Aid*

Christian Children's Fund*

Christian Disaster Response International*

Christian Reformed World Relief*

Church World Service*

Compassion International*

ConflictNet

Direct Relief International

Doctors Without Borders

Episcopal Relief & Development*

European Committee Humanitarian Office

Feed the Children USA

Fondation Hirondelle

Food for the Hungry

Food for the Poor

Friends of the World Food Program

Global Impact

Hadassah*

Heart to Heart International

Heifer International

HelpAge International

Help the Children

Friends—Quaker Organizations*

InterAction

International Aid*

International Medical Assistance

International Rescue Committee

International Orthodox Christian Charities*

International Relief Friendship Foundation

Japanese Red Cross Society

Lutheran Disaster Response*

MAP International*

Medical Teams International

Mennonite Disaster Service*

Mercy Corps

National Emergency Response Team

National Organization for Victim Assistance

Nazarene Disaster Response*

Nippon Volunteer Network

Northwest Medical Teams International

One World Organization

Operation Blessing*

Operation Compassion*

Opportunity International

Oxfam

PAHO

Exhibit 10.2. (*continued*)

PeaceNet	Tear Fund
Presbyterian Disaster Assistance*	Trocaire
Project HOPE	UJA Federations of America*
REACT International	UNICEF
Red Crescent	United Methodist Relief*
ReliefWeb	UN Foundation
Salvation Army*	UN World Food Programme
Samaritan's Purse*	Volunteers in Technical Assistance
Save the Children	Volunteers of America
Seventh Day Adventist*	William J. Clinton Foundation
Society of St. Vincent de Paul*	World Emergency Relief
Southern Baptist Disaster Relief*	World Relief
Swiss Disaster Relief Unit	World Vision*

*NGOs with religious affiliations or links.

ARC is an independent nonprofit that relies on financial support from donors but does have the ability to access government funds "when funding requirements are beyond that supported by the charitable public." To some businesses, this caveat is reason enough to steer clear of the organization. "If ARC is that cozy with the feds, then let Washington pick up the bill," is the rationale. That logic falls short because the organization's broad mission would be severely compromised if it were too deeply dependent on federal support (which it isn't and never has been).

In 2007, Congress revised the ARC charter and authorized several reforms largely aimed at making the organization's governing body more efficient and strategic. The fifty-member ARC board is being whittled down to between twelve and twenty members. Several other steps are being taken that are designed to shape the organization for the next several decades.

It is during this reconstruction phase when the private sector should be at the table with the right people offering the right kind of ideas. Company employees, retirees, and at least some senior executives will continue to give preference to the Red Cross—and will make it impossible for corporations to avoid supporting ARC. Rather than continuing to complain about the organization's shortcomings, a better option is to *help turn ARC into the kind of nimble first responder that can work with government agencies, businesses, and other nonprofits to provide people with aid and assistance when they need it most.*

Another point to keep in mind is that like the United Way, the ARC is sometimes unfairly attacked because of the inadequacies of a few operating units and the widely publicized problems that have plagued its national office. A majority of local ARC chapters (there are nearly seven hundred throughout the United States) are effective and provide a valuable service to those communities where they are located. It is especially inappropriate to use governance challenges at the national office as an excuse not to support a local ARC chapter if it is in line with the conditional charitable interests of the corporation.

It all boils down to this: companies—even small to mid-sized businesses—should consider thinking through how they will react to a nearby or distant disaster *before* a crisis actually occurs. It is far more difficult to address sometimes thorny issues (such as the mixed opinions regarding the ARC support) during a tempest than when conditions are calm.

IN SUMMARY

Question 10: How should a company respond to a disaster?

Answer: Develop a general disaster response strategy *ahead* of a crisis and use it in the aftermath of any future domestic or international catastrophes that warrant a company reaction. Other steps to take include (a) working with company human resource managers to design employee and retiree assistance policies; (b) selecting NGO disaster-response partners *before* a disaster; (c) exploring ways to react swiftly after a crisis with a provision to "bank" some or all cash support for future relief and rebuilding efforts; and (d) determining specifics for any special employee matching gift initiative that may be offered following a disaster.

11

Can a Company Measure
What Works?

"True genius," Winston Churchill said, "resides in the capacity for the evaluation of uncertain, hazardous and conflicting information."

If this is the case, the corporate philanthropy field is loaded with geniuses. There are plenty of managers who have the *capacity* to evaluate grants. Here's the problem: when it comes to gauging the value of a corporate contribution or a community relations initiative, *that capacity is rarely unleashed.* Which brings us to the next question bundled into our baker's dozen list:

Question 11: Can a company measure what works?

Answer: Yes, it can. But to do so effectively means figuring out what exactly needs to be measured and then determining how to evaluate by beginning the measurement process sooner rather than later.

Winston Churchill could have been a master corporate contributions manager. He would have understood how attempts to measure the impact of a grant can spin a company into a sea of uncertainty and generate a databank full of conflicting information. The entire process can even be hazardous to a manager's long-term career plans.

Measuring a grant's effectiveness is too often an exercise based on mixed expectations. Many times the evaluation process totally circumvents the questions company executives most want answered. The trick to effective measurement is to (a) get clarity on *what* the company wants to know about a grant's impact and (b) begin the assessment process at or before a contributions commitment is made.

The Measurement Foursome

Carried out properly, measurement and grant-making strategic planning are joined at the hip. It's bad practice to start thinking about assessment a couple of months before a three-year grant period is about to end. The right time to begin the evaluation process is *before* the company makes a donation to a nonprofit organization.

Here are four tips that should improve the way any company takes a hard look at what it expects a grant to accomplish—and what outcomes are secondary when it comes to measurement.

Decide Before Not After

As noted, the time to decide *what* a corporation expects a grant to accomplish is before funds are donated to a nonprofit organization—not after the fact. Assume a business agrees to make a cash contribution to the Nature Conservancy. The contributions committee or company foundation board goes on record at the time the donation is made with the following statement:

> Approved as a general support grant to the Nature Conservancy with no restrictions applied to the donation.

The only expectation the company has for this unrestricted grant is a notice from the Nature Conservancy that it actually received the contribution and an assurance that the organization provided no goods or services in exchange for cash. But suppose the corporation were to make a conditional grant:

> Approved: grant to the Nature Conversancy for the organization's green acres program based on the Conservancy's request to secure

funds for the acquisition of property adjacent to our company's headquarters location.

Unlike an unrestricted grant, this commitment comes with a clear expectation that the Nature Conservancy will use company funds for a very specific purpose—and the grant should be monitored accordingly. Now assume the company's senior management goes one step further by instructing the contributions office that in addition to awarding the grant, it should do the following:

> Secure as much exposure as possible for the grant to the Nature Conservancy in conjunction with ongoing efforts to obtain local official approval for a zoning variance for a plant expansion.

Far too often, expectations directly or indirectly associated with a grant aren't specified until long after a company's money is out the door. Outcome measurement requirements come in the form of an after-the-fact question such as, "Oh, by the way, did the land near our plant get picked up by the Nature Conservancy as part of its green acres program?" That's the wrong time to focus on grant deliverables. Asking after the fact why a company's Nature Conservancy grant didn't generate more local media coverage isn't the same as making it clear at the outset that pushing for media coverage is a high expectation.

Get Real

Full-scale, highly quantitative evaluations are simply not practical or affordable for 99 percent of the contributions a company elects to make. They are too expensive and time consuming. More general qualitative reviews are usually sufficient for most company grants. The few contributions that do warrant heavy-duty evaluation should be handpicked carefully and subjected early on to these two questions: (a) Why do we want this kind of detailed information? (b) How will it be used?

Data collection is costly, and if the expense only buys research that ends up in a file drawer, the company has made a bad investment. If, on the other hand, the information fulfills an important objective that is clearly stated when the grant is awarded, then the extra cost is justified.

Engage the Nonprofit Organization

Relying on a grant recipient to conduct a self-evaluation isn't perfect, but in most cases, it is the only sensible way to acquire information about what impact a corporate grant may have had. Asking a nonprofit to report on how it used company funds should be standard fare when making a grant—even a small one. Put a different way, for *routine* evaluations, let the nonprofit organization do a giant's share of the work.

Even when a much more in-depth independent evaluation is required, a company can pay for some or all of the cost for a third-party grant evaluation by channeling the expense through a nonprofit organization.

THE MEASUREMENT ``ADD-ON´´

Widget International makes a $100,000 cash grant to a charity. After the check is awarded, the head of Widget's contributions program pulls the nonprofit's CEO aside and says, "How would you like another $20,000 donation?"

The CEO is ecstatic. "What's the catch?" she says.

"Send us a note asking for $20,000 to evaluate the $100,000 grant we just gave you."

"And Widget will okay that amount?"

"Yes—if the request makes it clear that most of the money is to be channeled through you to an outside, independent evaluator who will report results to your organization and Widget simultaneously."

The CEO's enthusiasm wanes but she agrees to take the money once it is understood the independent evaluator will be a university business school professor who will be paid $15,000 for the project. That will leave $5,000 to cover overhead costs incurred by the CEO's organization.

There's a limit to when and where this funding technique can be used. If a company wants quantifiable research that yields evidence about whether or not a grant caused a spike in sales or provided the company with some other direct benefit, then research should be paid directly by the business—not as a nonprofit organization pass-through.

Get a Seat at the Cause-Marketing Table

Since "cause marketing" gets saddled with different definitions, let's open with the most common explanation of this concept:

Cause marketing (or sometimes called cause-related marketing) involves a collaborative relationship between a company and a nonprofit organization that yields mutual benefits. Corporations leverage a visible tie-in with a nonprofit as a way of generating sales or pumping up awareness about the business, brand, or both. On the flip side, the NGO capitalizes on the partnership by reaching a wider audience and strengthening its own name recognition—not to mention also receiving a payment from the corporation (which a company usually records as an ordinary business expense and not as a charitable donation).

Because so many cause-marketing commitments are made using marketing or advertising department funds, the corporate contributions or company foundation manager might not be invited to take part in the planning, execution, and evaluation of cause-marketing campaigns. That's a mistake. The effectiveness of a cause-marketing initiative is all about hooking up with the right nonprofit organization.

Evaluating which nonprofit organization is best suited for a highly visible connection with a corporation should be—at least in part—a responsibility shouldered by the company's contributions professional(s). Predictably, marketing or product directors may push back with this line: "Listen, this is strictly a marketing program that we're carrying in our budget—so bug off." That's the wrong approach. The program shouldn't belong "strictly" to a marketing department. Corporate contributions should own part of the deal.

There's no arguing that cause marketing is popular. Businesses are attracted to the concept because, according to recent opinion research data, nine out of ten consumers think it's important for companies to support causes and charities. But it isn't just the private sector that has a love affair with cause marketing. When Kurt Aschermann was the head marketing guru for Boys & Girls Clubs of America, he was known as the most successful cause-marketing dealmaker in the nation. As one of his "Ten Commandments of Cause-Related Marketing," this was his message to nonprofit organizations:

Where's the big money in a corporation? Bingo—it's in sales and marketing. The charity side may have some money for you, but the potential is much higher in sales and marketing. That means if you can convince your corporate partner your collaboration will benefit their business, you have a leg up (and the potential for a lot more money!)

Aschermann urged nonprofits to follow the big money, and if they did, the trail would often lead them to a company's marketing department. It is at that point when both the charitable organization and the corporation need to think carefully about the intended and non-intended consequences of a cause-marketing affiliation. Yes, there are mutually beneficial opportunities that can sprout from a cause-marketing arrangement. But there can also be not-so-pleasant surprises. I speak from experience.

A CAUSE MARKETING FIASCO

In 1994, while I was parked in Johnson & Johnson's corporate offices, one of the company's affiliates (McNeil Consumer Products Company, best known for its Tylenol line) entered into a cause-marketing arrangement with the Arthritis Foundation (AF). At the heart of the deal was an agreement that McNeil would produce what would be called a line of Arthritis Foundation Pain Relievers. The plan guaranteed AF a payment of $1 million and other benefits. As for McNeil, it would capture a lot more shelf space in the pain reliever section of your local pharmacy and grocery store—translation: big money.

The AF plan was largely the inspiration of two young, smart, and creative product directors. Coupling MBA talent with high energy can put an idea on a very fast track, which is exactly what happened inside McNeil's marketing department.

Located sixty miles from J&J's headquarters, the McNeil marketers were far enough out of sight and mind to escape Big Brother's second guessing. The pact was sealed between McNeil and AF before J&J's corporate contributions office caught wind of the agreement. In fact, information passed along to the contributions office was a mere courtesy since the McNeil deal was to be bought and paid for out of the affiliate company's marketing budget.

It wasn't long before all hell broke loose. The new pain reliever line drew the ire of competitors and the attention of regulators. Attorneys general of sixteen states and Washington, D.C., ended up charging McNeil (and J&J) with deceptive business practices. In the midst of the firestorm, McNeil announced it was discontinuing the line, claiming the pain relievers didn't meet sales projections.

The decision led to a $1.3 million payment to AF and a very costly settlement with attorneys general, including a $90,000 payment to each of the complainants, $250,000 to the National Institutes of Health for arthritis research, plus some additional costs. What was supposed to be a win-win for McNeil and AF turned out to be a multimillion-dollar blunder for J&J.

There was a lot of soul searching after the Arthritis Foundation partnership went south. From a contributions manager's perspective, I gave myself poor marks for not pushing my way into the deal when I caught the first scent of the cause-marketing collaboration. While the business metrics plugged in and around the AF plan were all about how many more pain relievers the company could sell, there was also something else that needed to be taken into account: the impact of the partnership on the reputation and image of both Johnson & Johnson and the Arthritis Foundation.

As noted, cause-marketing payments are generally considered ordinary business expenses and are not taken as charitable deductions. However, for purposes of *public reporting*, I encourage companies to *add* cause-marketing payments made to nonprofits as part of their donation totals—*if* the company doesn't require the nonprofit to render any services beyond lending its name to the cause-marketing campaign.

This is a large pill to swallow for tax purists who don't want any expense categorized a charitable donation unless it can pass the "no quid pro quo smell test." However, just as businesses publicly report the fair market value of product donations rather than the much lower tax value of such contributions, there are circumstances when numbers tracked inside the company should be reported differently to the outside world. As a general rule, company payments that end up on a nonprofit's revenue line should also be folded into a corporation's report of overall support for these outside organizations—including most cause-marketing commitments.

These four pointers are worth folding into any strategy designed to probe the effectiveness of a corporation's grant making.

Flimsy or Worthless Evaluation Reports

Companies may claim they do indeed measure the effectiveness of their contributions but do so in a way that provides minimal or no value to the company. A quick return revisit to Widget International will help make this point.

THE ``SAY LITTLE OR NOTHING´´ EVALUATION

Remember Widget's decision to make a product donation to the global relief organization called ABC (Chapter Seven)? The nonprofit wanted a cash contribution but instead agreed to accept the company's donation of five thousand about-to-be-phased-out widgets so they could be used for vocational training in China.

Here are commitments the ABC president made when agreeing to take the donation:

- "The product contribution will give thousands of Chinese citizens the kind of hands-on training that will make them more employable in a much shorter amount of time than is currently possible. A year's vocational education might easily be reduced to six months."
- "I can guarantee you those state-owned enterprises and ministry officials who could make or break your business in China are going to think Widget International walks on water."

Nine to twelve months after the ABC grant is made, Widget CEO Chuck Gilfant wants to know whether the $100,000 product donation (fair market value) did what the nonprofit said it would do. The company VP who oversees Widget's philanthropy program asks the ABC president for a status report. The nonprofit responds with a three-page "Evaluation and Impact Analysis" that includes these points:

- Donated widgets have been provided to directors of vocational programs in Xi'an and Guandong.
- Numerous Chinese are trained annually in these provincial facilities.
- Notice of Widget International's donation was sent to the Ministry of Commerce (Beijing) and the Chinese Ministry of Foreign Trade and Economic Cooperation.

The report comes with a cover letter that ABC uses to ask Widget to "expand this very successful program" by funding two other vocational education projects in Jiangsu and Fujian provinces. The nonprofit asks the company for $50,000 – in cash, not product – to underwrite ABC's expenses that will be incurred in growing the program.

Widget's VP summarizes the report in a two-paragraph email to Gilfant who, in turn, tells the VP to reject the $50,000 cash request but to "let the ABC president down easy." The VP circles back to ABC and explains Widget International is "unable to assist at this time but we are hopeful that we might be in a position to offer help next year by possibly continuing some type of product donation relationship . . . ."

The ABC Evaluation and Impact Analysis is then filed and forgotten.

This same scenario is played out many times over by companies that claim they "evaluate" or "measure" their donations and grants. Unfortunately what this process accomplishes is—very little. The only relevant information Widget International got, for instance, is confirmation by ABC that the organization shipped donated products to China. Notice the nonprofit skirted around making a flat-out statement about the number of students who used widgets as part of their vocational training. Did the widgets make the training more effective? No information. ABC stated that it alerted key trade and commerce ministries in China about the Widget donation. Exactly what does that mean? And do these ministries have more awareness—and a more positive impression—of Widget International now than they did before the product donation was made? We don't know.

Unless required to do otherwise, nonprofits generally churn out grant "evaluations" heavy on *qualitative* information and very short on *quantitative* data. Generalizations and anecdotes are plentiful but numbers and statistics are usually hard to find. Even if nonprofits do produce first-rate, data-based reports, such information may only get scant attention by corporate contributions managers.

And for good reason.

Unlike many big independent foundations that have large numbers of professionals with the training and time to review grantee reports, corporate contributions offices are lightly staffed. Forecasting budgets, meeting compliance requirements, dealing with a steady influx of requests, and carrying out a host of other duties suck up working hours. Evaluation doesn't often make it to the top of the priority pile *except* when the company CEO or some other high-level executive demands, "Tell me why we made that grant and let me know what impact it had." Translation: get answers to these two questions:

1. Is there hard evidence that shows if the company's cash or product grant made any kind of measurable difference to the program or project we funded?
2. What did we (our company) get out of this deal?

These questions usually tend to get asked when (a) a nonprofit that received a large donation in the past begins campaigning for another round of funding or (b) senior management starts prepping for an annual shareholder meeting or some other event at which philanthropy might be a topic of discussion.

So what is the most effective way to sort through—as Winston Churchill would say—"uncertain information" in order to come up with an acceptable answer to either query?

Measuring Social or Programmatic Impact

Getting hard evidence about the social impact of a grant can be tricky depending on *what* a company wants to know. For example, the Hershey Company partners with the United Negro College

Fund (UNCF) to provide scholarships to selected high school seniors who choose to attend any of a dozen Pennsylvania colleges. Hershey (the Pennsylvania-based chocolate and confectionery company) spends $100,000 a year on the scholarship program. Annually it gets a list of scholarship winners along with information about the higher education institutions where they are enrolled. The company also is told how much scholarship aid each student received (the maximum award is $5,000).

Simple.

But what if Hershey (or any of the other forty or so companies that also partner with UNCF) wants to evaluate these awards using different criteria? To get the following information, the measurement becomes more complex—and costly:

- Do students who receive the company-sponsored scholarships view the company differently after getting the award?
- What about the families of student scholars—how are their impressions of the company influenced by the award?
- Has the confectionary buying behavior of students, families, and friends been affected by the program?
- What kind of media exposure does the company receive as a result of this scholarship program?
- Are public officials, regulators, and other stakeholders important to the company aware of the corporation's scholarship support and, if so, are their attitudes affected by the company's largess?

These questions pull back the covers on the biggest flaw in the corporate contributions measurement process. *You don't know how far you traveled if you don't know your starting point.*

Using the UNCF scholarship example, unless we have survey data about how students and their families regard a company before a scholarship is awarded, it's not possible to measure accurately any changes in impressions that may have been triggered by the scholarship program.

If senior management agrees this kind of pre- and post-assessment isn't important, fine. But if a business wants to compare before and after insights, then the grant strategy has to include a much-better-than-usual evaluation component—one that typically needs to get activated at the beginning of the funding cycle and not at the end. Of the multitude of corporations in the United States, you would be hard pressed to find more than a handful that view the evaluation process this way.

Measuring the social impact of corporate grants can be a *routine* undertaking or a *full-scale* procedure. Most evaluations fall in the *routine* category and often put the onus on a nonprofit grant recipient to do the work.

DTE Energy, a diversified energy company located in Michigan, is typical of businesses that call on grant recipients to do their own evaluating. The company requests grantees looking for repeat contributions to provide details (up to three thousand characters) about how support provided by DTE was used during the previous twenty-four months and to cite any and all outcomes.

Many businesses ask for similar end-grant information. The weakness here is that the evaluation is not an independent review but rather a self-generated report. Most corporations don't have the time or resources to validate the information.

An alternative is for businesses to do their own analysis of the societal impact of a grant (rarely done) or hire an outside resource to take on that responsibility. The Coca-Cola Foundation used an external grant evaluation team to do a thorough review of its extensive scholars program (a $3 million-a-year program that was launched in 1986 to commemorate the company's flagship brand) and the team reports are among the most comprehensive I have seen. But the Coca-Cola evaluation model is hardly commonplace.

If any grant measurement is done at all, most companies are satisfied with qualitative results tacked on to the tail end of a contributions payment. For these businesses, a *routine* method of grant assessment meets their needs. *Full-scale* measurement is a different story and, according to my observations, almost always reserved for an assessment of the business value (not the societal value) of a grant—which leads us to the next point.

Measuring a Grant's Business Benefit

Keep the company checkbook handy if a decision is made to push the "full-scale" measurement button, because this kind of assessment is generally expensive—so much so that it could outstrip the value of the grant itself.

Assume your company wants to know if a $10,000 grant made to a national mental health program leads to a more positive impression of the corporation on the part of psychiatrists, psychologists, and other mental health practitioners. You decide to do a baseline study before the grant is made and then repeat the study after the program has been funded. A statistically valid research undertaking that includes phone interviews of a random sampling of the medical community could easily cost $50,000 or more for the baseline study and another $50,000 for the back-end study. Depending on how much information the company wants, the cost could go considerably higher.

Obviously, spending $100,000 or more to assess the effects of a $10,000 grant is crazy. So corporations have to be picky as to when and where they invest in this kind of analysis, usually limiting the research to large and often multiyear grants. Also, since a corporation is looking to gauge what impact a contribution has on the business itself, the research cost is usually carried as an ordinary business expense—not as a company foundation or contributions program payment.

So when does a company typically lay out the kind of money needed to pay the bill for *full-scale* research focusing on a corporate contribution? Often it is to measure the impact of a *cause-marketing* campaign. An example follows.

ASSESSING THE BUSINESS IMPACT OF CAUSE MARKETING

The Atlanta-based Sun Trust Bank launched a fourteen-month cause-marketing initiative. The bank—which has consumer banking operations throughout the Southeast—made the following offer: open a new personal or business checking account and Sun Trust will donate $100 to a charity designated by the customer. (The deal also included a provision by which the customer could claim a $50 gift card in lieu of the bank's donation.)

To figure out if the Sun Trust campaign drove up the number of new accounts, the bank could easily compare account traffic during the cause-marketing period with account startups at other times. Assuming the bank didn't factor in any other variables, Sun Trust could determine if its charitable giving promotion worked or didn't.

The bank could even dive deeper and check to see if cause marketing was more effective at some of its sixteen-hundred-plus retail branches but not at others. That information might lead bank marketers to consider launching new cause-marketing promotions in targeted locations while using different business development tactics in other regions.

Ever since 1983 when American Express showed how it could link up with a popular cause (Statue of Liberty restoration) to generate sales, cause marketing has been all the rage. Largely that's because the *measured effects* of a cause-marketing campaign as they relate to a business are so apparent. When American Express announced that it would make a cause-related donation to help spruce up Lady Liberty for her hundredth anniversary in 1986, card usage surged and the number of new card holders grew by an astounding 45 percent. Since then, businesses have cut scores of deals with nonprofits fueled by a desire to find different ways to sell everything from yogurt to Hamburger Helper.

Today there are dozens of other examples of contributions-linked marketing efforts that lend themselves to full-scale analysis. Recently, a few corporations have pushed cause marketing into cyberspace—and these ventures also are good candidates for full-scale research. Here are some examples:

- *PepsiCo* added a twist to the more common type of cause-marketing project by shifting its multimillion-dollar Super Bowl TV ad budget to fund a $20 million Internet-based social networking campaign in 2010. The "Pepsi Refresh Project" solicited grant requests from "people, businesses and nonprofits with ideas that have a positive impact on their communities." Then the social networking world was asked to cast votes to determine which of the thousand ideas collected each month should receive between $5,000 and $250,000 in funding. Pepsi's goal? Among other objectives, to widen its reach to the Internet audience—which made sense since rival Coca-Cola had a much stronger Internet presence at the start of the campaign.

- *Target* is another one of several businesses that plugged cause marketing into the social networking world. The company ran a brief campaign called "Super Love Sender" that gave Target's 750,000 Facebook fans an opportunity to determine how $1 million should be allocated to five national charities. The company termed the project a "fun, interactive and viral giving campaign that has the power to positively impact the educational programming of these five deserving charities."

These Internet-based campaigns are new wrinkles in the cause-marketing world but are as equally subject to careful measurement (perhaps even more so) than more typical non-web-based cause-marketing undertakings.

Commonsense Evaluations

It doesn't always take a formal measurement process to determine the effectiveness of a grant. There are times when the obvious is so apparent that it becomes invisible. This is especially true when companies fund a program or organization for years at a clip—grant making becomes a habit and businesses just don't bother with those *what* and *why* questions.

This lack of carrying out even the most cursory evaluation caused me a lot of grief while I was steering Johnson & Johnson's contributions program. For years, J&J spent a *huge* amount of money underwriting the full cost of a two-year MBA program for minority students. The company shouldered the tuition, housing, and related expenses for several young men and women to attend the Wharton School at the University of Pennsylvania and several other grade-A business schools. J&J also provided each scholar with a paid summer internship. The program chugged along with very little scrutiny until one day, someone in the corporation's executive stratosphere asked the obvious:

"What happens to these J&J scholars once they get their MBA degrees?"

The answer turned out to be a show-stopper. Not *one* of the young men and women had accepted a job offer from J&J. To the contrary. Most had been snapped up by our competitors (Merck, Bristol-Myers Squibb, and others) that patiently waited until J&J finished paying for the scholars' graduate education and then used handsome signing bonuses and bumped-up salary offers to lure them into their organizations. This late-in-the-game "evaluation" showed that Johnson & Johnson's philanthropy was educating the best and brightest to compete against our own company.

It is commonplace for corporations to fund scholarship programs that help swell the number of qualified graduates who can benefit all businesses in any industry category. But it is near insanity to underwrite the education costs of people who consistently are hired away by companies that want to eat your lunch. It was no surprise that once J&J took a hard look at the end result of its MBA scholars program, the corporation decided there were better ways to use its philanthropy to support minority education.

The moral of the J&J story is that for large grants (particularly those that are envisioned as long-term commitments), it is well worth a company's time to lay out all expectations for a grant before a check is cut. In a perfect world, it would be useful to subject every gift regardless of size to the same scrutiny but that's obviously unrealistic. It's also impractical to think the same kind of rigorous (and expensive) research a marketing department uses to evaluate a cause-related campaign can be applied to more than a very small number of grants.

Measuring Corporate America's Philanthropy

While companies might come up short in measuring the effectiveness of their grants, they are Winston Churchill geniuses compared to those trying to pull together data about corporate philanthropy as a whole. Why is it so difficult to paint a composite picture of the private sector's generosity? Mainly because there is no uniformity in the way businesses define and report corporate contributions.

This is a very frustrating reality that has cast a shadow over the corporate philanthropy field for decades.

I have worked with or profiled over two hundred companies during the past decade. A payment one business considers a contribution is stamped as a different kind of business expense by another. Some corporations include the dollar value of employee volunteer hours as part of their contributions total (which should be a no-no). Others include the full payment for dinners and special events—not just the portion that is earmarked for a nonprofit organization. As detailed in Chapter Seven, the valuation of product donations is all over the board.

While companies interpret the charitable deduction provisions of the tax law differently, that's small potatoes compared to what happens when it comes time to publicly report contributions. Remember, aside from company foundation information, businesses have no obligation to report their tax filing details (including charitable deductions) to the outside world. That leaves them with a lot of latitude to come up with a philanthropy number for public consumption. Any philanthropic claim made by a corporation is tough to validate.

The end result of this lack of uniformity is utter confusion about the size and impact of corporate philanthropy. Organizations such as the Conference Board, Committee Encouraging Corporate Philanthropy, Giving USA Foundation, and others report annual corporate contribution totals that differ wildly from one another. For example, in one year, the Committee Encouraging Corporate Philanthropy reported 136 companies donating a total of $11.2 billion. The exact same year, the Giving USA Foundation stated that *all* businesses in the United States contributed $13.8 billion. So does that mean just 136 corporations accounted for 81 percent of contributions made by hundreds of thousands of businesses that year? Hardly. The discrepancy is based on the kind of information collected by each monitoring organization.

Badly needed in the corporate philanthropy field is an agreed-upon formula for the annual *public reporting* of contributions information. A reasonable recommendation would be to report the following:

- Cash contributions made directly by the company or its foundation to organizations that qualify the business for a charitable tax deduction (501c3 nonprofits, certain public entities, and so on)
- Cash payments to qualified nonprofits for the full cost of nonprofit dinner and special event sponsorships (see Chapter Six)
- Cash payments made to qualified nonprofits as part of cause-marketing agreements, assuming no direct quid pro quo benefits are obtained by the company
- Qualified product and land donations at fair market value

To be *excluded* from this formula:

- Payments made by the company to its own foundation
- Payments to a nonprofit that yield direct benefits to the corporation
- Donation of depreciated products (used furniture, computers, and so on)
- Cash value of employee or retiree volunteer hours

History says that getting businesses to agree voluntarily to these standards won't work. Over the past thirty years, attempts have been made to encourage companies in the private sector to report their contributions exactly the same way. That hasn't happened. Imposing more government regulations isn't the answer either. So what needs to be done?

At least in respect to publicly held corporations, organizations such as the Financial Accounting Standards Board (FASB) could play an enormously helpful role in addressing this need. FASB's mission is to "serve the investing public through transparent information resulting from high-quality financial reporting standards developed in an independent, private sector, open due process." By adopting an accounting rule for tracking company payments that qualify for the public reporting of corporate contributions, the business community would—at last—have a uniform framework that could be used by all companies regardless of size or industry category.

By applying accounting principles to the corporate contributions field, it will be possible to make apples-to-apples comparisons among companies. Auditing firms—particularly the "Big Four" agencies PricewaterhouseCoopers, Deloitte Touche Tohmatsu, Ernst & Young, and KPMG—can then use agreed-upon accounting standards to

- Do away with the confusion as to what qualifies as a contribution for public reporting purposes and what doesn't
- Ensure that the public reporting of corporate contributions is fair and consistent
- Verify which companies are contributing cash equal to a minimum of 1 percent of estimated annual pretax net income by using our Sabsevitz Ante-Up Formula

Better measurement of the corporate contributions field in toto will provide the public with a much more accurate snapshot of the important role businesses play in addressing some of our most pressing social challenges.

IN SUMMARY

Question 11: Can a company measure what works?

Answer: Companies are best able to evaluate the effectiveness of their grant making if they decide *what* should be measured prior to making a contribution. Routine, nonquantitative evaluations are suitable for most smaller grants. Full-scale assessments that include data collection and analysis are suitable for some larger contributions including certain cause-marketing commitments.

How Should a Company Communicate Its Contributions Commitments?

One of the most often expressed frustrations in the corporate contributions field is the lack of attention given to a company's good works. "We fund a boatload of terrific programs but the local media couldn't care less!" is a familiar complaint.

Having once been on the other side of the media divide, I remember the constant onslaught of press releases all competing for ink or air time. But it was a rare editor or radio or TV programming director who would substitute "soft news" for a story about crime, politics, or a catastrophe. And since there was never a shortage of human misdeeds, electoral intrigue, and man-made and natural disasters, finding an opening to report an act of corporate social responsibility was close to impossible. Which is why business leaders so frequently struggle with our next baker's dozen question.

Question 12: How should a company communicate its contributions commitments?

Answer: Start by identifying who the most important audience is for what you want to say. Get a grip on why you want to dispense the information. Then put together a communications strategy and action plan using a rifle-shot approach whenever possible.

Too many businesses still promote (or try to promote) their grant making by firing off press releases with the hope that news about good works will somehow lead to a few column inches in the local paper or thirty seconds of air time on the hometown radio station. That is rarely the outcome.

Rifle-Shot PR

A far more effective strategy for corporations is to chop up the general public into clearly defined audience segments. Figure out which of these groups are most important to the business and come up with a communications strategy aimed at that audience. Once it's clear about *who* the company most wants to reach, *how* to make a connection gets easier. Following are some examples of ways certain communication tools can hit specific audiences.

Company Website–Prominence and Timeliness Are the Watchwords

An individual who is motivated enough to access a company website presents the business with an enormous advantage. The corporation has that individual's attention. So now what?

What a corporation posts on its own web pages represents one of its strongest—and oftentimes, most ineffectively used— communication opportunities.

If a company's website makes no mention at all about a corporation's social responsibility policies and activities, then here's what it's saying to its Internet visitors: "We have a self-absorbed, myopic approach to doing business."

If a corporation does make reference to its external affairs but buries that information deep in the bowels of its website, that's another not-so-great message.

But if a company's website shows there is a connection between its business interests and the rest of the world, it helps create a mind-set about the firm that can have an impact on investors, current and potential customers, employees, retirees, and other stakeholders.

Let's use an example of a website that does it right. Anheuser-Busch is the wholly-owned subsidiary of Belgium-based Anheuser-Busch InBev, the worldwide beer brewer. Go to the Anheuser-Busch web page, and you'll find eight menu picks:

- Home
- Company
- Environment
- Business Units
- Beer
- Community
- Press
- People

Two of the eight picks (environment and community) clearly deal with social responsibility issues. In other words, the company devotes 25 percent of its home page menu to corporate citizenship concerns. If the "Community" section is accessed, a detailed overview of Anheuser-Busch's charitable giving and community relations activities is presented, including its support for

- Education
- Economic Development
- Environment
- Disaster Relief
- Military
- Employee Giving
- Employee Volunteer Grants
- Matching Gifts
- Grant Guidelines

Under the same "Community" section, the company also adds a summary of its philanthropy philosophy along with news clips highlighting its social responsibility activities. Anyone scanning the corporate website is left with an impression that when it comes to practicing good corporate citizenship Anheuser-Busch "gets it." Want proof? In 2009, *Fortune* magazine's "Most Admired" poll ranked Anheuser-Busch above every other company in the nation in its social responsibility category. True, corporate philanthropy isn't the only ingredient that gets blended into a company's social responsibility batter. But for sure, the philanthropy information posted on the Anheuser-Busch website puts a lot of polish on the company's image as the nation's corporate responsibility leader.

Like Anheuser-Busch, a lot of corporations craft their websites to show how social responsibility commitments actually advance their business objectives. However, where far too many companies go wrong is that they don't keep their websites updated. When this happens, a positive first impression turns into a conclusion that the company is mostly spin and little substance.

For example, a company website (we'll keep the business anonymous) includes this statement: "Our corporate philanthropy spans the nation with diverse and sustained giving programs...." Click to the next web page for a list of contributions the company made and what you discover is an inventory of grants made three years ago. The company *claims* it places a high value on corporate contributions but the claim rings hollow when it can't (or forgets to) come up with current examples to back up its assertion.

This may come across as a petty issue. But according to feedback I get when speaking to nonprofit audiences, this is *really* irksome to a lot of people. Simply put, out-of-date website information reflects badly on a business; antiquated information about a company's philanthropy raises questions about just how much hot air is pumping up its claims.

Special Publications Are Expensive, So Use with Care

When WellPoint Health Networks, the nonprofit health plan serving the State of California, wanted to merge with the for-profit Blue Cross Blue Shield insurance giant called Anthem, it needed to convince California regulators and legislators that it had a history of social responsibility and that post-merger it was determined to continue its assistance to nonprofit organizations throughout the state. The merger plan ran into a near fatal roadblock when the California insurance commissioner voiced opposition. WellPoint had to generate a groundswell of grassroots support to get the plan back on track.

As part of its campaign to win merger approval (which finally happened late in 2004), WellPoint produced a social responsibility report that was distributed to key government, civic, education, health care, and business leaders throughout the state. The publication—loaded with references to WellPoint's substantive contributions efforts—has been credited as a vital resource in convincing California to okay the merger.

WellPoint understood *what* needed to be said to *whom*, which is *why* the company justified spending approximately $265,000 to print two hundred thousand copies of the publication. There's no arguing that reports like the one produced by WellPoint can be expensive. But consider the effectiveness of such a pointed communication compared, let's say, to a full-page, one-time insert in a publication such as the *Reader's Digest* national family edition, which would have cost WellPoint more than twice as much in 2004. It's highly unlikely a *Reader's Digest* ad could have matched the effectiveness of the WellPoint report.

Slick publications that tout a company's giving and volunteer efforts might not pass a cost-benefit test if answers to the *what, who,* and *why* questions come up short. Flipping through a posh booklet loaded with full-color photographs and overflowing with embellished copy that borders on the egocentric can easily lead to the question, "So why didn't you use the money spent on this publication to do more of the good works you claim you're funding?" But as the WellPoint example makes clear, there are times when special publications do make sense. Again, that's usually because a company has a definitive purpose in mind for whatever is being said.

A lot of businesses feel the need to publish a general year-end report intended for non-specific use or in response to public requests for information about the company's philanthropy. If that's the case, produce a simple brochure that includes succinct, truthful, and well-written information about the corporation's contributions and community relations activities.

Guidelines for Giving – A Communications Tool with a Small Window

As with company websites, businesses sometimes overlook the communications importance of a set of guidelines that most companies use as a general framework for making contributions decisions.

Remember there are hundreds of thousands of nonprofit organizations constantly foraging for funding and other kinds of assistance. Nonprofit volunteers, board members, and staff personnel regularly probe corporations in search of company giving guidelines. *What* businesses say about their philanthropy interests can influence how these organization representatives feel about a company regardless of whether they end up getting a donation.

Effective giving guidelines should accomplish two objectives. First, they should open the smallest possible window for unsolicited grant requests to fly into a corporation's inner sanctum. The goal is keep appeals that have no chance of being funded from ever showing up in the first place. By fending off these requests, the corporation isn't put in a position of having to send out a mountain of reject letters. Stated another way, a well-constructed guideline statement encourages submission of only those proposals that line up with a corporation's highest-priority giving interests.

Second, effective guidelines give businesses a way of explaining *what* their primary philanthropy or community relations interests are and *why*—even to those who have no chance of receiving a company donation. If after reading a corporation's guidelines a nonprofit concludes there is absolutely no hope for a contribution and yet is left with a high regard for the company because of the way its philanthropy "case" has been presented—then that's the true test of a top-notch guideline statement.

Shotgun PR

Communicating a company's contributions to well-defined audiences allows a corporation to rifle shot its messaging and circumvents the kind of problem described in the following case.

Senior VP: "Why aren't we getting more press coverage for the grant we just made to the World Wildlife Fund?"

Contributions Manager: "Our communications department sent out a national release to all print and electronic media last week. But it wasn't picked up."

Senior VP: "Damnit! We have shareholder resolutions on the table from two environmental activist groups. If our stockholders could see a TV news clip or at least read a story in the print media about the grant, we'd be getting a lot more mileage than from our own self-generated hype."

Contributions Manager: "It's the same old problem—the press couldn't care less about using ink or air time to cover a company's good works."

The company's senior VP is interested in getting the word out about the World Wildlife Fund grant to a very specific audience—institutional and individual stockholders. He would have much preferred a rifle shot at that audience. But the corporate communications office took aim at a much broader target—the general public. A PR shotgun was used to fire a media release at every newspaper, radio, and TV station on the company's contact list. Even if the release were to have been picked up by one of the wire services or earned a thirty-second mention on a network news broadcast, the likelihood is slim that the story would have registered with many of the people the senior VP wanted to reach.

Even when acknowledging that a rifle shot is effective, companies still are quick to look for a shotgun. With that reality in mind and the likelihood that wildly firing PR buckshot is going to continue no matter what, let's examine how to point and shoot so as to increase the chances of success. Here are two real (and really different) releases, each fishing for media attention with a slightly different "hook":

Release 1: Salesforce.com Named to Corporate Philanthropy Top 50

San Francisco, CA—Salesforce.com, the world leader in delivering software-as-service, announced today that the salesforce.com/foundation has been named to the San Francisco Business Times' annual ranking of the Bay Area's 50 largest corporate giving programs.

Release 2: MetLife Foundation Awards Grants to 20 Big Brothers Big Sisters Agencies for Hispanic Mentoring Program

Philadelphia, PA—Big Brothers Big Sisters of America has awarded MetLife Foundation Hispanic Mentoring grants to 20 local Big Brothers Big Sisters agencies nationwide. The grants are made possible through a $500,000 leadership contribution from MetLife Foundation.

How effective were these releases? We don't know for sure—but we can hazard a guess based on an analysis of other company promotional strategies. Before picking apart these examples, circle back to the answer to this chapter's question. We should have a clear understanding about

- *Whom* (specifically) we most want to reach with this information?
- And *Why?*

These two seemingly simple questions are very important even when using a PR shotgun. Answers will lessen the chances a corporation will fire its PR pellets willy-nilly. Even a shotgun needs to be aimed. Apply this thinking to our media release examples.

Release 1 is a self-generated announcement sent out by Salesforce.com, a San Francisco–based business. If the company's response to the "Whom do we most want to reach?" question happens to be "the general public," the press release probably missed its mark even if it did get picked up by the mass media. As noted earlier, researchers have found that only a small percentage of the public is impressed when a company gives away a large amount of money. Nine out of ten people think more highly of a company when it donates products or services—or when its employees volunteer their time. Consequently, the Salesforce.com (release 1) message probably didn't do much to move the corporate reputation needle.

But suppose Salesforce.com answered the "Whom do we most want to reach?" question differently. Suppose its strategy was to heighten employee morale. The company puts together a release that appears to be aimed at external media but is mainly targeted to workers. The eye-catching information cuts through the clutter of internal messaging, and employee pride goes up a notch or two.

Or suppose Salesforce.com asks itself, "Whom do we most want to reach?" and answers, "those polled as part of *Fortune* magazine's 'Most Admired Companies' survey." The company would then send a special mailing in early fall just before chief financial officers and other high-level executives at *Fortune* 1000 companies are asked to pick the most admirable businesses in America. (*Fortune* surveys approximately fifteen thousand senior executives, outside directors, and industry analysts for its annual listing of "most admired" businesses in sixty-four industry groupings.)

We don't know what Salesforce.com's intent was when issuing this release. But what we *do* know is that if the end goal was to impress the public at large, shotgun PR probably didn't get the job done.

Release 2 might seem to be a product of MetLife's PR department. Actually, the release was distributed by Big Brothers Big Sisters. Even if the release got scant general media attention, it probably registered with Big Brothers Big Sisters staff, volunteers, and donors. So if the *whom* the company most wanted to have an impact on was this audience, then the shotgun was a rifle shot in disguise.

Release 2 helps make another point: a business that self-promotes its own largesse has a higher believability hurdle to overcome than a company that gets stroked by a credible source standing outside the business. A crusty publisher once had a conversation with me that summed up how some in the media view any release that comes directly from a company: "If a business wants to thump its chest, send 'em our advertising rate card."

While working for a chain of weekly newspapers, I recalled those words and leaned on companies to think about advertising. Some actually did buy space. Today, some still do. And using paid advertising to shotgun a message about corporate responsibility isn't always a bad idea. There are ad campaigns that use a company's philanthropic and other social responsibility commitments as centerpieces for a broad-scale corporate image campaign. I learned how effective that approach can be when I was consulting for Xerox several years ago.

"For every $1 spent on public broadcasting, budget at least $2 to $3 for media promotion."

The VP for public relations knew what he was talking about. At the time, the Public Broadcasting Service listed Xerox as one of its most valued program underwriters.

"Yes, the TV productions Xerox sponsors do reach a target audience important to the company," the VP said. "But the number of viewers is low compared to the number of key people who read *The Wall Street Journal* and other papers where we advertise."

So Xerox placed ads in print publications that focused on the company's PBS support. It connected with high-end decision makers, many of whom probably never watched a Xerox-sponsored show on public television.

The take-away: using advertising to self-promote isn't necessarily a bad idea. But it's a decision that should rest heavily on the content the company wants to include in such ads. If there is an overload of chest-beating, the ad could backfire and leave audiences with a less-than-positive impression. And that gets us back to the preferred (and cheaper) method of reaching an audience—calling on a nonprofit grant recipient to promote the company name a la release 2, with which Boys Clubs Girls Clubs served as a PR messenger and ambassador for MetLife.

The Awards Concept as a PR Magnet

Finding a way to leverage a company's grant making so it gets public attention often requires thinking outside the "usual" PR channels. Unorthodox methods of delivering company information to clearly targeted audiences can yield big benefits. Using a company-sponsored award as a communications strategy is definitely one of those unorthodox ideas—and one that almost always delivers outstanding results. Here's an example.

J&J COMMUNITY HEALTH CARE AWARDS

Hundreds of community health centers scattered throughout the United States deliver badly needed medical and dental services to people living at or below the poverty line. While reliant mainly on public funding (for example, Medicaid reimbursement), centers also benefit greatly from private donations of products and cash.

Health centers sometimes buy medical supplies and pharmaceuticals at discounted prices. But they also solicit and receive free drugs and supplies from health care companies. Making contributions to these centers can prove advantageous to businesses in the medical field. Here's why.

First, about four thousand physicians, dentists, nurse practi-
tioners, midwives, and other clinicians work for the National Health
Service Corps (NHSC)—many providing medical services via community health centers. Because a percentage of NHSC clinicians
move on to private practice or other public health agencies, they
become more and more influential in product purchasing decisions.
Hence, their early impressions about companies and brands can
have long-term commercial consequences.

Second, companies are well aware that community health center patients also make their own pharmaceutical and general
medical supply purchasing decisions. Developing a company or
brand allegiance among these millions of consumers can translate
into an increase in sales and earnings.

Finally, corporations know that supporting certain community
health centers can be a very effective way to open doors to key
federal and state lawmakers.

Well aware of these advantages, Johnson & Johnson turned
to a nonprofit group called the National Association of Community
Health Centers (NACHC) to develop and administer a unique health
care awards program. NACHC solicited proposals from around
the country, and a blue-ribbon selection panel picked exemplary
programs that delivered quality care to people most in need.
Winners received J&J cash grants ($150,000 paid over two years)
in addition to a crystal trophy that became a visual symbol of health
care excellence (and a terrific photo-op for media covering award
ceremonies).

Similar to a tactic used to fund grant evaluation expenses (see
Chapter Eleven), J&J offered each award winner an "add-on" contribution to pay for an event to celebrate the achievement. Very
few nonprofits turned down the money. Winning organizations used
the supplemental contributions to underwrite extraordinary functions ranging from luncheon events with hundreds in attendance
to state house receptions with key lawmakers in the room. Without
exception, the festive events included a few speeches, and all of
them heaped praise on J&J, almost to the point of embarrassment.
Audiences, which always included high-level civic and health care
leaders, were left with an impression about the corporation that no
media story or paid advertisement could match.

In recent years, the J&J Community Health Care Program has undergone several changes. It is now administered by the prestigious Johns Hopkins Bloomberg School of Public Health, and the company grants eight awards of $200,000 each (over a two-and-a-half-year period) to a cross-section of 501c3 nonprofits that address critical health problems such as childhood obesity.

When it comes to putting a spotlight on a company, award programs can deliver. They take careful planning and the right nonprofit partner. Plus they require adequate funding. But if these ingredients are blended together properly, the end product can promote corporate citizenship in a big way.

Where to Get Help

"We're not communications experts, and there's no way the company's going to approve hiring any outside PR help," contributions managers complain when prodded to get more public exposure for the company's philanthropy efforts. They usually settle down when they learn there are free or inexpensive ways to communicate a corporation's grant-making activities.

Establish a Dotted-Line Link to Your Communications or PR Department

Here's what having a "friend" in the company communications or PR department can do for a corporate contributions staff:

- A business has a retainer with a prominent (and expensive) PR agency. The company is obligated by agreement to use the agency for a specific number of hours of service. As the contract period draws to a close, there are unused hours that the PR department hands over to the corporate contributions office. The agency runs out the clock by developing a powerful video about the company's philanthropy that gets featured at the company's annual shareholder's meeting.
- The manager responsible for employee communications writes several short stories about the impact of selected company grants. She uses the stories as "drop-ins" or

fillers when putting together employee e-bulletins throughout the year.

- A media relations consultant retained by the communications department arranges for TV coverage of employee volunteers participating in an inner-city house-building project run by Rebuilding Together (formerly Christmas in April). The story gets primetime local media exposure complete with pictures of workers wearing company vests and hats.

There are a lot of ways a communications professional can help get the word out about a corporate contributions program. The trick is to connect to a professional who is interested to the point of being passionate about the company's philanthropy. Locate that individual, and the word gets out.

The eye-care company Bausch + Lomb serves as a great example of what a competent internal communications team can do to buff up the image of a company.

BAUSCH + LOMB'S PEDIATRIC CATARACT INITIATIVE

"We need to reach ophthalmologists, optometrists, other health care professionals, and every Lions Club volunteer about this," said Mike McDougall, Bausch + Lomb's VP for communications and public affairs—and one of the brightest young corporate media executives in the country.

The *this* McDougall referenced was the company's decision to attack a little known but tragic medical problem affecting thousands of newborns—pediatric cataracts. Babies born with the condition—especially in medically underserved countries—are at risk of severe vision loss and blindness.

Teaming up with Lions Clubs International, the largest volunteer service organization in the world, B + L launched the Pediatric Cataract Initiative and put it at the top of its contributions priority list. The company awarded a major grant to the Lions foundation, which then channeled funding to groups working on prevention and treatment of the malady. But the program's success—from both a social and a business perspective—rested heavily on how extensively the Initiative could be communicated.

McDougall and his group put together an extraordinary promotion package that included

- Facebook and Twitter social networking pages that immediately attracted large audiences
- An exhibit booth display and materials designed for national eye-care professional organization conventions and conferences
- A powerful five-minute video for a plenary session at the Lions International annual convention in Australia (sixteen thousand attendees)
- A special program logo converted into lapel pins
- Media releases highlighting members of a blue-ribbon advisory council (internationally recognized eye-care experts)
- Interviews with industry and trade publications that led to a flood of feature articles
- Print and electronic media outreach in China, where first Pediatric Cataract Initiative grants were made (and where B + L has emerging business interests)
- A series of stories and information injected into B + L's internal communications system

The impact? One journalist covering the new Initiative summed it up: "B + L has put itself at the front of the corporate social responsibility pack."

Let Somebody Else Do the Communicating—Even Inside the Company

The average worker in a large corporation knows little about his or her employer's contributions activities. Corporate philanthropy is also a mystery to workers in most small to mid-sized businesses. There might be some familiarity with matching gifts if the company offers that benefit (although typically, the employee participation rate in a company matching gift program is only around 10 percent). But for the most part, corporate philanthropy and community relations just don't show up on an employee's radar screen.

Employees are part of the general public. So as research has shown, it should come as no surprise that they don't do backflips when informed their employer is doling out big checks to charities. Yet that's the headline most corporations use when reaching out to their workers. "Last year, your company donated $5 million to charitable organizations in communities where we live and work...." That doesn't cut it.

What *does* register with employees is the end result of a company's philanthropy. Here are a couple of examples:

- A lunch-and-learn session with a panel of young people who had their lives turned around because a company contribution backed up an employee volunteer initiative that made it possible for a local youth center to continue operating
- A robotics demonstration by high school students and company engineers who entered a science and technology competition sponsored by the company and run by the nonprofit organization, FIRST

These inventive ways of communicating a corporation's philanthropy will penetrate the information overload that burdens nearly every employee.

A note of caution: there may be occasions when too much exposure stirs up more negative than positive reactions to a company's grant-making efforts. Here's an example of why this sometimes can be a problem. In 2006, the Columbus (Ohio) Children's Hospital accepted a $10 million donation from Abercrombie & Fitch, the edgy specialty clothing retailer. As an acknowledgement of the contribution, the hospital put the company's name on its emergency department and trauma center. The decision unleashed nationally publicized protests from organizations critical of openly linking the hospital to a company known for its sometimes sexually charged advertising.

The takeaway from this story is the need to think through every conceivable reaction to any plan designed to aggressively communicate a company's social commitment. There are times—albeit few and far between—when companies should move forward without making a lot of noise.

Use but Don't Abuse College Interns

I am a big believer in college (particularly graduate-level) interns. With only a couple of exceptions over the years, I have found them to be highly energetic, absent of cynicism, and full of ideas. Young people studying journalism can be very helpful in getting the word out about a company's contributions program. These students can be especially valuable in helping a company access and benefit from social media. However, to capitalize fully on their talent and enthusiasm, interns need (and deserve) direction and guidance. Using an intern as a glorified file clerk is a waste of a valuable resource.

Consider "loaning" an intern to a nonprofit slated to get a grant from the company. Let the intern develop and execute a media strategy using the grant as a means of getting exposure for both the nonprofit and corporation. This "in the trench" experience will expose the intern to all aspects of promotion from press release writing to making contact with print and electronic media reporters.

Most interns are required to submit a report to their university advisers at the close of their experience. Asking an intern to include recommendations about how to improve a company's communications activities and methods can turn up some surprisingly interesting ideas.

Interns cost a company little or nothing—which is another reason why interns should be rewarded with rich experiences that will help mold them into high-performing professionals.

Think Creatively

Some advertising experts claim the average American is confronted with three thousand marketing messages each day. These include print, radio, TV, Internet, and billboard ads. Then there is the barrage of non-advertised information—from the evening news to office memos. By sheer necessity, people are forced to resort to a kind of mental triage system that sorts out information based on "need to know," "nice to know but really not that important," or "probably not worth knowing at all." Too often, information about corporate philanthropy and community relations ends up in the last bucket—*unless* it is fashioned in a way that makes what's being said a higher priority.

With some exceptions, mass producing media releases with the hope a company's contributions' achievements will make news is a waste of time and money. Instead, fall back to the fundamentals of deciding *who* is your primary audience, *what* you want them to know, and *why* you should bother telling them. Then look for a way to reach that audience, avoiding the "same old, same old" approaches.

Maybe it's leasing a blimp to flash messages about how a company is addressing critical social needs. (Horizon Blue Cross Blue Shield of New Jersey does just that as part of its effort to curb childhood obesity in the Garden State.)

Or maybe it's turning company trucks into mobile billboards for charity. (The trucking firm, YRC Worldwide, uses the sides of vehicles to promote programs such as "Back Snack"—an initiative that gives poor children snack-filled backpacks on Fridays to provide them food for the weekend.)

The trick is to focus on the *who, what,* and *why*. And for the *how,* get as inventive as you can.

IN SUMMARY

Question 12: How should a company communicate its contributions commitments?

Answer: Begin by deciding *who's* the most important audience for *what* you want to say. Be clear about *why* you want to dispense the information. Then put together a communications strategy and action plan. Think creatively, including ways (such as awards programs) to get outsiders to promote your philanthropy efforts. Use a "rifle-shot" approach to communicating grant-making information whenever possible.

13

What If a Company's Profits Tank?

Businesses and society can reap a host of mutually beneficial "deliverables" from strategies outlined in *Smart Giving Is Good Business* if a company is making money. Think of corporate philanthropy as the cart and company profitability as the horse. The horse had better be in good shape or the cart goes nowhere. As the late management guru Peter Drucker put it, "A business that does not show a profit at least equal to its capital is socially irresponsible." Then Drucker added this footnote:

"Economic performance is the first responsibility of business—without it, a business cannot discharge any other responsibilities, cannot be a good employer; a good citizen; a good neighbor."

So all is well when a company brings in more money than it spends. If profitable, a business has the financial wherewithal to make conditional contributions that, if pointed in the right direction, can actually enhance the company's ability to become even more profitable while also offering society a helping hand.

But what happens if a corporation is plagued by a serious downturn in earnings or, even worse, has a balance sheet that's in the red? Under these unfortunate circumstances, what happens to a company's conditional grant making? These concerns move us to unlucky number thirteen in our baker's dozen list:

Question 13: What if a company's profits tank?

Answer: If a corporation makes a profit, it should also be making conditional grants adhering to the Sabsevitz Ante-Up Formula. However, if a company projects a significant earnings loss, it should make prudent decisions about adjusting the ante-up budget through a temporary suspension of contributions allocations, a delay in contributions payments, or – as a last resort – a permanent reduction in the contributions budget for the year. Companies with foundations should consider making larger-than-planned annual payouts to offset any downturn in direct corporate support.

If a company's profit decline is not severe, any reduction in its contributions payout may not be advisable. But if the business is experiencing a truly significant dip in earnings, then pulling the budgetary emergency brake may be unavoidable.

The hard reality is that corporate philanthropy has its place in the pecking order of business basics, and there are circumstances when a company simply does not have the capacity to continue making contributions. On the other hand, when a corporation experiences a drop in profits *but is still making money*, conditional grant making should continue. Referencing our earlier analogy—as long as the horse has enough feed to keep pulling, the cart should keep on rolling. There are even a few instances when after the horse is on its knees and gasping for what could be its last breath, the cart still has some momentum. Take, for example, the Chrysler Corporation.

I was called to assist Chrysler late in 2008 as it was teetering on the brink of bankruptcy. While the corporation was begging Congress for financial help, it was also trying to sustain its engine and vehicle sales to the military—one segment of its business that was doing well. Chrysler asked that I help the company fulfill its commitment to veterans' organizations, especially those that worked to place former service personnel into decent-paying jobs. The corporation wanted to send a signal that even in the darkest of times, Chrysler placed a very high value on its relationship to all branches of the military.

Although Chrysler was hemorrhaging millions in losses each quarter, the company continued to make grants through its still-functioning foundation. The question loomed: given the company's perilous financial condition, was it now time to turn the philanthropy spigot off even if conditional contributions were clearly beneficial to the corporation?

For Chrysler, the answer was "no."

If strategically positioned contributions are advantageous to the corporation, they can be—at least in some instances—justified even when a business is operating in the red. However, under these circumstances, a company (particularly a publicly held corporation) had better make sure its contributions live up to the business relevance test in a big way.

Fortunately, very few of America's thirteen thousand publicly held corporations declare bankruptcy each year. And even among the millions of mid-sized and small businesses, the failure rates aren't so high as many believe. The U.S. Census Bureau reports about half the businesses it tracks are still operating five years after they open. And the National Federation of Independent Businesses estimates 69 percent of companies still in business are either profitable or breaking even.

Of course, there is another way of looking at these data—a half to a third of all smaller businesses either disappear in five years or operate in the red. But keep in mind that a portion of these companies are purchased by other businesses or are swallowed up in mergers—so the statistics are not so grim as they might first appear to be.

Even in the midst of a recession, most businesses continue to pound out a profit. They may be earning less than in years past, but they are not showing a loss. A knee-jerk reaction among many of those firms suffering from declining earnings is to cut or even eliminate contributions as a way to reduce costs and thereby help rebuild the profit line. That may not always be the right move. In fact, in many cases, it can be counterproductive. But before deciding what a corporation with diminishing profits should do with its contributions program, let's circle back to the fundamentals sketched out by Peter Drucker.

In rank order, a corporation's main obligations are to

- Legally and ethically make a profit
- Employ a workforce
- Pay taxes

Then to that list, let's add

- Be conditional in its grant making

Put yourself in the Berluti oxfords of Chuck Gilfant who, you'll recall, runs Widget Worldwide. The company's profits make an unexpected U-turn and begin heading south. The CEO's bonus, stock options, and reputation begin taking a hit. Returning Widget to the days when the company increased its revenue and earnings each year becomes a paramount concern for Gilfant. What does he do?

First, he looks for ways to pump up profits but is careful not to take any legal or ethical shortcuts. Adhering to environmental standards, producing goods or services that aren't dangerous or inferior, banning any practice that cheats investors, and playing by fair employment rules are "musts" for Widget Worldwide.

Next, Gilfant checks his business plan to make sure Widget is creating and maintaining the right kind of jobs. Gilfant is smart enough to know that when corporations are taken down to their core, most are nothing more than aggregations of people, all of whom should be rowing the company boat in the same direction—toward profitability. Gilfant is also aware of the peripheral societal benefits that come from employing people. Widget's employees earn wages that fuel commerce, offset costs of public services via tax payments, and fund nonprofit causes through personal donations. However, Gilfant is also a realist and knows there are occasions when shrinking the workforce is necessary. And for Widget, this is one of those times. The company will phase out five thousand jobs over the next two years, with attrition taking care of most of the shrinkage.

Third, Gilfant grimaces and takes a hard look at Widget's tax obligations. Widget Worldwide isn't ecstatic about paying taxes, but its management recognizes that in the United States, where most of its tax burden rests, the current federal tax code is quite lenient. Corporations are allowed numerous deductions, which take a lot of the pain out of what on paper looks to be a staggering 35 percent of taxable earnings. Widget's total adjusted bill for federal, state, city, and international taxes is in line with what other large companies pay (corporate tax rate examples from 2008 validate this point: Hewlett-Packard, 20 percent; Procter & Gamble, 25 percent; and Dell, 23 percent). Gilfant instructs Widget's tax department to take full advantage of all deductions and credits. But on the flip side, he makes it clear that Widget shouldn't cross the line—the tax man mustn't be left short.

Finally, Chuck Gilfant examines Widget's contributions program and other expenses linked to community relations and employee volunteerism. He places a call to his vice president for public relations, to whom Widget's office of corporate contributions reports. What follows is a likely scenario.

WIDGET'S QUANDARY: TO CUT OR NOT TO CUT

"Should we cut our corporate giving budget or not?" Gilfant asks the VP. Actually, the CEO isn't anxious to reduce Widget's philanthropy payout—but he needs a defensible reason for not doing so.

"Maybe we should consider bringing it down a notch," the VP responds. He misreads his boss, thinking that Gilfant is searching for an excuse to shave contributions expenses. "After all, we're doing away with five thousand jobs and our profits are down. If we continue doling out a lot of money to charity, it could rankle some people."

Although this isn't the response Chuck is hoping to hear, the VP has put his thumb on why it's risky *not* to trim Widget's philanthropy allocations. "How much is our corporate giving costing us now?" asks Gilfant.

"We used the Sabsevitz Formula to calculate our current budget, which is based on 1.2 percent of our pretax earnings the year before last."

Gilfant recalled agreeing to the new ante-up method of establishing a contributions spending target for the company. "Go on."

"Two years ago, our profits were higher than what we expect in earnings for this year. While we thought our contributions would end up at around 1 percent of pretax profits this year, that percentage is going to be higher *if* we don't cut the budget for grants."

"How much higher?"

"Could end up at around 2 percent of pretax earnings."

The VP pauses, waiting for Gilfant's response. Several seconds pass before the CEO asks, "How are we making grant decisions these days?"

"Excuse me?"

"Aren't you checking to make sure every contribution that goes out the door has relevance to the company?"

"Yeah," the VP confirms. He isn't sure where Gilfant is heading. "About a year ago, we started making conditional contributions. We make grants on the condition they can be backed up with a business rationale of some kind."

"So we're using our contributions program to solve certain kinds of business problems—"

"Or create opportunities," the VP interrupts. "Like basic research projects we're funding that could open the door to new product development down the line."

"For now, let's stick to our problems," Gilfant says. "We have people who'll be out of a job in a few months. Can we fund programs that re-train workers for other kinds of employment?"

The VP had discussed a similar strategy with Widget's head of human resources earlier in the week. "We can if the programs aren't limited to our own people. The community college just sent us a proposal that might work."

"What about vandalism?" asks Gilfant.

"Vandalism?"

"Security says there's been a 20 percent increase in property damage over the past three months. We're paying a lot more money than we anticipated. After-school programs have been shut down, night-time recreation is history—isn't there a way we can do something about this?"

"Maybe a special grant to the United Way," the VP suggests.

"Here's where I come down on this one," concludes Gilfant. "Don't cut the contributions budget. Stay focused on our biggest problems. And wherever possible, use our grant money to hit those problems hard. Make every contribution count."

Chuck Gilfant has come a long way since Chapter Two, when Widget's CEO found little difference between a contribution and a tax. Keeping the company's contributions budget intact even when the corporation's profit projections aren't rosy is a wise move—*if* Widget continues to practice conditional corporate philanthropy. However, if Widget's profit picture turns *very* gloomy, put yourself in Gilfant's chair and sort through your options. Would you start trimming the company's contributions program—and if so, how deep a cut would you make? Following are a few guidelines that should help you arrive at the best possible decision.

The Under 5 Percent of Pretax Net Income Rule

Let's assume your company is practicing our "ante up" budgeting system. Your business has a conditional contributions spending plan equal to 1 percent of this year's likely pretax profits, which you have estimated by using the Sabsevitz Ante-Up Formula. Now your company has run into a fiscal wall and earnings are plunging. When matched up against lower forecasted profits for this year, your giving will equal nearly 5 percent of that amount! What to do?

If at all possible, nothing.

Remember, a business is allowed to deduct up to 10 percent of its pretax income for charitable donations. Very few businesses hit the 10 percent mark, but spending 5 percent of pretax profits—while unusual—is not unprecedented. In fact, some businesses regularly set their yearly contributions allocation at that level. So it is certainly defensible to keep your budget at or slightly below 5 percent of pretax earnings *if* your giving is conditional. Be mindful, though, that when contributions consume a greater percentage of profits, validating that every contribution has relevance both to society *and* to your business is very important.

The Over 5 Percent of Pretax Net Income Rule

Assume you get even more bad news about your company's finances. The profit projection for the year is so ominous that your current budget will probably end up *higher* than 5 percent of this year's earnings. This is where a downward adjustment may be inevitable.

Worth remembering is that it usually takes a dramatic plunge in profits to get to the 5 percent watermark. Let's say your company set its current year's contributions budget by calculating 1.2 percent of $100 million in before-tax earnings two years ago. Using that formula, you anticipated the company's grant making would end up at 1 percent of the current year's pretax profits—which would mean a contributions payout of $1,200,000. Your finance VP delivers the really bad news that this year's revised earnings forecast will put your company's pretax profits at $10 million—a tenfold drop from two years ago. It also means that your planned giving total of $1.2 million will exceed 10 percent of earnings for the year. This is the kind of freefall that is likely to take its toll on every aspect of a company's operations—including its contributions program.

Before putting a scalpel to your company's contributions budget, there are a couple of options you may want to consider that could make radical surgery a bit less excruciating.

Drop-Back Strategy

If a company's contributions payout falls dramatically from one year to the next, it sends a strong signal that the business truly is in trouble. That may not be the kind of flag a company wants to fly in front of investors and customers, since it only serves to reinforce the firm's financial troubles. A more reasonable strategy—and one more easily explained to nonprofit organizations, shareholders, and other stakeholders—is to drop back to last year's level of giving (assuming last year's spending was less than what is budgeted for the current year). If a business is experiencing a falloff in profits, holding contributions even to what was allocated a year earlier is generally viewed as a sensible and understandable decision.

Deferred Payment Option

I have worked with businesses that have developed a contingency budget reduction plan based mainly on deferred payments. Under this approach, many nonprofit organizations in line to get grants are informed that no grant decisions will be made until year end—and possibly not until next fiscal year. In some instances, pessimistic earnings forecasts turn brighter and the company finds it is able to pay out more donations in the fourth quarter than anticipated earlier in the year. In other cases, philanthropy obligations are pushed into the upcoming fiscal year. Of course, this latter course of action means a hefty portion of next year's budget will be eaten up by these carry-forward obligations. Nevertheless, the tactic gives the corporation one more year to rebound financially, which may allow it to increase its philanthropy budget to accommodate these previous year expenses.

The Give-While-Downsizing Dilemma

One of the most perplexing questions facing any company when dealing with contribution decision making is, Should our corporation continue giving away money when we're firing people?

The answer is in many cases, "yes" *if* (a) conditional grant making is sharply focused on programs and causes that enhance a company's ability to do business *and lessen the probability that more people will be let go* and (b) the corporation can communicate clearly the business importance of sustaining its contributions activities.

I consulted with Starbucks during a difficult period when the company was forced to shutter a number of its stores. Many of Starbucks' "baristas" found themselves without jobs. Reputed for its corporate responsibility, Starbucks was in a bind. How could it defend cutting checks to nonprofit organizations when it was also cutting its workforce? The company answered the question by strategically placing contributions that helped stabilize its business and limit or eliminate additional layoffs. It leveraged a portion of its philanthropy program to bolster customer confidence and reinforce the Starbucks' brand, particularly among its core customers. What's more, it communicated clearly what it was doing and why.

Starbucks' philanthropy actions can't be solely credited for the company's turnaround from 2007, when its stock lost 42 percent of its value, to 2010, when revenue and same-store sales started climbing. Still, it is apparent conditional contributions were a factor.

When Taproot Foundation (the largest nonprofit consulting group in the nation) surveyed four hundred business professionals to probe attitudes about how companies should handle charitable contributions during the throes of a recession, here is one of its findings:

> Philanthropy and community service during workforce reductions should be maintained but positioned carefully.

Only one out of four people surveyed by Taproot said businesses should *not* be giving away money to charities while at the same time cutting staff. Another 29 percent were neutral on the issue. Slightly less than half the respondents agreed that it is okay to continue making contributions if the company is laying off employees.

The divided opinion about the ethics of giving away money or product while downsizing staff underscores why it is so critical to have a solid explanation as to the reason(s) a corporation is continuing its *conditional* grant making at a time when the company is also shedding jobs. Effective communication (Chapter Twelve) is imperative.

Recession Reaction

Answers to this chapter's question primarily apply to situations when a corporation's earnings drop because of some singular business problem. But what should a corporation do with its contributions program if there is an economic slump that ripples through the entire private sector?

The recession that began infecting the world in 2007 was a phenomenon that tested businesses throughout the nation and across the globe. The Charlotte Community Affairs Professionals (CCAP) in Charlotte, North Carolina, gives us insight on how some companies reacted to that economic firestorm.

Charlotte was among the hardest hit urban communities following the nation's banking implosion. Two of the city's largest corporate donors—Bank of America and Wachovia (now part of Wells Fargo)—are headquartered in the city. The recession ate into the earnings of other companies that had a large presence in Charlotte. Nonprofits soon were stung by a deep reduction in donations, with the situation made even worse by a highly publicized local United Way brouhaha.

Recognizing that Charlotte and surrounding communities were in jeopardy, many of the CCAP member companies (including Goodrich, Duke Energy, Piedmont Natural Gas, Food Lion, LS3P, Lowe's, Harris Teeter, AT&T, TIAA-CREF, Wachovia, and Bank of America) rallied behind a special "Critical Need Response Fund." Extra funding poured into the region's social infrastructure.

On the surface, it might seem as if business donations aimed at providing Charlotte area residents with shelter, food, heat and electricity, and other basic necessities fell outside the conditional contribution parameters advocated in this book. But consider this: corporations that have their headquarters or major operations in a city usually have *huge* property interests that could quickly fall in value if the community were to disintegrate. It makes sense for businesses to direct their conditional contributions toward programs and organizations that can protect these expensive investments *if*

- The company sends a clear message to those inside and outside the corporation walls as to the social *and* business purpose of these donations.
- Nonprofit organizations are informed that these short-term commitments are unlikely to continue once a recession begins to ease.

IN SUMMARY

Question 13: What if a company's profits tank?

Answer: Continue to make conditional grants adhering to the Sabsevitz Ante-Up Formula if the company is profitable. If a corporation faces a significant earnings loss, adjust the ante-up budget through a temporary suspension of contributions allocations, a delay in contributions payments, or–as a last resort–a permanent reduction in the contributions budget for the year. Companies with foundations should consider making larger-than-planned annual payouts to offset any downturn in direct corporate support.

14

Conclusion:
The Nun's Tzedakah

On my office wall, I have a plaque that quotes Thomas Jefferson. It reads,

> I deem it the duty of every man to devote a certain portion of his income for charitable purposes; and that it is his further duty to see it so applied as to do the most good of which it is capable.

This should be a guiding principle not just for each individual, but also for each corporation. For a company to use a donation "to do the most good of which it is capable," means pointing cash, product contributions, and employee time in a direction that addresses a social need—but in a way that keeps such a commitment in line with a corporation's interests and mission.

Businesses are far more likely to carry out Jefferson's "further duty" if they can get past thirteen obstacles that too often clot the corporate philanthropy pipeline. I've recast the baker's dozen list of potential roadblocks into a checklist that any company can (and should) use to determine if it is living up to the standards and expectations of a *comprehensive* corporate citizen.

SMART GIVING CHECKLIST

☐ Make conditional contributions.

Properly designed and managed, contributions should always be made on the condition that they meet both social *and* business objectives. While there are moral and ethical reasons for companies to carve out a small percentage of their profits to support nonprofit causes, there need to be solid business reasons as well.

☐ "Ante up."

If a corporation is *really* a comprehensive corporate citizen, it uses the Sabsevitz Ante-Up Formula to budget its contributions spending—1.2 percent of last year's pretax net income equals the minimum cash giving budget for next year. Product donations, extra cash support, employee volunteer activities, and so on are all over and above the ante-up minimum. It's that simple.

☐ Let *senior executives own* part of the company contributions program.

The more top-level executives are fully engaged in a company's conditional grant making (helping to chart a course, taking the lead in carrying out high-impact programs), the more powerful and successful the contributions program is going to be.

☐ Enlist the *CEO* to set the tone.

Especially when it comes to corporate philanthropy and employee volunteerism, the chief executive is a pied piper. The workforce takes its cue from the front office. Here are the two essentials for the CEO: (a) assign the right senior managers to map out and oversee a conditional contributions program and (b) constantly cheerlead.

☐ Make sure the *contributions manager* is an effective company spokesperson.

Most corporate contributions directors also wear community relations hats. They interface *a lot* with key community and regional stakeholders. Is the manager the kind of corporate representative who should be waving the company flag? Corporations need to choose wisely.

☐ Establish or maintain a company *foundation*—but only if justified.

Corporations sometimes give birth to a foundation for show more so than purpose. There are situations when a foundation is beneficial. But in many instances, foundations are cumbersome funding spigots that don't add much to a corporation. Launch or maintain a foundation only if it adds value and doesn't get in the way of conditional grant making.

☐ Maximize *product-giving* opportunities.

Fair or not, tax laws make the donation of products a lot more attractive than the contribution of cash. In addition, research shows the public is more impressed by product giving than by large cash donations. So a company owes it to its owners to at least explore all possible product-giving options.

☐ Control dinners and special events.

Few companies can dodge the barrage of dinner, walkathon, golf outing, and auction requests. But firms should stay in control of these kinds of charitable commitments—and define the business relevance of every special-event investment the company makes.

☐ Support the *United Way*—if warranted.

There may be a few bad apples among the nation's eighteen hundred local United Ways. But for the most part, the United Way and similar "umbrella" fundraising organizations warrant limited corporate support.

☐ Get ahead of a *disaster*.

Concocting a plan and vetting the best possible nonprofit crisis-management partner(s) are two good ways to get a handle on a catastrophe—before it happens.

☐ Know what, what not, and when to *measure*.

Figure out what to evaluate before making a grant. Getting a clear understanding of expected "deliverables" before a nonprofit receives a contribution is the pathway to effective measurement.

☐ Tell the story.

But tell it to audiences that count. Pinpoint the people who should be informed about a company's support of a nonprofit program or cause. Then pierce the information "clutter" by using innovative and sometimes unorthodox communication strategies.

☐ Don't let an *economic downturn* bury company
    contributions.

Strategic grant making should be part of a larger corporate plan to combat the effects of a rocky economy. Even in the face of lower earnings and job layoffs, conditional contributions can be critically important.

If the private sector gives this checklist serious attention, corporate philanthropy will experience a much-needed rebound. But it's worth reminding ourselves that such an infusion of new conditional grant making is only a means to a far more important end. The real measure of the value of any contribution is what difference it ultimately makes. No one helped me remember that point more than a tiny woman with a gigantic heart and indefatigable resolve. Here's the story.

SISTER ISOLINA'S TZEDAKAH

The nun stood a notch below five feet but she was a giant in Ponce, the second largest city in Puerto Rico. Once reputed for its bars and prostitutes, Ponce now drew tourists by the drove for its restored neoclassical buildings, imposing fountains, and plazas. "This way," the nun said and led me through the front entrance of the *Centros Sor Isolina Ferré*.

I did a quick scan of the place. "Huge!" I blurted out.

The nun smiled back at me. "Used to be a cement factory."

"How does a cement factory turn into—this?" I asked. The building's interior was crowded with women, some working behind rows of sewing machines and others clacking at keyboards hooked to what looked to be new personal computers.

"My father's company donated the building," the nun explained.

Everyone in Puerto Rico knew the nun's father. Until his death, Antonio Ferré headed one of the most affluent and influential families on the island. Why his daughter, a woman born into wealth and status, chose to trade what could have been a life of privilege and comfort for the sake of a cause was still a mystery to some.

"Most of the rest of what you see in here," the nun said, motioning to the furniture and equipment that filled the room, "was also donated."

"And the women—who are they?"

"More to the point" the nun replied, "is who they *would* have been without this center. Prostitution is still a career choice for young women who have no skills."

"So this is a vocational training center—"

"It's more than that. It's a place where we build character and self-confidence. We give women what they need to become productive citizens. Our main product is human dignity."

That "product" is what the nun marketed to many of the 161 *Fortune* 500 corporations with operations in Puerto Rico. She had a way of explaining the business benefits of human dignity—about how personal pride was the cornerstone for a strong work ethic. She didn't beg for donations; she proposed cash and product "investments" that companies could write off as charitable commitments. Her business savvy, determination, wit, and—most of all—passion convinced most corporations to contribute generously to the nun's *Centros,* sometimes going over budget to fulfill their obligations.

In 1999, the nun was awarded the Presidential Medal of Freedom—America's highest civilian award. The news didn't come as any great surprise. She had already received the Albert Schweitzer Prize for Humanitarianism and was commonly referred to as "Puerto Rico's Mother Teresa." She died a year later, leaving behind five "human dignity centers" staffed by 350 workers who provided job training and high school equivalency programs to over 10,000 Puerto Ricans a year.

"Amazing how much value she could wring out of a donation," Roger Fine reflected when learning about Sister Isolina Ferré's death. Fine was a veteran Johnson & Johnson executive who was about to become the corporation's general counsel. Among the framed pictures in his office was a snapshot of the petite nun sandwiched between the two of us.

"She knew how to shake every corporate tree in Puerto Rico," I said. "Got money and materials out of companies that normally wouldn't part with a dime."

"Do you know why?" Roger asked.

"Yeah—because she didn't have a tin cup mentality. With her, it was never an appeal but always a deal. Whatever she put in front of a company was a win-win for the business and for her centers."

"True," Fine agreed and then added, "but she had something else going for her."

"What?"

"*Tzedakah*."

Roger was a devout Jew who over the years had taught me a limited number of Hebrew words. "A Catholic nun driven by the Judaic principle of charity?" I asked.

"Exactly," Roger answered. "She told businesses that they had a *duty* to be charitable. It wasn't optional. It was *tzedakah*."

I thought about Fine's observation. "There'd be a lot more money and donated product on the table if every corporation saw it the same way."

"Unfortunately, that's a big *if*," Roger noted. "To get that to happen, businesses are going to have to be helped over a lot of hurdles."

Smart Giving Is Good Business has earmarked thirteen of those hurdles—and offered thirteen ways companies can go around or over them.

If put into practice, our baker's dozen list of questions-turned-recommendations will make a huge difference to many of those Sister Isolinas who continue to wrestle our most serious social challenges. The impact on the nonprofit sector as a whole will be significant. Should it be adopted by just the leading-edge group of corporate donors, the Sabsevitz Ante-Up Formula is expected to generate an *additional $7 billion to $8 billion in corporate funding for nonprofits each year,* with most of that new giving in cash.

Let's be clear—none of this added money should be provided ahead of intelligent forethought. Businesses need to *get smart* before unleashing their generosity. If and hopefully when that happens, companies will indeed extract "the most good" from their *tzedakah*.

Bibliography

Introduction

Association of Corporate Contributions Professionals. http://www.accprof.org; accessed October 15, 2010.

Committee Encouraging Corporate Philanthropy website. http://www.corporatephilanthropy.org; accessed October 15, 2010.

Corporate Income Tax Returns—2006 Statistics of Income. Internal Revenue Service, U.S. Department of the Treasury. http://www.irs.gov/pub/irs-soi/06coccr.pdf.

Corporate Profits. National Bureau of Economic Research. http://www.nber.org/palmdata/indicators/corporate.html#TotalProfits (beforetax<ahref='#N_1'>\1\</a>)<ahref='#N_2'>\2\</a>; accessed October 15, 2010.

"Corporate-Driven Aid: $147.8 Million." Business Civic Leadership Center, U.S. Chamber of Commerce, March 9, 2010. http://www.uschamber.com/bclc/haiti_corporatedonations.htm.

Isodore, Chris. "It's Official: Recession Since Dec. '07." CNNMoney.com, December 1, 2008.

Nonprofit Almanac 2007. National Center for Charitable Statistics at the Urban Institute, 2007.

"Our Credo Values." Johnson & Johnson. http://prod-www.jnj.com/connect/about-jnj/jnj-credo; accessed October 15, 2010.

"Press release: 2009 Corporate Profits." Bureau of Economic Analysis, U.S. Department of Commerce, March 26, 2009. http://www.bea.gov/newsreleases/national/gdp/2009/pdf/gdp408f.pdf.

Small Business Administration, Office of Advocacy. http://www.sba.gov/advo; accessed October 15, 2010.

SOI Tax Statistics—Integrated Business Data. Internal Revenue Services, U.S. Department of the Treasury. http://www.irs.gov/pub/irs-soi/80ot1all.xls; accessed October 15, 2010.

Chapter One

Banks, Paula. "Social Responsibility on a Global Scale." Speech by Paula Banks, BP Vice President Global Social Investment to New Academy of Business Conference on Corporate Responsibility. London, April 2002.

Bardes, Philip, Petrovits, Christine, and Radhakrishnan, Suresh. "Is Doing Good Good for You? Yes, Charitable Contributions Enhance Revenue Growth." Research paper, New York University, Stern School of Business, July 2006.

"Berkshire Hathaway, Inc. News Release." Berkshire Hathaway, July 3, 2003. http://www.berkshirehathaway.com/news/jul0303.pdf.

BP Annual Report 2002. BP Corporation. http://www.bp.com/liveassets/bp_internet/globalbp.

"Business of Philanthropy." *The McKinsey Quarterly,* January 2007.

Deming, W. Edwards. *Out of the Crisis.* Cambridge, MA: MIT Press, 1986.

ExxonMobil 2009 Corporate Citizenship Report. ExxonMobil Corporation, 2010.

Himmelstein, Jerome L. *Looking Good and Doing Good: Philanthropy and Corporate Power.* Bloomington: Indiana University Press, 1997, pp. 80–88.

ISO 26000. International Organization for Standardization. http://www.iso.org/iso/home.html; accessed October 15, 2010.

Karnani, Aneel. "The Case Against Corporate Social Responsibility." *The Wall Street Journal,* August 23, 2010.

Muller, Tom, and Bogner, Judith. "Nestle Chairman Opposes Company Philanthropy as Misuse of Funds." *Bloomberg Businessweek,* June 6, 2010.

Newman, Paul, and Hotchner, A. E. *In Pursuit of the Common Good.* New York: Nan A. Talese, 2003.

Quick Facts About Charitable Giving from the Center on Philanthropy Panel Study. Center on Philanthropy at Indiana University, 2005. www.philanthropy.iupui.edu.

STAGING/global_assets/downloads/A/Annual_Report_2002_Full_volume.pdf.

"Three Gulf Research Institutions to Receive First Round of $500 Million Funding." Press Release: BP Corporation, June 15, 2010.

Chapter Two

"Charitable Giving at 105 Big Companies." *The Chronicle of Philanthropy,* July 2, 2009.

Collins, Jim. *From Good to Great: Why Some Companies Make the Leap and Others Don't.* New York: HarperCollins, 2001.

Friedman, Milton. "The Social Responsibility of Business Is to Increase Its Profits." *The New York Times Magazine,* September 13, 1970.

Giving USA. Glenview, IL: Giving USA Foundation, 2008.

Kanter, Rosabeth Moss. *Supercorp.* New York: Crown Business, 2009.

Karnani, Aneel. "The Case Against Corporate Social Responsibility." *The Wall Street Journal,* August 23, 2010.

Miller, Rich. "Recession Hits U.S. Corporate Profit: Will Overall Economy Be Next?" *International Herald Tribune,* December 3, 2007.

"News Release: Gross Domestic Product and Corporate Profit Report." Bureau of Economic Analysis—U.S. Department of Commerce, June 25, 2010. http://www.bea.gov/newsreleases/national/gdp/2010/pdf/gdp1q10_3rd.pdf.

Nocera, Joe. "Emerald City of Giving Does Exist." *The New York Times,* December 22, 2007.

North American Classification System. U.S. Census Bureau. http://www.census.gov; accessed October 15, 2010.

Nutting, Rex. "Profits Surge to 40-Year High." *Marketwatch,* March 30, 2008.

Target Corporate Fact Card. Target Corporation, n.d. http://sites.target.com/images/corporate/about/ pdfs/corp_factcard_101107.pdf.

"U.S. Charitable Giving Falls 3.6 Percent in 2009 to $303.75 Billion." Press release: Giving USA Foundation, June 9, 2010.

Weeden, Curt. *Corporate Social Investing.* San Francisco: Berrett-Koehler, 1998.

Chapter Three

"The Corporate Contributions Program at Roche." Roche Pharmaceuticals, Nutley, NJ. http://www.rocheusa.com/portal/usa/charitable_funding_guidelines; accessed October 15, 2010.

"Grant Application Guidelines." The Coca-Cola Company. http://www.thecoca-colacompany.com/citizenship/foundation_guidelines.html; accessed October 15, 2010.

"Guidelines." UPS. http://www.community.ups.com/Diversity/ Supplier+Diversity/Guidelines?srch_pos=1&srch_phr=grant+ guidelines&WT.svl=SRCH; accessed October 15, 2010.

"Guidelines for Grant Applications." Boeing Community Relations. Seattle, WA. http://www.boeing.com/companyoffices/aboutus/ community/elig_excl.html; accessed October 15, 2010.

"Medtronic Grant Programs." Medtronic Corporation. http://www .medtronic.com/foundation/programs.html; accessed October 15, 2010.

"Unrelated Business Income Defined." U.S. Department of Treasury, Internal Revenue Service, August 20, 2010. http://www.irs.gov/ charities/article/0,,id=96104,00.html.

Chapter Four

"CECP Report Proposes New Approach for Businesses to Solve Societal Challenges in Coming Decade." Press Release: Committee Encouraging Corporate Philanthropy, June 17, 2010.

"Donald M. Kendall, Co-Founder, Former Chairman & CEO, PepsiCo." Beverage Forum. http://www.beverageforum.com/ bevforumbios2004.htm; accessed October 15, 2010.

Glod, Maria. "U.S. Teens Trail Peers Around World on Math—Science Test." *The Washington Post*, December 5, 2007.

Iwata, Edward. "To Split or Not to Split." *USA Today*, March 14, 2008.

Kanter, Rosabeth Moss. *Supercorp*. New York: Crown Business, 2009.

Kowitt, Beth. "Captains of Education." *Fortune*, December 8, 2008.

Malakian, Anthony. "To Split or Not to Split: That Is the Top Question." *American Banker*, July 2008. http://www.americanbanker.com/usb_ article.html?id=20080625LLFN42AU.

McNeil, Donald G., Jr. "Ally for the Poor in an Unlikely Corner." *The New York Times*, February 9, 2010.

"More Firms Split CEO and Chairman Roles: Study." Reuters release, June 16, 2008.

Rockefeller, David. "America After Downsizing: Maximizing Society's Profits." Speech to the New York Economics Club, September 12, 1996.

Weeden, Curt. "Big Oil Is a Big Cheapskate to Charity." *BusinessWeek*, November 25, 2008.

"When Chairman and CEO Roles Split." *Directorship*, January 14, 2008. http://www. directorship.com/when-chairman—ceo-roles-split.

Chapter Five

ACCP Guide to Compensation, Benefits & Staffing. Association of Corporate Contributions Professionals, 2005.

Barbaro, Michael. "Embattled Chief Executive Resigns at Home Depot." *The New York Times*, January 3, 2007.

Department of the Treasury, Internal Revenue Service, *2005 Statistics of Income*. http://www.irs.gov/pub/irs-soi/05coccr.pdf.

Freddie Mac Audit Committee Report, June 2005. http://www.freddiemac .com/investors/pdffiles/proxy_061405_2.pdf.

Healy, James R., and Woodyard, Chris. "Choice for Chrysler CEO Blasted." *USA Today*, August 8, 2007.

Internal Revenue Service Data Book 2008. http://www.irs.gov/pub/irs-soi/ 08databk.pdf.

"Most Small Companies Make Charitable Donations, Survey Finds." *The Chronicle of Philanthropy*, November 20, 2008. http://philanthropy .com/news/prospecting/6349/most-small-companies-make-charitable-donations-survey-finds.

"New Survey Shows Great Enthusiasm for Charitable Giving by Small Businesses." *PRNewswire*, October 16, 2008.

Chapter Six

Pfizer 1999 Annual Report. Pfizer Corporation. http://www.google.com/ search?hl=en&q=pfizer+1999+annual+report+%24300+million+ contribution

Schwartz, John. "Viagra's Hidden Risks." *Washington Post*, June 9, 1998.

"Top Funders: 50 Largest Corporate Foundations by Asset Size." Foundation Center, July 2010. http://foundationcenter.org/findfunders/ topfunders/top50assets.html.

"Top 100 U.S. Foundations by Total Giving." Foundation Center, July 2010. http://foundationcenter.org/findfunders/topfunders/ top100giving.html.

Chapter Seven

ARAMARK/Building Community. Business Civic Leadership Center— 2009 Corporate Citizenship Awards.

"Charitable Giving at 83 Big Companies." *The Chronicle of Philanthropy*, August 21, 2008.

"Corporate Contributions Holding Steady." Press release: Conference Board, December 17, 2008. http://www.conference-board.org/utilities/pressDetail.cfm?press_ID=3542.

Corporate Reputation Report. Hill & Knowlton and Yankelovich Partners. Hill & Knowlton, 1998.

Direct Relief 2008 Annual Report. Direct Relief International. http://www.directrelief.org/uploadedFiles/Our_Finances/Related_Documents/AR_low.pdf.

"GSK Global Policy Issues—Product Donations." GlaxoSmithKline website, March 2009. http://www.gsk.com/policies/GSK-on-product-donations.pdf.

"Madison Avenue Magic: Study Reveals Positive Effects of Unconscious Exposure to Advertisements." Press release: Rensselaer Polytechnic Institute, December 9, 2008.

Motorola. "Global Day of Service." http://responsibility.motorola.com/index.php/society/comminvest/employeevolunteer/globaldayservice; accessed October 15, 2010.

Procter & Gamble, "Children's Safe Drinking Water." http://www.pg.com/en_US/sustainability/social_responsibility/childrens_safe_water.shtml; accessed October 15, 2010.

"Swaziland Wellness Centre Innovative and Effective Response to Health-care Worker Crisis." Press release: BD, April 23, 2008.

Wake Forest—The Quarterly Magazine of Wake Forest, March 2005. http://www.wfu.edu/magazine/archive/wfm.2005.03.pdf.

"WHO Calls for Good Drug Donation Practice During Emergencies as It Issues New Guidelines." Press release: World Health Organization, September 3, 1999.

Chapter Eight

"The Growth of Cause Marketing." Cause Marketing Forum, 2010. http://www.causemarketingforum.com/page.asp?ID=188.

Nober, Jane. "Hands On—That's the Ticket." *Foundation News & Commentary*, May-June 1998.

Panepento, Peter. "Critics Dispute Claim That Charities Lose Money on Special Events." *The Chronicle of Philanthropy*, May 10, 2007.

"Sponsorship Spending to Total $16.78 Billion in 2008." IEG website, January 2008. IEGSponsorship.com. http://www.sponsorship.com/About-IEG/Press-Room/Sponsorship-Spending-To-Total-$16.78-Billion-In-20.aspx.

Tri-Cities Guild Golf Classic, May 2007. http://tcchguilds.org/pdf/sponsorshipform07.pdf.

Chapter Nine

ACCP Guide to Employee Worksite Giving Programs & Campaigns. Association of Corporate Contributions Professionals. Mount Pleasant, South Carolina, 2008.

Barrett, William P. "United Way's New Way." *Forbes,* January 1, 2006.

Giving USA 2008. Giving USA Foundation.

Greenwall, Megan. "21 Regional Nonprofits Withdraw from United Way." *The Washington Post,* April 29, 2009.

Johnston, David Cay. "Private Sector; In My . . . Suitcase." *The New York Times,* October 4, 1998.

Lewis, Nicole. "United Way of America CEO Has Spent Two Decades as a Local Leader." *The Chronicle of Philanthropy,* November 29, 2001.

Patterns of Household Charitable Giving by Income Group, 2005. Bloomington: The Center on Philanthropy at Indiana University, Summer 2007.

Sinclair, Matthew. "William Aramony Is Back on the Streets." *Nonprofit Times,* March 1, 2002.

2007 Annual Report of United Way of America. United Way of America, Alexandria, Virginia.

"United Way Asks Gloria Pace King to Resign." WCNC News Channel 36, August 26, 2008.

"Walmart Foundation Tax Preparation Partnership Expects to Yield More Than $1 Billion for Consumers." Press release: Walmart Foundation, January 28, 2010.

Chapter Ten

"Chevron Announces Opening of Vocational Training Center in Tsunami-Affected Indonesian Province." Press release: Chevron Corporation, August 20, 2008.

"Excel Delivers Water from Miller Brewing Co. to Hurricane Victims." *Outsourced Logistics,* August 27, 2004. http://outsourced-logistics .com/logistics_ services/outlog_story_6163/.

Federal Charter of the American Red Cross, May 2007. http://www.redcross .org/www-files/Documents/Governance/charter.pdf

Hurricanes Katrina and Rita: Coordination Between FEMA and the Red Cross Should Be Improved for the 2006 Hurricane Season. U.S. Government Accounting Office, 2008. http://www.gao.gov/new.items/ d06712.pdf.

"New CEO Named to American Red Cross." Press release: American Red Cross, April 16, 2008.

Ross, Brian. "Red Cross President Resigns; Questions Remain." *ABC News,* December 13, 2005.

Rucker, Phillip. "President of Red Cross Is Forced to Resign." *The Washington Post*, November 28, 2007.

Sontag, Deborah. "Who Brought Bernadine Healy Down?" *The New York Times Magazine*, December 23, 2001.

Storm, Stephanie. "Red Cross Fires Its President, Citing Relationship." *New York Times*, November 29, 2007.

Chapter Eleven

"Applying for Support." DTE Energy Foundation. http://www.dteenergy.com/dteEnergyCompany/community/foundation/applyForGrants.html; accessed October 15, 2010.

Aschermann, Kurt. "The Ten Commandments of Cause-Related Marketing." Cause Marketing Forum. http://www.causemarketingforum.com/page.asp?ID=103; accessed October 15, 2010.

Cause Marketing Forum website. http://www.causemarketingforum.com/page.asp?ID=188; accessed October 15, 2010.

Common Report Form Format. Council of Michigan Foundations. http://www.michiganfoundations.org/s_cmf/bin.asp?CID=516&DID=10468&DOC=FILE.DOC; accessed October 15, 2010.

Financial Accounting Standards Board website. http://www.fasb.org; accessed October 15, 2010.

"Giving in Numbers 2007." Committee Encouraging Corporate Philanthropy, 2008.

"Grantee Perception Report FAQs." The Center for Effective Philanthropy. http://www.effectivephilanthropy.org/index.php?page=alias; accessed October 15, 2010.

Lee, Jaimy. "A Good Time to Give." PRWeek/Barkley Public Relations Cause Survey, October 27, 2008. http://www.prweekus.com/pages/Login.aspx?retUrl=/A-good-time-to-give/article/119965/&PageTypeId=28&ArticleId=119965&accessLevel=2.

Lim, Terence. *Measuring the Value of Corporate Philanthropy*. New York: Committee Encouraging Corporate Philanthropy, 2010.

Pepsi Refresh Project. PepsiCo 2010. http://www.refresheverything.com/.

Student Scholarship Detail Information. United Negro College Fund, 2009. http://www.uncf.org/forstudents/scholarDetailSGA.asp?id=301.

"Target Launches $1 Million Contest for Charities." Press release, Target Corporation, February 1, 2010. Note: the five organizations that received "Super Love Sender" grants were St. Jude Children's Research Hospital, United Through Reading Military Program, Kids in Need Foundation, Teacher Resource Centers, and the United Way.

Chapter Twelve

Anheuser-Busch website. http://www.anheuser-busch.com; accessed October 15, 2010.

Deutsch, Claudia. "Keeping the Promise to Help Children." *The New York Times*, November 10, 2008.

Elliott, Stuart. "When a Corporate Donation Raises Protests." *The New York Times*, March 12, 2008.

"*Fortune* Most Admired Companies." Website by Hay Group, n.d. http://www.haygroup.com/ww/Best_Companies/Index.aspx?ID=1582.

Heller, Lorraine. "Target Hispanics Early to Keep Brand Loyalty, Says Market Researcher." Foodnavigator-USA.com, September 25, 2007. http://www.foodnavigator-usa.com/Financial-Industry/Target-Hispanics-early-to-keep-brand-loyalty-says-market-researcher.

"MetLife Foundation Awards Grants to 20 Big Brothers Big Sisters Agencies for Hispanic Mentoring Program." Press release: Big Brothers Big Sisters. PRNewswire, January 27, 2009. http://news.prnewswire.com/DisplayReleaseContent.aspx?ACCT=104&STORY=/www/story/01-27-2009/0004961407&EDATE=.

The Phantom Cause. Cone LLC, February 27, 2009. http://www.coneinc.com/whatdoyoustandfor.

"RESPONSEability: Leading the Way to Social Responsibility." WellPoint Corporation, 2004. http://www.wellpoint.com/pdf/WellPoint_SRAR_final.pdf.

"Salesforce.com Named to Corporate Philanthropy Top 50." Press release: salesforce.com, July 13, 2003. http://www.salesforcefoundation.org/node/55.

Taylor, William. "Permission Marketing." *Fast Company*, December 18, 2007.

"World's Most Admired Companies 2009: Best in Social Responsibility." *Fortune* magazine, 2009. http://money.cnn.com/magazines/fortune/mostadmired/2009/snapshots/5009.html.

Chapter Thirteen

The Charlotte Critical Need Response Fund. Launched by the Leon Levine Foundation and run in partnership with the Mecklenburg Ministries, Foundation For the Carolinas, United Way of Central Carolinas, and the Charlotte Chamber of Commerce.

Drucker, Peter F. *The Practice of Management.* New York: Harper & Row, 1954.

Klein, Karen E. "What's Behind High Small-Biz Failure Rates?" *Business-Week*, September 2009. http://www.businessweek.com/smallbiz/news/coladvice/ask/sa990930.htm.

Chapter Fourteen

"Business Professionals' Attitudes Toward Corporate Philanthropy and Service During a Recession." Taproot Foundation, February 2009.

"Corporate Philanthropy Inspires Trust: Does It Also Prompt Higher Profits?" *Knowledge@Wharton Network*-Wharton School, University of Pennsylvania, January 10, 2007.

"Puerto Rico Profile: Sra. Isolina Ferre." *Puerto Rico Herald*, January 14, 2000.

Quick Facts About Nonprofits. National Center for Charitable Statistics, 2009. http://nccs.urban.org/statistics/quickfacts.cfm.

"The Sector's Economic Impact." *Independent Sector Nonprofit Almanac.* http://www.independentsector.org/economic_role?s=employment%20in%20nonprofit%20sector; accessed October 15, 2010.

Wharton School Publishing, February 16, 2007. http://www.ftpress.com/articles/article.aspx?p=694698.

About the Author

Curt Weeden is recognized as one of the nation's leading experts in the philanthropy and social responsibility fields. He speaks frequently to nonprofit and business audiences on philanthropy trends and how business-nonprofit alliances can generate social change while also addressing private sector interests. *Book of Nathan*, Weeden's debut novel (written with publishing executive Richard Marek), has received wide acclaim, as have his earlier nonfiction books, which include *Corporate Social Investing* (published by Berrett-Koehler with introductions by the late Paul Newman and investment guru Peter Lynch) and *How Women Can Beat Terrorism* (Quadrafoil Press).

Weeden is president of Business & Nonprofit Strategies, Inc., a consulting group providing management guidance to some of the nation's largest corporations and charities. Weeden founded and served as chief executive of the Association of Corporate Contributions Professionals (ACCP), a national professional organization representing corporate contributions, community relations, and employee volunteer managers from over 150 companies. Member companies are responsible for over $20 billion in annual corporate cash and product contributions.

In 1999, Weeden launched the Contributions Academy, which became the principal management education resource for corporate grant makers in the United States and in many countries abroad. The Academy became part of ACCP in July 2005.

Prior to launching the Academy, Weeden served as vice president for Johnson & Johnson and managed that corporation's contributions program. Before joining J&J, he headed a consulting firm that provided external relations and merger and acquisition services to several of the nation's largest businesses, including Bank of America, General Motors, Merck, and Xerox.

Weeden writes extensively about corporate philanthropy. Articles have appeared in *Business Week, USA Today,* the *Miami Herald,* the *San Francisco Examiner,* the *Christian Science Monitor, Across the Board,* the *Financial Times,* the *Chronicle of Philanthropy,* and the *Los Angeles Times.*

Weeden and his wife live in Mount Pleasant, South Carolina.

Businesses Index

Page references followed by *t* indicate a table.

Nonprofit Organizations Index

Page references followed by *t* indicate a table; followed by *e* indicate an exhibit.

Subject Index

Page references followed by *fig* indicate an illustrated figure; followed by *t* indicate a table; followed by *e* indicate an exhibit.